The Epistles of John

The Epistles of
John

Walking in the Light of God's Love

A Verse-by-Verse Commentary
by
Zane C. Hodges

GES

Grace Evangelical Society
Denton, Texas

To my friends
Robert and Barbara Calhoun
and their children,
LaShonda, Tameka, Robert, and Richard

The Epistles of John
Copyright ©1999 by Grace Evangelical Society
Printed in the United States of America

Second Printing

Requests for information should be addressed to:
Grace Evangelical Society
publications@faithalone.org

Cover Design: Rachel Goss
Typesetting: Cathy Beach

Library of Congress Cataloging-in-Publication Data

Hodges, Zane C., 1932 - 2008
The Epistles of John: Walking in the Light of God's Love
by Zane C. Hodges
p. cm. –(the Grace New Testament Commentary)
Includes bibliographical references
ISBN 978-0-9788773-5-4
Library of Congress Catalog Card Number: 99-97136
1. Bible. N.T. John–Commentaries.
I. Bible. N.T. John. English. Hodges. 1999. II. Title. III. Series.

The Epistles of John
Walking in the Light of God's Love

Contents

First John

Second John

Third John

Abbreviations
and Bibliography

LIST OF ABBREVIATIONS

AB   Anchor Bible

AUSS   *Andrews University Seminary Studies*

BDF   Blass, Debrunner, Funk. *A Greek Grammar of the New Testament and Other Early Christian Literature*

BGD   Bauer, Gingrich and Danker. *A Greek-English Lexicon of the New Testament and Other Early Christian Literature*

BT   *Bible Translator*

BTB   *Biblical Theology Bulletin*

BV   *Biblical Viewpoint*

EJ   *Evangelical Journal*

ET   *Expository Times*

EQ   *Evangelical Quarterly*

GTJ   *Grace Theological Journal*

H.E.   *Historia ecclesiastica.* Eusebius of Caesarea (ca. 262–ca. 339). Translation by Christian Frederick Cruse. Baker Book House edition, 1955.

Herm	Hermeneia—A Critical and Historical Commentary on the Bible
HNTC	Harper's New Testament Commentaries
HTKNT	Herders Theologischer Kommentar zum Neuen Testament
ICC	International Critical Commentary
IVPNT	InterVarsity Press New Testament Commentary Series
JB	The Jerusalem Bible
JBL	*Journal of Biblical Literature*
JOTGES	*Journal of the Grace Evangelical Society*
JSNT	*Journal for the Study of the New Testament*
JTS	*Journal of Theological Studies*
KJV	The Authorized King James Version
MajT	*The New Testament According to the Majority Text*
MM	Moulton and Milligan. *The Vocabulary of the Greek Testament Illustrated from the Papyri and Other Non-Literary Sources*
MNTC	Moffatt New Testament Commentary
NACE	New American Catholic Edition
NASB	New American Standard Bible

Neot	*Neotestamentica*
Nestle-Aland	*Nestle-Aland: Greek-English New Testament,* 27th ed.
NICNT	New International Commentary on the New Testament
NIDNTT	*The New International Dictionary of New Testament Theology*
NIV	New International Version
NKJV	New King James Version
NoT	*Notes on Translation*
NRSV	New Revised Standard Version
NTS	*New Testament Studies*
RevExp	*Review Expositor*
RQ	*Restoration Quarterly*
TDNT	*Theological Dictionary of the New Testament*
TNTC	Tyndale New Testament Commentaries
UBS	*The Greek New Testament.* United Bible Societies, 4th ed.
WBC	Word Biblical Commentary
ZNW	*Zeitschrift für die Neutestamentliche Wissenschaft*

BIBLIOGRAPHY

I. Commentaries

Brooke, A. E. *A Critical and Exegetical Commentary on the Johannine Epistles.* International Critical Commentary. Edinburgh: T. & T. Clark, 1912.

Brown, Raymond E. *The Epistles of John.* Anchor Bible. Garden City, NY: Doubleday, 1982.

Bruce, F. F. *The Epistles of John: Introduction, Exposition and Notes.* Old Tappan, NJ: Fleming H. Revell, 1970.

Bultmann, Rudolf. *The Johannine Epistles: A Commentary on the Johannine Epistles.* Trans. by R. Philip O'Hara, Lane C. McGaughy, and Robert W. Funk. Ed., Robert W. Funk. Hermeneia. Philadelphia: Fortress Press, 1973.

Burge, Gary M. *The Letters of John.* NIV Application Commentary. Grand Rapids: Zondervan Publishing House, 1996.

Dodd, C. H. *The Johannine Epistles.* Moffatt New Testament Commentary. New York: Harper & Row, 1946.

Hodges, Zane C. "1 John," "2 John," and "3 John," in *The Bible Knowledge Commentary: An Exposition of the Scriptures by Dallas Seminary Faculty.* New Testament edition. Ed. by John F. Walvoord and Roy B. Zuck. Wheaton, IL: Victor Books, 1978.

Houlden, J. L. *A Commentary on the Johannine Epistles.* Harper's New Testament Commentaries. New York: Harper & Row, 1973.

Marshall, I. Howard. *The Epistles of John.* New International Commentary on the New Testament. Grand Rapids: Wm. B. Eerdmans Publishing Co., 1978.

Plummer, Alfred. *The Epistles of St. John.* Cambridge: University Press, 1886 [reprint ed., Grand Rapids: Baker Book House, 1980].

Schnackenburg, Rudolf. *Die Johannesbriefe.* Zweite, neubearbeitete Auflage. Herders Theologischer Kommentar zum Neuen Testament. Freiburg, Germany: Herder, 1963.

Smalley, Stephen S. *1,2,3 John.* Vol. 51: Word Biblical Commentary. Waco, TX: Word Books, 1984.

Stott, John R. W. *The Letters of John: An Introduction and Commentary.* Tyndale New Testament Commentaries. Revised edition. Grand Rapids: Wm. B. Eerdmans Publishing Co., 1988.

Thompson, Marianne Meye. *1-3 John.* The IVP New Testament Commentary Series. Downers Grove, IL: InterVarsity Press, 1992.

Westcott, Brooke Foss. *The Epistles of St John: The Greek Text with Notes.* New Introduction: Johannine Studies Since Westcott's Day, by F. F. Bruce. Grand Rapids: Wm. B. Eerdmans Publishing Co., 1966 [1st ed., 1883].

II. Reference Works and Special Studies

Aland, Barbara and Kurt; Karavidopoulos, Johannes; Martini, Carlo M.; and Metzger, Bruce; eds. *Nestle-Aland: Greek-English New Testament.* 8th ed. rev. English text: 2nd ed. of the Revised Standard Version. Greek text: Novum Testamentum Graece, 27th ed. Stuttgart, Germany: Deutsche Bibelgesellschaft, 1994.

_____. *The Greek New Testament.* 4th rev. ed. Stuttgart, Germany: Deutsche Bibelgesellschaft and United Bible Societies, 1994.

Bauer, Walter. *A Greek-English Lexicon of the New Testament and Other Early Christian Literature.* Trans. and adapted from Bauer's 4th ed. by William F. Arndt and F. Wilbur Gingrich. 2nd ed. rev. and augmented from Bauer's 5th ed. by F. Wilbur Gingrich and Frederick W. Danker. Chicago: University of Chicago Press, 1979.

Blass, F., and Debrunner, A. *A Greek Grammar of the New Testament and Other Early Christian Literature.* A translation and revision of the ninth-tenth German edition incorporating supplementary notes of A. Debrunner by Robert W. Funk. Chicago: University of Chicago Press, 1961.

Brown, Colin (gen. ed.). *The New International Dictionary of New Testament Theology.* 3 vols. Translated with additions and revisions from the German, *Theologisches Begriffslexikon zum Neuen Testament,* ed. by Lothar Coenen, Erich Beyreuther, and Hans Bietenhard. Grand Rapids: Zondervan Publishing House, 1975-78.

Bruce, F. F. *The Acts of the Apostles: The Greek Text with Introduction and Commentary.* 2nd ed. Grand Rapids: Wm. B. Eerdmans Publishing Co., 1952.

Bullinger, E. W. *Figures of Speech Used in the Bible: Explained and Illustrated.* London: Messrs. Eyre and Spottiswoode, 1898 [reprint ed., Grand Rapids: Baker Book House, 1968].

Capra, Fritjof; and Steindl-Rast, David. *Belonging to the Cosmos: Explorations on the Frontiers of Science and Spirituality.* With Thomas Matus. San Francisco: HarperSanFrancisco, 1991.

Carson, D. A.; Moo, Douglas J.; and Morris, Leon. *An Introduction to the New Testament.* Grand Rapids: Zondervan Publishing House, 1992.

Bibliography

Greene, Brian. *The Elegant Universe: Superstrings, Hidden Dimensions, and the Quest for the Ultimate Theory.* New York: W. W. Norton & Company, 1999.

Hatch, Edwin and Redpath, Henry A. *A Concordance to the Septuagint and the other Greek Versions of the Old Testament (Including the Apocryphal Books).* Graz, Austria: Akademische Druck-U Verlagsanstalt, 1954.

Hodges, Zane C. *Absolutely Free! A Biblical Reply to Lordship Salvation.* Grand Rapids: Zondervan Publishing House, 1989.

_____. *The Gospel Under Siege.* 2nd ed. Dallas: Redención Viva Publishers, 1992.

_____. *Grace in Eclipse.* 2nd ed. Dallas: Redención Viva Publishers, 1987.

_____and Farstad, Arthur L. *The Greek New Testament According to the Majority Text.* 2nd ed. Nashville: Thomas Nelson Publishers, 1985.

Kennedy, George A. *New Testament Interpretation through Rhetorical Criticism.* Chapel Hill, N.C.: University of North Carolina Press, 1984.

Kittel, Gerhard and Friedrich, Gerhard, eds. *Theological Dictionary of the New Testament,* 10 vols. Translated and edited by Geoffrey W. Bromiley. Grand Rapids: Wm. B. Eerdmans Publishing Co., 1964-76.

Law, Robert. *The Tests of Life: A Study of the First Epistle of St. John.* 3rd ed. Edinburgh: T. & T. Clark, 1914 [reprint ed., Grand Rapids: Baker Book House, 1968].

Lieu, Judith M. *The Second and Third Epistles of John: History and Background.* Edinburgh: T. & T. Clark, 1986.

Metzger, Bruce M. *A Textual Commentary on the Greek New Testament.* 2nd ed. Stuttgart, Germany: Deutsche Bibelgesellschaft and United Bible Societies, 1994.

Moulton, James Hope and Milligan, George. *The Vocabulary of the Greek Testament Illustrated from the Papyri and Other Non-literary Sources.* Grand Rapids: Wm. B. Eerdmans Publishing Co., 1960.

Richards, W. L. *The Classification of the Greek Manuscripts of the Johannine Epistles.* No. 35: Society of Biblical Literature Dissertation Series. Missoula, MT: Scholars Press, 1977.

Robinson, J. A. T. *Redating the New Testament.* Philadelphia: Westminster Press, 1976.

Ross, Hugh. *Beyond the Cosmos.* Colorado Springs: NavPress, 1996.

Scrivener, F. H. A., ed. *The New Testament in the Original Greek according to the Text Followed by The Authorized Version together with the Variations Adopted in The Revised Version,* new ed. Cambridge: University Press, 1894.

Zerwick, Maximilian. *Biblical Greek: Illustrated by Examples.* English edition adapted from the fourth Latin edition by Joseph Smith. Rome: Scripta Pontificii Instituti Biblici, 1963.

III. Periodical Articles

Achtemeier, Paul J. "*Omne Verbum Sonat*: The New Testament and the Oral Environment of Late Western Antiquity," *Journal of Biblical Literature* 109 (1990): 3-27.

Anderson, John and Joy. "Cataphora in 1 John," *Notes on Translation* 7 (1993): 41-46.

Black, D. A. "An Overlooked Stylistic Argument in Favor of *panta* in 1 John 2: 20," *Filologia Neotestamentaria* 5 (1992): 205-208.

Caddock, John. "What Is Contemplative Spirituality and Why Is It Dangerous? A Review of Brennan Manning's *The Signature of Jesus*," *Journal of the Grace Evangelical Society* 10 (1997): 3-25.

Court, John M. "Blessed Assurance?" *Journal of Theological Studies* 33 (1982): 508-17.

Curtis, Edward M. "The First Person Plural in 1 John 2:18-27," *Evangelical Journal* 10 (1992): 27-36.

Custer, Stewart. "The Doctrine of Christ: II John," *Biblical Viewpoint* 27 (1993): 63-65.

Custer, Stewart and Barrett, Michael P. V.; *et al.* "Bibliography on the Epistles of John," *Biblical Viewpoint* 27 (1993): 85-101.

de Jonge, M. "An Analysis of 1 John 1, 1-4," *The Bible Translator* 29 (1978): 323-30.

du Preez, J. "'Sperma Autou' in 1 John 3:9," *Neotestamentica* 9 (1975): 105-12.

Feuillet, André. "The Structure of First John: Comparison with the Fourth Gospel; The Pattern of Christian Life," *Biblical Theology Bulletin* 3 (1973): 194-216.

Francis, Fred O. "The Form and Function of the Opening and Closing Paragraphs of James and 1 John," *Zeitschrift für die Neutestamentliche Wissenschaft* 61 (1970): 110-26.

Grayston, Kenneth. "'Logos' in 1 John 1.1," *Expository Times* 86 (1975): 279.

The Epistles of John

_____. "The meaning of *PARAKLETOS*," *Journal for the Study of the New Testament* 13 (1981): 67-82.

Hodges, Zane C. "Fellowship and Confession in 1 John 1:5-10," *Bibliotheca Sacra* 129 (1972): 48-60.

_____. "Problem Passages in John's Gospel, Part 2: Untrustworthy Believers—John 2:23-25," *Bibliotheca Sacra* 135 (1978): 139-52.

Hoffman, Thomas A. "1 John and the Qumran Scrolls," *Biblical Theology Bulletin* 8 (1978): 117-25.

Kubo, Sakae. "1 John 3:9: Absolute or Habitual?" *Andrews University Seminary Studies* 7 (1969): 47-56.

Leedy, Randy. "The Structure of 1 John," *Biblical Viewpoint* 27 (1993): 11-19.

Lieu, Judith M. "Authority to Become Children of God: *A Study of 1 John*," *Novum Testamentum* 23 (1983): 210-28.

Louw, J. P. "Verbal Aspect in the First Letter of John," *Neotestamentica* 9 (1975): 98-104.

Mazak, Gregory J. "Following the Right Example: III John," *Biblical Viewpoint* 27 (1993): 67-77.

Mitchell, Margaret M. "'Diotrephes Does Not Receive Us': The Lexicographical and Social Context of 3 John 9–10," *Journal of Biblical Literature* 117 (1998): 299-320.

Moody, D. "God's Only Son: The Translation of John 3:16 in the Revised Standard Version," *Journal of Biblical Literature* 72 (1953): 213-19.

Richards, W. Larry. "Test Passages *or* Profiles: A Comparison of Two Text-Critical Methods," *Journal of Biblical Literature* 115 (1996): 251-69.

Bibliography

Robinson, J. A. T. "The Destination and Purpose of the Johannine Epistles," *New Testament Studies* 7 (1960-1961): 56-65.

Storm, Melvin R. "Diotrephes, A Study of Rivalry in the Apostolic Church," *Restoration Quarterly* 35 (1993): 193-202.

Thomas, J. C. "The Order of the Composition of the Johannine Epistles," *Novum Testamentum* 37 (1995): 68-73.

Vorster, W. S. "Heterodoxy in 1 John," *Neotestamentica* 9 (1975): 87-97.

Ward, Tim. "Sin 'Not Unto Death' and Sin 'Unto Death' in 1 John 5:16," *Churchman* 109 (1995): 226-37.

Washburn, David L. "Third Class Conditions in First John," *Grace Theological Journal* 11 (1990): 221-28.

Watson, Duane F. "Amplification Techniques in 1 John: The Interaction of Rhetorical Style and Invention," *Journal for the Study of the New Testament* 51 (1993): 99-123.

Weir, J. Emmette. "The Identity of the Logos in the First Epistle of John," *Expository Times* 86 (1975): 118-19.

The Epistles of John

Introduction

The New Testament epistles that we know as First, Second, and Third John offer us an important glimpse into the life of the early Christian church, particularly as it struggled with teachers of false doctrine. Of the three, the only one which does not focus on false teachers is Third John, where the problem was an apparently orthodox church leader named Diotrephes, who had managed to become the first known church "dictator."

In modern times, however, these epistles have *themselves* been alleged to support a false doctrine. They have been used in this way chiefly for the purpose of teaching that a Christian's assurance of eternal salvation must rest, at least in part, upon his or her good works subsequent to regeneration. Although this doctrine is widely popular today and is spread across many denominational lines, it is in direct conflict with the Gospel of John, written by the same author. For this reason, there is an urgent need that the epistles be re-examined and understood to be consistent with the theology of John's Gospel.

This requires us to challenge many of the assumptions that are the basis of a widespread misreading of these significant epistles. The following Commentary, therefore, is designed not only to expound the meaning of these letters, but also to correct many misapprehensions about them which are current today.

I. Authorship

The author of First John does not mention his name; perhaps it was on the outside of the scroll in which his letter was written. In any case, that the recipients knew from whom the letter had come and the apostolic identity of the author seems apparent from 1:1-4 and 4:6 (see Commentary). Ancient tradition in the main assigns the epistles to John the son of Zebedee, one of the twelve apostles. Although efforts have been made to evade the implication that an eyewitness wrote 1:1-4, these efforts are an attempt to avoid the natural sense of the text. Equally, the statement of 4:6 ("We are of God. He who knows God hears us; he who is not of God does not hear us. By this we know the spirit of truth and the spirit of error") would be pompous, to say the least, if it was not penned by an apostle.

In Second and Third John the writer introduces himself as "the Elder." A theory that traces back to ancient times holds that a statement made by a certain Papias (ca. A.D. 60–ca.130), bishop of Hieropolis in Phrygia, known to both Irenaeus (fl. ca.175–ca.195) and Eusebius (ca. 262–ca.339), differentiates the "elder John" from the apostle of that name. This conclusion, drawn from the quotation of Papias, is highly doubtful, and he can easily be read as giving the title of "elder" to the apostles themselves. The oft-quoted statement is as follows:

> For I have never, like many, delighted to hear those that tell many things, but those that teach the truth, neither those that record foreign precepts, but those that are given from the Lord, to our faith, and that come from the truth itself [a possible allusion to 2 John 12]. But if I met with any one who had been a follower of the elders any where, I made it a point to enquire what were the declarations of the elders. What was said by [Greek: *eipen*] Andrew, Peter or Philip. What by Thomas, James, John, Matthew, or any other of the disciples of our Lord. What was said by [Greek: *legousin*] Aristion, and the presbyter [= elder] John, disciples of the Lord; for I do not think that I derived so much benefit from books as from the living voice of those that are still surviving.[1]

Scholars have often noted the imprecision of this statement. Yet, clearly it is possible to conclude that both the terms "elder" and "disciple of the Lord" could be applied to apostles, and that perhaps both could *not* be applied to the otherwise unknown Aristion, who is only designated as a disciple. This seems quite possibly to be confirmed when Eusebius himself, a little later in this section, repeats Papias's phrase "the declarations of the elders" in the form "the declarations of the apostles."

Eusebius does this despite the fact that he wanted to make "the elder John" a different man and also the author of the Book of Revelation. The change of tense in the Greek text of Papias (as quoted by Eusebius) from *eipen* to *legousin* implies that both Aristion and the elder John were still alive. It is certainly conceivable, though carelessly worded, that Papias mentioned the apostle John twice, once among the other elders, all of whom were now dead, and again as a continuing witness along with Aristion. There is no adequate basis here for Eusebius's guess that a man known as "the Elder John" wrote Revelation. Still less is there a basis for the modern conjecture that this alternative John wrote the epistles. Indeed, Eusebius in the same section informs us that Papias used "testimonies from the first epistle of John."[2]

The efforts made by critical scholarship to find non–apostolic authors for the Fourth Gospel and the epistles are perhaps not surprising, due to scholarship's usual bias against apostolic eyewitness accounts. But the attempt to differentiate the authorship of the Gospel from that of the epistles and even, sometimes, that of First John from Second and Third John, is a stunning display of tunnel vision. It would be hard to find four books anywhere in Greek literature that exhibit a style more likely to stem from one mind than does the style of the Gospel and the epistles. Even the English reader can detect this, but in Greek the impression of a single writer is overwhelming. This being the case, the strong support given by ancient tradition to authorship by John the son of Zebedee for both the Gospel and the epistles should be seen, not as two sets of evidence but as a single voice.[3]

C. H. Dodd was prominent among twentieth-century writers in denying that the epistles and the Gospel were from the same author. But upon examination, the alleged differences that support this authorial diversity appear to be both minuscule and picayune, and do not really affect the overwhelming impression of single authorship upon anyone who reads these documents in the original. The identity of authorship for the Gospel and epistles may be regarded as quite certain, despite the capacity of some New Testament scholars to challenge even the most evident conclusions in the biblical field.

The near unanimity of ancient opinion that the apostle John wrote them must therefore carry its full weight. In the case of the Gospel, internal evidence strongly suggests that the unnamed disciple "whom Jesus loved" must be regarded as the author and that this disciple is John the son of Zebedee. If he is not, the absence of any mention of John in the Gospel is exceedingly hard to explain. In the light of all this, the title

The Epistles of John

"the Elder" (used in Second and Third John) is perhaps simply the author's self-effacing way of saying "the elderly one" or "the old man." (See Paul's reference to himself as "being such an one as Paul, the aged" [more literally, "old man Paul"]: Philemon 9.) The apparent use of the term "elder" by Papias as a designation for the apostles themselves might well have grown out of the apostle's own usage here. On the other hand, it is also possible that "the older ones" (or, "elders") had already become such a designation. If so, the term in Second and Third John could be a claim to apostolic authority. The content of both letters is very suitable to such a claim and this claim would reinforce the admonitions these letters contain. A choice between the two options for the meaning of "the Elder" is difficult to make.

Brown's conclusion about the alleged stylistic differences between the Gospel and epistles is, in itself, fairly devastating:

> Overall, then, it seems that the variation of minute stylistic features between GJohn and 1 John is not much different from the variation that one can find if one compares one part of GJohn to another part. In particular, the Johannine Jesus *speaks* as the author of the Johannine Epistles writes.[4]

This is clear enough, and we might even suppose John picked up to a considerable extent the oral style of his Lord, just as today students in homiletics often pick up the preaching style of their favorite preacher or even of the homiletics professor himself. After all, First John is really a homily in written form, and intended to be read to a congregation.

But Brown is not fully content with this conclusion, since he goes on to say:

> I am persuaded that there is a marked difference between the two works in terms of clarity of expression. Having translated both GJohn and 1 John, I found the first relatively simple while the obscurity of the second was infuriating. If one studies my Notes…where I point out the number of scholars divided over the grammar and meaning of almost every verse in 1 John, one might conclude that, simply from the viewpoint of translating correctly, there are more difficulties in

any two chapters of 1 John than in the whole of the much longer GJohn…Today granted the fact that we know little about the identity or age of the evangelist and/or the epistolary writer, the greater obscurity of the Epistles becomes an argument for difference of authorship.[5]

Hardly. On the contrary, contemporary theological thought is so far out of step with the theology of the Fourth Gospel and the epistles that it is little wonder that the tight didactic style of the latter creates difficulties for interpreters. In any body of literature, empathetic interpreters are always the best. That the First Epistle is not easy, all will no doubt admit. But that the epistle by itself is to blame for Brown's frustration is another matter. John A. T. Robinson gives an extremely able defense (by a liberal writer!) of John the son of Zebedee as the author of all four books.[6]

In conclusion, the implicit claims to apostleship found in 1 John 1:1-4 and 4:6, and the possible claim to this in Second and Third John (i.e., elder = apostle), concurs with our other available data. Thus the authorship of the three Johannine Epistles by John the apostle may be regarded as extremely well supported and incapable of cogent refutation.

II. Audience, Date, and Destination

There are no clear internal indications of the date at which the Johannine Epistles were written. It is likely that they were written after the Fourth Gospel, but this cannot be definitely proved. It is also likely, but unprovable, that they were written before the Book of Revelation.

The date of the Gospel is most likely prior to A.D. 70. As J. A. T. Robinson pointed out in *Redating the New Testament,* if the destruction of the Jewish temple in 70 had already occurred, the Gospel's silence about this is puzzling. More importantly, the statement of John 5:2 that "there is in Jerusalem by the Sheep Gate a pool" argues powerfully that Jerusalem was still standing when the Gospel was written. This is the kind of instinctive statement that one who knew the pool was still there would make. It has been excavated only in modern times. In the light of this, even if the epistles were written after the Fourth Gospel, they could have been written before A.D. 70. A date prior to the outbreak of the Jewish War (A.D. 66–70) seems most likely for the Gospel, since the fear of

The Epistles of John

Roman intervention expressed in John 11:48 has no obvious connection with the events of 66 and following. Indeed, the Gospel could have been written quite a few years before that war.[7]

To the same effect is the consideration of the date of the Book of Revelation. Here especially, Robinson's observations are effective that a silence about the destruction of the Jewish temple is far from likely in this book. In addition, the mention in Revelation 17:10 of five fallen Roman emperors is most naturally taken as referring to Augustus, Tiberius, Caligula, Claudius, and Nero, bringing us to A.D. 68. In that case, Galba was the reigning emperor (cf. "one is" in Revelation 17:10) and Otho would be "the other" who "has not yet come" and "must continue a short time" (Revelation 17:10). Galba ruled from June 68 to January 69 (Otho only until April of 69), so that the date of the Book of Revelation may with some confidence be placed during the period of Galba's rule, i.e., in late 68 or very early 69. The epistles do not seem likely to have been written after Revelation, though nothing definitively excludes this possibility. Still, their stylistic resemblances to the Gospel incline one to date them not too far from the time of that book.

We are thus left with a relatively wide window of time during which the Gospel and epistles might have been written, that is, from within a few years after the resurrection of Christ to the outbreak of the Jewish War in A.D. 66. Before attempting to narrow the date further, we must consider the origin of both the Gospel and epistles.

That John went to Ephesus in later life is widely accepted. According to Eusebius, when the apostles were scattered after the outbreak of the Jewish war, John received Asia as his sphere of ministry, "where, after continuing for some time, he died at Ephesus."[8] According to Irenaeus (fl. ca.175–cca.195), "John, the disciple of the Lord…published the gospel while living at Ephesus in Asia."[9] We have no particular reason to doubt this statement, but we need to ask *when* this might have occurred.

With Robinson,[10] I think Galatians 2:9 is an excellent place to start. There we are told that "when James, Cephas [= Peter], and John, who seemed to be pillars, perceived the grace that had been given to me, they gave me and Barnabas the right hand of fellowship, that we should go to the Gentiles and they to the circumcised." This "new concordat for missionary policy," as Robinson calls it,[11] must in all probability be dated in the late 40s, based on any viable chronology of Paul.

24

We may take A.D. 33 as a firm date for the crucifixion of our Lord, a date that I believe was established in an article by Paul L. Maier entitled, "Sejanus, Pilate, and the Date of the Crucifixion."[12] In order to accommodate the chronological notices found in Galatians 1:18 and 2:1, we should place Paul's conversion no later than A.D. 34. If the fourteen years of Galatians 2:1 are inclusive of the three in 1:18, which seems likely, then this "concordat" took place about A.D. 48. Since the Jerusalem Council (Acts 15) is not mentioned in Galatians, where it certainly seems relevant, an early date for Galatians, prior to the Council, seems necessary—probably A.D. 49.

By A.D. 51, Paul was in Corinth, since the commencement of the proconsulship of Gallio (Acts 18:12) can be dated with considerable confidence to A.D. 51.[13] By this time, the Jerusalem Council was over, and Paul's missionary journey into Europe, recorded in Acts 16:6–18:18, was nearly over. But it is at the *beginning* of this evangelistic incursion into Greece that we are informed that Paul was "forbidden by the Holy Spirit to preach the word in Asia" (Acts 16:6). Why? We are not told.

It seems quite possible, however, that the reason Paul was not allowed to preach in the province of Asia at this time was that the apostle John already had a mission there focused on the Jewish synagogues in Ephesus and elsewhere. Indeed, though it is an argument from silence, the last time John is mentioned as an *actor* in the narrative of Acts is at 8:14, when he joins Peter to visit the converts in Samaria. Peter, we know, was in Antioch shortly after the "concordat" (cf. Galatians 2:11) and had been at Corinth, apparently prior to the writing of First Corinthians (cf. 1:12; 3:22). A trip by John to Asia, in particular Ephesus, prior to 51 cannot be ruled out.

On the whole, it seems that the most likely date for the composition of the Gospel of John at Ephesus (as per Irenaeus) would be somewhere in the period A.D. 48–52. During this time frame, we may suppose that John's own converts were primarily, though not exclusively, drawn from the Jewish population in Asia. Indeed, we might even think of John as the de facto founder of the seven churches of Asia (Revelation 2 and 3). No doubt these early, chiefly Jewish, converts furnished the later Pauline churches with their core membership as well as with the finest prospects for their leadership. When John returned to Jerusalem, or wherever else he might have gone, he left behind his Gospel as an evangelistic tool to be used by his converts with particular, though not exclusive, reference to the Jewish community. The deeply Jewish coloring of the Fourth Gospel is now evident thanks to the finds at Qumran, but these finds have not eliminated the Hellenistic flavor of that book. Composition and publication in Ephesus fits all the internal factors in the Gospel.

At the time of the writing of his First Epistle, our best surmise is that John was now back in Jerusalem with a number of other apostles (cf. 2:19 and Commentary). The antichrists against whom he warns the readers (1 John 2:18ff.) are false teachers who "went out from us" (2:19). That is the same expression used to describe the legalists who are repudiated by the apostles and elders in Acts 15 (see "Since we have heard that some who *went out from us* have troubled you with words…" Acts 15:24; italics added). John already is well acquainted with at least one of the churches addressed (see Second John and Commentary). His paternal concern for them, marked by his repeated term of address, "little children," also suggests that he felt a real pastoral responsibility for these believers. All this comports easily with what has been suggested about John's previous relationship to the churches of Asia, especially Ephesus.

We do not know how much time elapsed between the composition of the Fourth Gospel and the writing of the epistles, which seem often to presuppose the teaching found in the Gospel. But it could well have been quite a few years. In 2 John 12 and 3 John 10 and 14, the apostle clearly seems to think it possible that he might come to the recipients soon. This may well be due to a decision to make another trip in person to this region where he had converts. Alternatively, as suggested in the Commentary, he may have anticipated that the Lord's prophecies about Jerusalem were about to be fulfilled, and that he and the other apostles would soon leave to take up new spheres of ministry (as per Eusebius, cited above). In the latter case, if all three were written at about the same time, the date of the epistles might be in the middle 60s, say 64 to 65. In the former case, they could be quite a bit earlier, even in the middle to late 50s, perhaps even as early as A.D. 55. Robinson's dates for the epistles, in the sequence Second, Third, and First John, are A.D. 60–65.[14]

The phrase "from the beginning" refers to the readers' earliest days in the Christian faith (cf. 1 John 2:7, 24; 3:11; 2 John 6; see Commentary). Therefore, it seems better to assume a longer rather than a shorter interval between the Gospel and the epistles. While admitting that it is a guess,

I prefer a date circa 64 to 65 to an earlier date for these epistles, if they were written at the same time and thus sent out together. Of course, they *could* have been written at separate times, but the concerns of Second John at least are essentially those of First John. (Third John admittedly is different in its focus.)

I believe that First, Second, and Third John were all written from Jerusalem and sent out for delivery by someone headed for the province of Asia, probably Demetrius (3 John 12). First John was a circular letter (hence no specific addressees are mentioned), and was intended to be passed around the circuit of churches for which John felt special responsibility, perhaps the seven churches of Asia. It is even possible that First John might have actually been intended for the leaders of the various churches to which it went. There are indeed indications within the epistle (2:12-14; 2:20; see Commentary) that the readership is regarded as spiritually mature. In that case, the First Epistle was intended to fortify the leaders who would bear the major burden of resisting the false teachers. At the same time, John would have expected the letter to be read to the congregation(s) and, when that was done, the apostle's expression of confidence in the competence of the leaders would enhance the esteem in which the believers held them. It would strengthen their hand against the false teachers. (For additional comments on this possibility, see the Commentary.)

Second John is a cover letter intended for one of these churches, probably Ephesus, with which John was well acquainted (cf. verses 1, 4). Third John is a personal letter to Demetrius's hoped-for host, Gaius, who stands at the end of his journey.

Demetrius's route of travel could be essentially the reverse of Paul's journey from Ephesus to Jerusalem, described in Acts 18:21-22. From Jerusalem he would go down to Caesarea where he could find a suitable ship headed for the Ionian coast (modern Turkey) on which Ephesus lay. Of course, a slower ship with several stops might be financially more feasible (cf. Paul's voyage from Miletus, south of Ephesus, to Caesarea: Acts 21:1-8). Once he arrived at Ephesus, he would drop off First and Second John and proceed onward to the house of Gaius, probably in another locality in Asia. This locality was likely inland from Ephesus since, if he was an evangelist, Demetrius would have been looking for a field less well plowed with the gospel than Ephesus was. (Paul who came later than John, had spent two years in that city: Acts 19:10.) Though the word had been widely disseminated in Asia (Acts 19:10), after an interval of perhaps at least a decade since Paul's mission in that province, there was plenty for Demetrius to do.

This reconstruction, of course, must remain conjectural, even though it seems to account for all the facts available to us. But fortunately, such is the content of John's letters, that we do not need to know the precise scenario surrounding their composition and destination in order to profit greatly from their message.

III. Early History of the Epistles

The limitations on our specific knowledge of the original destinations of First, Second, and Third John make it impossible to say much about the history of their circulation. The ancient evidence suggests that First John was more widely known than Second and Third John at the earliest stages of their history. But this is natural, given the size and general character of First John over against the brevity and more specific character of the other epistles.

In fact, if First John *was* a circular letter delivered to several churches in succession, it would be natural for it to be copied by most or all of these churches, from which other copies would be made as occasion dictated. Hence, First John probably got off to a rather rapid circulation, at least in the area of the Greco-Roman world to which it was first sent, most likely the Roman province of Asia which is now western Turkey. In contrast, Second and Third John might have remained in the hands of the original recipients for some time, perhaps even until an interest in collecting the apostolic writings arose.

We need not suppose, however, that such an interest developed only in the second century or later, as some have thought. On the contrary, Second Peter shows us that in all probability a collection of Pauline writings already existed in Peter's day (2 Peter 3:16). Of course, liberal New Testament scholars almost universally deny the authenticity of Second Peter, but the grounds for this rejection are quite subjective and far from compelling. Without arguing the case here, I take the authenticity of Peter's second letter for granted. Thus, Peter himself is a witness to an early interest in collecting the inspired writings, and we may appropriately surmise that the spread of John's Gospel and his first epistle might themselves stimulate a search for any other writings from his pen. No doubt the church addressed in Second John, and Gaius who received Third John, were only too pleased to provide copies once this search was underway.

But hidden as are these earliest movements of our three epistles, the fact remains that they have come down to us in approximately 600 Greek manuscripts of varying ages. A papyrus fragment of First John (with text 4:11-12, 14-17) is located in the Houghton Library at Harvard University and is known by the designation $\mathbf{P}^9$. Dated by Kurt Aland as from the third century A.D., it is perhaps the oldest surviving portion of John's First Epistle.

The standard editions of the Greek New Testament (Nestle-Aland [27th ed.] and UBS [4th ed.]) present a text of the three epistles which frequently differs in details from the form of text exhibited by a large majority of the surviving Greek manuscripts. As is well known, these editions prefer the form of text found in the ancient Egyptian uncial manuscripts, written in what are now called capital letters. Chief among these in the Johannine Epistles are Codex Sinaiticus (Aleph, 4th century), Codex Alexandrinus (A, 5th century), and Codex Vaticanus (B, 4th century), all three of which contain the entirety of John's three Epistles. Modern translations like NASB, NIV, NRSV, JB, etc., tend to follow the text found in these mss. But a very large percentage of the surviving minuscule or small letter manuscripts exhibit the type of Greek text which underlies the KJV and the NKJV.

A major study of the surviving manuscripts of the Johannine Epistles has been undertaken by W. L. Richards and published in his book, *The Classification of the Greek Manuscripts of the Johannine Epistles*.[15] Out of a total of some 600 manuscripts containing these epistles, in whole or in part, Richards selected eighty-one for thorough investigation and he feels confident that these "adequately represent the total number."[16] We have often cited his data in our notes where we are discussing textual problems in the epistles.

As the late Dr. Arthur Farstad and I argued in our edition of the Greek New Testament,[17] a case can be made that we should prefer the large majority of extant manuscripts. These represent one text form. Their large number indicates a high probability that this text form is more ancient and closer to the original than rival text forms found in a much smaller number of documents. Thus, the readings of this ancient, majority text form, are to be generally preferred to those represented in smaller numbers of manuscripts, even when some of the rival manuscripts themselves are of older date than the majority representatives. But our view is *not* that we must merely count manuscripts. Instead, we maintain that final decisions on some matters in the original text of the New Testament books must be made on the basis of genealogical work of the type we have already attempted in the Book of Revelation. Significant interaction from the larger scholarly community in regard to this central feature of our textual position has been slow in coming. This may in part be due to the contrary assumptions made by most scholars in regard to textual criticism. But no field progresses when it is stifled by premises which its practitioners refuse to reexamine.

Where necessary, therefore, I have discussed significant differences between the text of First, Second, and Third John adopted in the Hodges/Farstad edition, and the rival text in the critical editions. This is not done exhaustively because this book is a commentary, not a text-critical study. When I do discuss textual issues, it is my practice to give reasons, other than mere numbers, why one might prefer the majority reading.

But such discussions have a simple background premise: it is easier to understand why a spurious reading (rather than an original reading) is found in only a small number of documents. The normal transmission of manuscript texts usually results in later, spurious readings being found in fewer manuscripts than the older, original readings. To reverse this and say that the original readings are more often found in a smaller number of manuscripts than spurious readings presupposes a highly abnormal transmission of the text. Though Westcott and Hort argued in the nineteenth century for their famous "Syrian" recension of the New Testament text, this theory of abnormal transmission has found little or nothing to support it in twentieth century text-critical study, especially in the last few decades. The sooner this or similar theories are totally discarded, the better.

The English text in this commentary is the New King James Version.

IV. Literary Character

The Epistles of Second and Third John are clearly letters, although Second John employs the metaphor of a woman and her children as a literary device for addressing a church and its members (see Purpose below). First John, on the other hand, is not, strictly speaking, a personal letter, but the traditional designation "epistle" is suitable, since this genre of literature can be regarded as covering what we might call today a treatise, discussion, or even a sermon on a theological or moral theme.

Many writers have despaired of finding any kind of "ground plan" in First John. Typically, Leedy has written:

> The most helpful suggestions regarding the structure of 1 John begin by setting down the fact that John does not develop a careful scheme of logical reasoning. Any attempt to find a line of argumentation building one point upon the proof of another is doomed to fail. First John simply does not develop its ideas argumentatively, as most of the other epistles do. Walter Conner has expressed this fact most strikingly by observing that John's thought processes resemble those of a woman more than those of a man.[18]

This frustration is unwarranted. Although it is obvious that the author does not deploy the wide range of connective words so common in Paul's writings, this does not mean that no scheme or ground plan underlies the composition of First John. On the contrary, what we know today about the rhetoric taught and practiced in the Greco-Roman world inclines me to think that John did think in structural terms about his epistle.

We may profitably consider the general structure that might be used by a "deliberative orator" in the world of John's day, as described by George A. Kennedy.[19] It must always be remembered that the New Testament epistles were designed to be read aloud in the gatherings of believers and thus are functionally sermonic in character. Thus First John might with real reason be regarded as a "speech" set down in writing. Obviously the apostles spoke more than they wrote. They would naturally be concerned about how their epistles were "heard" by the congregations addressed (1 Timothy 4:13, "Till I come, give attention to *reading,* to exhortation, to doctrine" [italics added]). Thus Kennedy's outline of the parts of an address may be considered as a possible structural approach to First John.

The parts of a deliberative oration, as described by Kennedy, are a formal "proem" or preface, followed by the "proposition, proposal, or thesis of the speaker." This is followed by supporting material in the form of the "central body of the speech." This "body" is called "the 'headings' (*kephalaia*) since the orator often groups his arguments to demonstrate that the action he supports is possible and that it will be expedient, or just, or honorable, or consistent with the values of the audience, or the only possible course of action."[20] This in turn is followed by an "epilogue" which "in classical theory" was primarily used "to recapitulate the points the speaker had made and to arouse the emotions of the audience to action." Also helpful in analyzing First John's structure is Fred O. Francis's study of the "double form" of epistolary openings in Hellenistic letters.[21]

The general format that seems to have been in the apostle's mind, as he composed his epistle, is not a slavish reproduction of the one presented by Kennedy. Instead, we seem to stand within the broad parameters of recognized stylistic conventions, making oral comprehension of the letter easier for its hearers when it was read in church meetings.

What we have called a Prologue (1:1-4; see under Outline) may be considered, in Kennedy's terms, a formal "proem," which takes the place of the expected epistolary greeting (as found in James 1:1). The Prologue announces the subject matter and its goal: fellowship with God. There follows an extended section that elaborates on the nature of fellowship with God. I have called this section a Preamble (1:5–2:11). Though in Kennedy's analysis, proem and preface are interchangeable terms, it is not going too far to say that First John exhibits both a proem (prologue) *and* a preface (introduction). In form, this introduction closely resembles James's introduction to the theme of "trials" in James 1:2-18 (a fact not noted by Francis in the *ZNW* article mentioned above). Like James's own introduction, John's has a twofold division (1 John 1:5–2:2 and 2:3-11; cf. James 1:2-11 and 12-18).

The section that follows 1 John 2:11 may be regarded as roughly parallel to the orator's proposition or proposal and covers verses 12-27 (called Purpose in my outline). Here for the first time the apostolic author discloses the reason he is writing, in terms of his specific concerns.

The apostle does not write because of any perceived deficiency in his readers (2:12-14), but because of the ever-present danger of being seduced by the world and its representatives, the antichrists (2:15-27). His bottom line in this unit is that the readers should continue in the truth as they were originally taught it and thus continue their fellowship with the Father and the Son (2:27).

The central body of the epistle, corresponding to the headings in Kennedy's scheme, is found in 2:28–4:19 (called Body in my outline). This turns out to be a carefully structured unit leading the reader to the pinnacle of experience in the abiding life of fellowship. As suggested in the Commentary itself, 2:28 serves as a thematic statement for the body of John's letter. But it could almost equally be argued that it is a thematic proposal for the entire letter for which the sections on fellowship with God (1:5–2:2) and on the dangers of the antichrists (2:12-27) have prepared the way. If so taken, 2:28 is roughly parallel to the theme statement found in James 1:19-20. For purposes of outlining I have elected to include the verse within the epistle's core section. But I do so with some diffidence, which is always appropriate when dealing with hinge verses that seem to refer backward as well as forward.

First John 4:20–5:17 is a unit whose flow of thought can be easily traced and it has been called Conclusion in this Commentary. As in the scheme presented by Kennedy, John's conclusion has clear elements of recapitulation while driving home both the urgency and the viability of obedient action. I have reserved the term Epilogue for the final unit, 5:18-21. In terms of size, this section is comparable to the Prologue, and both Prologue and Epilogue are marked by the knowledge/experience of a collective subject ("we"). Thus the Epilogue, by virtue of these resemblances to the Prologue, imparts to the epistle a feeling of balance and completeness.

The opinion so often stated in the past, that John lacks clear development and structure in his first epistle, turns out, upon careful examination, to be unfounded. The final proof of this must be in the Commentary itself, of course. Nevertheless, I have no hesitation in saying that the author of First John was a man whose simplicity of language in no way indicates that his concepts and thought structure were simplistic. On the contrary, no book of the New Testament—not even Romans—has been structured with more care than the Epistle of First John.

V. Purpose

In First John the apostle writes out of a concern that certain false teachers may be given a hearing in the church or churches he is addressing. Since they essentially deny the fundamental truth of the Christian faith, namely, that Jesus is the Christ come in flesh (1 John 2:22; 4:3), their doctrine strikes right at the heart of all Christian experience. The readers, who are clearly Christians themselves (2:12-14, 21; 5:13), are therefore not in danger of losing eternal life—which cannot be lost—but are in danger of having their fellowship with God the Father and with Jesus Christ His Son seriously undermined. Thus, the stated general aim of the epistle is *fellowship* (1 John 1:3).

In the process of discussing the terms, conditions, and experiences connected with genuine fellowship with God, the apostle also takes time at appropriate points to deal with the false teachers and their fellowship-threatening doctrines. Thus, a statement of purpose for First John could also include the thought that he writes to sustain and promote fellowship with God in the face of the theological errors that constitute an attack on this fellowship.

In the past it was often suggested that the false doctrine in view in First John was so-called Gnosticism. But since our knowledge of Gnosticism is largely dependent upon sources later than First John itself, this is a somewhat precarious proposition. If one wishes to postulate a kind of pre-gnostic Gnosticism, this might be true, but we would still have to look to First John itself for any real knowledge of the heresies John seeks to refute. In this regard, it is not always clear in First John whether the false statements condemned can be positively ascribed to the errorists or whether they simply represent false ideas which are common enough among Christian people.

What we *can* say about the errorists of First John is that they denied that Jesus was the Christ who had come in flesh. Exactly what form this denial took is not absolutely clear, but the statements in 1 John 5:6-8 suggest the possibility of an error similar to the one ascribed in ancient Christian literature to a certain Cerinthus, who is presented as an adversary of the apostle John at Ephesus. Cerinthus is said to have held that the man Jesus and the divine Christ were two distinct beings, and that the Christ descended on Jesus at His baptism, but left Him prior to His death.

Thus the divine Christ might be said to have come "by water" but not "by blood" (see 5:6 and Commentary). The denial that Jesus was the Christ may have involved a division of His Person into two distinct beings, in order to divide His experiences and assign some to the human person only.

If this were the case, it would imply that some aspects, at least, of physical experience were considered by the false teachers to be inappropriate or meaningless for a divine being. This may have involved the concept that any real physical contact with such a being was also impossible and that people could have contact only with the human Jesus. If this claim was made, it is denied in 1:1-4 where the apostles are said to have had physical contact with "that *eternal life* which was with the Father and was manifested to us" (1:2, italics added).

It would be a small step from a doctrine like this to a general rejection of the importance of God's commands related to physical experience. Thus prohibitions against immorality, for example, might be dismissed as of no concern to those with "spiritual insight" who realized the separation between the divine, or spiritual, realm and the realm of physical experience. John's apparent concern that the commandments of the Lord should be taken seriously would thus be relevant to any such teaching as this (1 John 2:3, 4, 7; 3:23; 4:21; 5:2-3). The errorists could have affirmed, for example, that the *spiritual* person did not actually commit sin when he was involved in immorality, since he was fundamentally above or separate from all physical experience.

Particularly relevant is the final command of the epistle: "Little children, keep yourselves from idols" (5:21). As the letters to the seven churches in Revelation reveal, the problem of Christian compromise with pagan idolatrous practices was very much alive in these churches (Revelation 2:14, 20). The cultural situation made such compromise particularly seductive. Artisans, for example, might belong to a particular guild that had a specific pagan god as its patron. Guild meetings could be held in the idol's temple and such feasts often featured the availability of meat offered to idols as well as the opportunity for immorality with temple prostitutes. A Christian who refused to attend such meetings might well fear expulsion from his guild and the loss of his means of livelihood. Any doctrine rationalizing participation in such activities could well attract adherents.

The Epistles of John

The climactic place that the command of 5:21 has at the very end of the epistle strongly suggests that the heresy John was combating did, in fact, tolerate, or even encourage, some form of compromise with pagan practices. The indications within the epistle suggest that the rationalization for this involved a carefully articulated distinction between the physical and spiritual realms.

This also leads to the observation that the text of First John contains hints that the apostle is combating a view of God that allowed for *both light and darkness* as part of the divine nature. For example, when John writes, "God is light and in Him is no darkness at all" (1:5), the Greek statement about "no darkness" is emphatic, as the English words "at all" rightly suggest. Again, at 2:29 where John writes, "If you know that He is righteous…" he uses a Greek conditional form that does not take such knowledge for granted. One might almost say in English, "If you know (though some do not) that He is righteous…"

This suggests that the false teachers may have taught that ultimately both good and evil, light and darkness originated with God Himself. For this assertion they may have found support from a statement like Isaiah 45:7, "I form the light and create darkness: I make peace and create evil. I the Lord do all these things" (KJV). (For the probable Jewishness of the false teachers, see below.) From that base, the errorists could claim that the Divine Being had experience of both good and evil, and thus human participation in His spiritual nature could involve participation in what seemed like "good" or "evil" from an unenlightened point of view. Indeed, some such idea as this appears to lie behind the discussion of the sinlessness of the regenerate person's nature, which is found in the famous text in 3:6-9 (see Commentary).

John also stresses the idea of "original truth," and repeatedly uses the phrase "from the beginning" in connection with what Christians were taught or believed (see 1:1; 2:7; 2:24; 3:11). Although the doctrines of the errorists involved denials of previously revealed truth (e.g., 2:22), it seems certain that they did not simply deny Christianity in its totality, but rather reinterpreted Christian history and doctrine. This is most evident in a text like 5:6, where it is natural to infer that in some sense they held that Jesus Christ came "by water" (baptism) but denied that He came "by blood" as well (see reference to Cerinthus above). For this reason these false teachers are often referred to in the Commentary as "the Revisionists," those who brought a *new version* of Christianity.

I have refrained from calling them Gnostics because there is no trace of the later Gnostic mythologies in First John (with the possible exception of the reference to Cain, in 3:12). It is conceivable that the false teachers could be called Proto-Gnostics, but in the present state of our knowledge, the term *Revisionists* seems more appropriate. I admit to being influenced here by Brown's term for the antichrists, whom he calls "secessionists" based on 2:19.[22] But this commentary takes a different view of 2:19 (see next paragraph; see also the Commentary discussion), and the word Revisionists seems more appropriate. Nevertheless, I do not wish to deny that they probably reflected some of the concepts that were formative in later Gnostic thought.

It is also important to note that the false teachers evidently were at one time connected with the apostolic circle. This is by far the most natural reading of 2:19 where a "they-us-you" sequence begins (for the "you," see 2:20; and see Commentary for fuller discussion). If, as we suggest under Date, the epistles were written in the 60s (or even in the 50s), the Jerusalem church was still very much alive and influential, being as it was, the Mother Church. Naturally, false teachers who wished their doctrines to be heard in the churches among the Gentiles would be only too glad to claim connections with the Mother Church. Indeed, the legalists who came to Antioch from Judea (Acts 15:1) apparently made such claims, which the apostles and elders at Jerusalem felt compelled to deny (Acts 15:24). From 2:19 we can infer similar claims by the false teachers, and 1 John 2:19 is an apostolic denial of these.

Although the complete theology of the antichrists cannot be reconstructed from the Johannine Epistles, the hints that First John affords us about their doctrine are both interesting and timely. At present there is a movement gathering momentum, one related to so-called "contemplative spirituality," in which Roman Catholic and Buddhist mysticism are merged. Within this system of thought, Jesus is stripped of His uniqueness as "the only begotten" Son of God and is ascribed a divinity which in character is no different than the divinity belonging to all men. According to this perspective, each and every individual is "one" with God and Jesus simply realized this oneness to a greater degree than others. He is thus not *the Christ* in the Johannine sense of mankind's one and only Savior (John 1:29; 4:42).

The literature being produced by this "new wave," sometimes called New Age II, is copious. It tends to regard the ancient Gnostics as wrongly marginalized by an increasingly Hellenized Christianity. It is not at all accidental that a periodical that reflects this new system is called *Gnosis: A Journal of the Western Inner Tradition,* published quarterly by the Lumen Foundation in San Francisco.

It is striking that this system has a place for "darkness" as the contemplative person meditates wordlessly and reaches down into the darkness of his own inner self in search of a rediscovery of his oneness with Ultimate Reality from which humanity has become estranged. Man's "fall" is the loss of a realization of this oneness, while his "salvation" is "enlightenment" in the sense of a renewed realization of his union with God and with the cosmos. Western rationalism is said to have corrupted the immediacy taught by the great masters of the inner life, such as Jesus and Buddha, and to have created antinomies, like good and evil, which hinder humanity's experience of unity with one another and with the cosmos. Among the seminal thinkers identified with this general movement are Teilhard de Chardin, Thomas Merton, Fritjof Capra, David Steindl-Rast, Thich Nhat Hanh, Matthew Fox, Beatrice Bruteau, and many others.[23]

Such ideas could easily form the basis of a universal synthesis of mankind's religions (an undertaking its practitioners acknowledge). It could clearly also become the basis for the new world religion sponsored by the Man of Sin, the Beast of Revelation 13:1-10 (2 Thessalonians 2:3-12) and by the False Prophet (Revelation 13:11-17). Since this latter figure is best understood as the Antichrist referred to by John (see 2:18 and Commentary), it would be ironic if the contemporary system closest to the false doctrine of the "many antichrists" (2:18) should turn out to be the final form of religious deception. As Paul states it, this is "the lie" men will be deluded into believing when the Man of Sin appears (2 Thessalonians 2:11-12).

Like First John itself, Second John is chiefly concerned with the Revisionists, or antichrists. At first glance, Second John might seem like a personal letter, but by most commentators today it is taken as written to a particular Christian church which is personified under the designation of "the elect lady." (For such personifications in biblical times, see the Commentary discussion.) The address itself has been treated in various ways: (1) "To the lady Electa," taking Electa (Greek: *eklectē*) as a proper name. But then it is odd to find this word repeated in verse 13 in the phrase "your elect sister," so that the term in verses 1 and 13 is most likely an adjective, "elect," in both verses (two sisters, both named Electa, is hardly likely). (2) "To the elect Kyria," taking the word for "lady" (Greek: *kyria*) as a proper name. Though Kyria is known as a proper name, the absence of an article before the word "elect" in Greek seems unnatural for this proposed meaning. (3) "To an elect lady" (something like "dear lady"), assuming that no proper name is included. But this is contrary to the usage of Third John in which not only the recipient is named (Gaius, verse 1), but also two other individuals are mentioned by name (Diotrephes, verse 9, and Demetrius, verse 12). Although John claims to know this lady's "children" (verses 1, 4) and her sister (verse 13), none of these is named in Second John.

The fluctuation between second person singular and plural verbs in Second John also argues that "the elect lady" is a personification. If a real woman and her children are addressed, why is only the woman addressed in verse 5, "And now I plead with you [singular], lady, not as though I wrote a new commandment to you [singular]..."? Isn't the command relevant for the children, too? But then immediately, in verse 6, the apostle speaks of "...the commandment, that as you [plural] have heard from the beginning..." Similarly, why does he say, verse 12, "having many things to write to you [plural]," whereas he says, verse 13, "The children of your [singular] elect sister greet you [singular]"? Why do not these "children" also greet the elect lady's children who would be their cousins? And why do only the children of the elect sister greet the elect lady? Is the sister away? Is she dead? But all such questions vanish when we understand "lady" as a corporate designation for a church, and the "children" as the members of that church. John simply shifts from singular to plural because either way he is referring to the entire body of believers. The "elect sister" is then obviously a "sister church," no doubt the one from which John writes. Since, as I suggest above, this was probably the Jerusalem church, it is a gracious touch that this famous "mother" church should be regarded by John as simply the "sister" of the congregation he is addressing.

The view that the elect lady is the *whole* Christian church falters on the obvious question of the identity of her "sister."[24]

Finally, Third John is a personal letter. There is no hint of doctrinal problems in this epistle, and Diotrephes seems nothing more than the first known church tyrant in Christian history. But this epistle is all the more important for its uniqueness in addressing a problem which has replicated itself in Christian history too many times to count.

Given the invaluable insight into Christian experience afforded by First John, and the warnings against even seeming complicity with false teachers in Second John, Third John caps a trio of letters which we could not afford to be without. Containing only seven chapters as they do, these chapters are still among the most challenging in the Bible.

Outline of First John

I. PROLOGUE: THE CALL TO FELLOWSHIP (1:1-4)

II. PREAMBLE: LIVING IN FELLOWSHIP WITH GOD (1:5–2:11)
   A. Staying on the Path: Walking in God's Light (1:5–2:2)
   B. Reaching the Goal: Knowing the God of Light (2:3-11)

III. PURPOSE: THE READERS MUST RESIST THE ANTICHRISTS (2:12-27)
   A. By Recognizing Their Spiritual Assets (2:12-14)
   B. By Recognizing Their Spiritual Adversaries (2:15-27)
      1. Resisting the World (2:15-17)
      2. Resisting the Antichrists (2:18-27)

IV. BODY OF THE EPISTLE: THE LIFE THAT LEADS TO BOLDNESS BEFORE CHRIST'S JUDGMENT SEAT (2:28–4:19)
   A. The Theme Verse: Abide to Be Bold (2:28)
   B. By Learning to See God's Children (2:29–3:10a)
   C. By Learning to See Christian Love (3:10b-23)

1. What Love Is Not (3:10b-15)
2. What Love Is (3:16-18)
3. What Love Does for Believers (3:19-23)
D. By Learning to See the God of Love (3:24–4:16)
   1. God's Indwelling Affirmed (3:24)
   2. God's Spirit Recognized (4:1-6)
   3. God's Indwelling Recognized (4:7-16)
E. Conclusion: Having Boldness at the Judgment Seat (4:17-19)

V. CONCLUSION: LEARNING HOW TO LIVE
OBEDIENTLY (4:20–5:17)
   A. What Loving Our Brothers Means (4:20–5:3a)
   B. What Actually Empowers Our Love (5:3b-15)
   C. What Faith and Love Can Do for Our Brother (5:16-17)

VI. EPILOGUE: CHRISTIAN CERTAINTIES (5:18-21)

Outline of Second John

I. SALUTATION (1-3)

II. BODY OF THE LETTER: PROTECTING THE TRUTH BY
REJECTING ERROR (4-11)
   A. Practice the Truth as Originally Given (4-6)
   B. Protect Your Work by Rejecting Error (7-11)

III. FAREWELL (12-13)

Outline of Third John

I. SALUTATION (1)

II. BODY OF THE LETTER: UPHOLDING THE
    TRUTH BY SUPPORTING ITS REPRESENTATIVES
    (2-12)
    A. Commendation of Gaius's Walk in the Truth (2-4)
    B. Encouragement of Gaius's Support for Those Who Proclaim
        the Truth (5-8)
    C. Exhortation to Continue This Support in Regard to
        Demetrius (9-12)

III. FAREWELL (13-14)

ENDNOTES

[1]Eusebius, *H.E.* 3.39.

[2]Ibid.

[3]For data, see the survey of this evidence in D. A. Carson; Douglas J. Moo; and Leon Morris, *An Introduction to the New Testament* (Grand Rapids: Zondervan Publishing House, 1992), pp. 139-43, 446-50.

[4]Raymond E. Brown, *The Epistles of John,* AB (Garden City, NY: Doubleday, 1982), p. 24.

[5]Brown, *Epistles,* pp. 24-25.

[6]John A. T. Robinson, *Redating the New Testament* (Philadelphia: Westminster Press, 1976), pp. 254-311.

[7]Ibid.

[8]Eusebius, *H.E.* 3.1.

[9]Irenaeus, *Adversus haereses* 3.1.1.

[10]Robinson, *Redating,* p. 304.

[11]Ibid.

[12]Paul L. Maier, *Church History* 37 (1968): 3-13.

[13]F. F. Bruce, *The Acts of the Apostles: The Greek Text with Introduction and Commentary.* 2nd ed. (Grand Rapids: Wm. B. Eerdmans Publishing Co., 1952), p. 346.

[14] Robinson, *Redating*, p. 307.

[15] W. L. Richards, *The Classification of the Greek Manuscripts of the Johannine Epistles*. No. 35: Society of Biblical Literature Dissertation Series (Missoula, MT: Scholars Press, 1977).

[16] Ibid., p. 13. See also his "Test Passages *or* Profiles: A Comparison of Two Text-Critical Methods," *JBL* 115 (1996): 251-69.

[17] Zane C. Hodges and Arthur L. Farstad, *The Greek New Testament According to the Majority Text*, 2nd ed. (Nashville: Thomas Nelson Publishers, 1985), pp. ix-xliv.

[18] Randy Leedy, "The Structure of I John," *BV* 27(1993): 13.

[19] George A. Kennedy, *New Testament Interpretation through Rhetorical Criticism* (Chapel Hill, NC: University of North Carolina Press, 1984).

[20] Ibid., p. 48.

[21] Fred O. Francis, "The Form and Function of the Opening and Closing Paragraphs of James and 1 John," *ZNW* 61 (1970): 110-26.

[22] See Brown's discussion in *Epistles*, pp. 69-115.

[23] For a typical expression of the system summarized above, cf. Fritjof Capra and David Steindl-Rast, *Belonging to the Cosmos: Explorations on the Frontiers of Science and Spirituality* (San Francisco: HarperSanFrancisco, 1991). For an effective conservative critique, see John Caddock, "What Is Contemplative Spirituality and Why Is It Dangerous? A Review of Brennan Manning's *The Signature of Jesus*," *Journal of the Grace Evangelical Society* 10 (1997): 3-25.

[24] For a review of the whole problem of the address, see Brown, *Epistles*, pp. 651-55.

The First Epistle of John

Abiding in the Truth Produces
Confidence at His Coming

CHAPTER 1

The Call to Fellowship

(1 John 1:1-4)

I. PROLOGUE: THE CALL TO FELLOWSHIP (1:1-4)

> **¹That which was from the beginning, which we have heard, which we have seen with our eyes, which we have looked upon, and our hands have handled, concerning the Word of life—**

The apostle John begins with a prologue that announces both the subject matter and the purpose of his letter. The subject matter is clearly stated in the opening verse.

The original word translated "**concerning**" (Greek: *peri*) was often used to introduce topics of discussion (1 Corinthians 7:1, 25; 8:1, 4; 12:1; 16:1; 1 Thessalonians 5:1). That is exactly what John's opening verse does. The apostle is going to talk about **that which was from the beginning…concerning the Word of life**.[1]

It is significant that this original information is neither vague nor uncertain. On the contrary, what **was from the beginning** has the support of firsthand observation and experience. This original information has been **heard, seen, looked upon,** and **handled**. And this was not done by John alone, but by a group with which he associates himself in the repeated use of the word **we**.

If the traditional authorship by John, the son of Zebedee is accepted (see Introduction), then the obvious reference of the **we** is to the apostolic circle of witnesses who were designated for this role by the Lord Jesus Christ Himself (see Acts 1:8, 21; 3:15; 5:32, etc.).[2] To be part of this select group of witnesses, one had to have been in the company of the disciples from the very beginning of our Lord's public ministry (Acts 1:21). Thus the writer here is linking himself with these specially chosen witnesses whose testimony goes back to **the beginning** of the Christian revelation (see also Mark 1:1).

As the author will later show us, he is concerned about a group of professed teachers who are Revisionists. Their message does not accord with the truths originally manifested to the apostolic circle of witnesses. If the readers were to adopt any of the distinctive doctrines brought by these men, it would destroy their fellowship with the apostolic circle and with God (verse 3).[3]

It is important to notice that the apostle does not begin with the phrase, *He who was from the beginning* but **that which was from the beginning**. The impersonal form is deliberate.[4] To be sure, he is thinking of the Lord Jesus as the One who was **heard, seen, looked upon,** and **handled**. But the *Person* of Christ, per se, is not his theme here. Rather his theme is "that eternal life which was with the Father and was manifested to us" (verse 2). Of course Jesus *is* "the true God and eternal life" (5:20). But the apostle wishes to stress the realities that concern eternal life itself. This is a life which his readers share (see 5:13 and discussion there). They cannot lose this life, of course, but they can certainly lose the experience and enjoyment of it. If they are beguiled by the Revisionists, that is exactly what they *will* lose.

John does not want this to happen. His epistle will therefore stress the truths about eternal life which have been revealed in and by the Lord Jesus. The reaffirmation of these truths is the key to ongoing fellowship with the apostolic circle and with the Father and the Son (verse 3). The readers must "let that abide in [them] which [they] heard from the beginning" (2:24a). If that happens, then they "also will abide in the Son and in the Father" (2:24b).

It is often forgotten in our day that revealed truth is the basis for all fellowship with God and for true fellowship with one another. One who departs from the original truths which the Lord revealed to His appointed witnesses will by so much depart from true fellowship with God. God will not have fellowship with a lie or with any form of spiritual darkness (1:5-6).

Therefore, it is vital to John that the readers maintain their commitment to what has been made known **from the** very **beginning…concerning the Word of life.**

The phrase **the Word of life** in this verse would be better read as "the word of life" or even as "the word of Life." Commentators need to resist the temptation to interpret this text by analogy with John 1:1. It is clear from verse 2 that the subject matter is not "word" but "life." Thus the phrase **concerning the word of life** means "concerning the message about life." As Raymond Brown observes, "The numerical use of *logos* in the Johannine writings overwhelmingly favors 'message' (some 25 times), not a personified Word."[5] But since Jesus Christ Himself is that life (5:20), we might also say it means "concerning the message about *Life.*" In all likelihood John did not distinguish these two meanings, since eternal life itself cannot be effectively distinguished from God's Son who *is* Eternal Life!

It would be difficult to stress too much the importance of getting the subject matter of First John clearly in mind. The incarnate life of Christ on earth definitely forms the core of the truth that John is addressing. But the specific, historical details of that life are not under consideration in this epistle. In fact, a major contrast between the Gospel and the epistle is precisely the absence of historical information from the latter. Instead, in this letter, John is addressing precisely those principles of the earthly life of our Savior, which are to find recapitulation in the life of his Christian readers. As he will show us, when Christians truly experience this life, there is a sense in which Jesus Himself—the *Life*—is once again "reincarnated" among them!

> **[2]The life was manifested, and we have seen, and bear witness, and declare to you that eternal life which was with the Father and was manifested to us—**

The New King James Version (hereafter, NKJV) leaves untranslated the Greek word *kai* that begins this verse. John is fond of this word and his frequent use of it no doubt reflects his Hebraic background. But it does not follow from this that his usage is stereotyped and meaningless. As an author he seems well aware of the flexibility of the Greek *kai* (just as the Hebrew equivalent, *waw*, is equally flexible). In the present verse the initial *kai* most likely has an ascensive force[6] and could be translated "and indeed." John emphatically asserts the manifestation of the divine life (or, Life) to which he and the other apostles can give firsthand testimony. The reality of the incarnate Life is, for these witnesses, beyond question.

The word **manifested**, used twice here, is an important word for John. It occurs a total of nine times in this brief epistle. (Its final use, in 4:9, comes at a climax point in this letter.) The word is skillfully chosen for the writer's purposes, since eternal life can be "manifested" in more than one way. Historically it was **manifested** in the life, death and resurrection of the incarnate Son of God. But John wants to show his readers how it can be **manifested** among them as well (4:9-16).

This **manifested** life, therefore, can be talked about! The apostles **have seen** it, **bear witness** to it, **and declare** it to the readership. As eyewitnesses of this life (Life) they can give testimony to its reality. But this is not something they do only when called upon to do so. Instead, they actively **declare** it, that is, proclaim it, to the readers. This intensity of communication is fully justified by the profound importance of the subject matter, since this life is nothing less than **that eternal life which was with the Father and was manifested to us.**

To be noted are the last words of this verse: **to us.** The full-orbed revelation of this life was made only to the selected witnesses, the apostles themselves. As Peter himself once said, "Him God raised up on the third day, and showed Him openly, not to all the people, but to witnesses chosen before by God, even *to us* who ate and drank with Him after He arose from the dead" (Acts 10:40-41, italics added). Thus John and his apostolic fellow witnesses were uniquely equipped to share with the readers their knowledge of this **manifested** life.

> [3]**That which we have seen and heard we declare to you, that you also may have fellowship with us; and truly our fellowship is with the Father and with His Son Jesus Christ.**

As John has now made clear, his subject matter in this epistle is the truth about eternal life that was revealed from the beginning of the Christian message to the chosen apostolic witnesses. John now states the purpose, or goal, of the epistle. That purpose, simply stated, is **fellowship.** Fellowship translates the word *koinōnia*, which basically means "sharing." As in English, it can indicate shared experiences, undertakings, possessions, etc. The related noun (*koinōnoi*) is used in Luke 5:10 of business "partners."[7]

But the **fellowship** John speaks of is no ordinary kind of fellowship. To begin with it is **fellowship with us**—that is, with the apostolic witnesses who have "heard... seen...looked upon...and...handled" the original manifestation of eternal life (verse 1). One might be tempted to ask whether such **fellowship** is truly possible, since the experience of the apostles with God's incarnate Son seems so unique and so unrepeatable. Yet clearly John believes that it *is* possible.

In addition, the **fellowship with us** into which John invites the readers involves sharing the apostles' own **fellowship...with the Father and with His Son Jesus Christ**. This is a stunning claim. The author of the epistle is stating that he is part of a circle so intimate with God that if one has **fellowship with** his circle, one also has **fellowship with** God **the Father and with His Son**! But the claim is no more amazing than the one he also makes in 4:6: "We are of God. He who knows God hears us; he who is not of God does not hear us."

The modern world, with its skepticism and unbelief, has virtually lost its respect for apostolic authority. To the modern and postmodern scholar, the apostles were mere creatures of their own, prescientific age. Their viewpoints have no more authority than the modern mind feels willing to grant them, and the enlightened scholar of today always knows more than these "ignorant and unlearned" men did.

But the biblical point of view is different. In the Christian faith, all claims to truth must be tested at the bar of apostolic authority. What the apostles said as representatives of a Risen Lord carried all the authority of the Lord Himself. To refuse to hear the *apostles* was to refuse to hear *God Himself*. In the same way, to be "out of fellowship" with apostolic thought and practice was to be "out of fellowship" **with the Father and the Son**. There is no form of true Christian **fellowship** outside of apostolic truth, since the New Testament message is nothing more nor less than the truth which the Lord Jesus revealed to His apostles and which He commanded them to teach to us (John 14:25-26; Matthew 28:18-20).

It is noteworthy, however, that in offering to share the apostolic experience with his readers, John mentions only **that which we have seen and heard**. He does not repeat two ideas found in verse 1, namely, "which we have looked upon, and our hands have handled." The word translated "looked upon" (Greek: *etheasametha*) can suggest "the thought of attentive, careful regard, as in Mt 11:7."[8] Since here this word follows the more common word, "seen," it is likely that John intended the more intensive sense, as we might say, "which we gazed at." Of the four words in verse 1 ("heard...seen...looked upon...handled"), the first two, which are repeated in verse 3, are in the Greek perfect tense, while the last two, not repeated in verse 3, are in the aorist tense.

Although commentators are often guilty of overrefinement in handling the Greek tenses, the change of tense in verse 1 appears to be deliberate. The thought of "sharability" most likely underlines this shift of tense.[9] In this context the verbs in the perfect imply the ongoing sharability of the experience of the apostles, while the two aorist verbs carry no such connotation. This explains why, in the present verse, John speaks only of **that which we have seen and heard** as the basis of his shared **fellowship** with the readers.

Thus the apostles really could not share the experience of "gazing at" and "handling" the manifested Life. But they *could share* whatever was **seen** or **heard**. And while all Christian **fellowship** with God must lie within the parameters of what the apostles saw and heard, the apostolic experience as a whole cannot be fully shared in this life. We must wait until we are in the presence of the Lord to "gaze at" or "handle" Him! But that is clearly something to look forward to.

> **4And these things we write to you that *our*[10] joy may be full.**

The apostle states that he has chosen to write about the things he has just mentioned in order to make possible a fullness of **joy** within the apostolic circle. There are only three references to **joy** in the three Johannine Epistles: here, in 2 John 12, and in 3 John 4. In 2 John 12, the apostle hopes to visit the readers and "speak face to face, that our joy may be full" (the Greek is identical to that in this verse). In 3 John 4, he states that, "I have no greater joy than to hear that my children walk in truth" (3 John 4).

In these epistles, then, the theme of **joy** surfaces as an expression of apostolic love for Christian believers. John and the other apostles are delighted when those they have led to Christ, or nurtured in the faith, are true to the faith and demonstrate this by "walking" in the truth they have been taught. Indeed, according to 3 John 4, this represents a maximum degree of happiness for the apostle (see discussion there). Thus if the present letter succeeds in encouraging the readers to "let that abide in [them] which [they] heard from the beginning" (2:24), the apostles will feel that the **joy** they already have in these believers will **be full**. That is, they will have a full cup of spiritual **joy** because of the fidelity of the readers to the truths they were taught at the very beginning of their Christian experience.

Obviously such an emotional investment in their readers is a clear sign of the pastoral heart which the apostles of our Lord, like the Savior Himself, possessed so richly. Completely absent here is the modern tendency not to be too concerned about doctrine, as long as the flock attends the meetings of the church with regularity and participates in the church's aims and goals. What the contemporary church urgently needs is a revival of its respect for the importance of divine truth, along with a rejection of doctrinal error as dangerous to God's sheep.

Insofar as pastors and other leaders ignore the relevance of truth to spiritual growth and personal conduct, they will endanger the flock's fellowship with "the Father and with His Son Jesus Christ" (verse 3). John refuses to ignore such issues, and cannot even have fullness of **joy** if his beloved brothers fall prey to the doctrinal errors to which they are being exposed.

The epistle is written to rebuke these errors, to keep the readers abiding in the original truths they have learned, and to secure for the apostles themselves a loving **joy** over the spiritual well-being of their brothers and sisters in Christ.

The Prologue ends in verse 4, with this appealing hint of the apostles' personal attachment to, and concern for, the readers.

ENDNOTES

[1] The three major Greek New Testament texts, Nestle (27th), UBS (4th), and the Majority Text (see *Bibliography*), treat 1 John 1:1 as a broken structure (*anacoluthon*) which is interrupted by verse 2 and resumed in verse 3. This could be correct, but given the simplicity of Johannine style, an introductory *anacoluthon* does not seem probable. It is more likely that the statement of verse 1 should end with a period because the verse serves as a title for the book, as do Matthew 1:1 and Mark 1:1 for those books, and Revelation 1:1 for that book (also authored by John). This use of an introductory phrase for a title is a convention well established in the Hebrew and Greek Old Testament. Compare (in Rahlf's edition of the LXX) Ecclesiastes, Song of Solomon, Isaiah, Hosea, Joel, Amos, Obadiah, Nahum, Habakkuk, Zephaniah, plus the apocryphal Bel and the Dragon.

The First Epistle of John

[2] Stephen S. Smalley (*1,2,3, John,* WBC [Waco, TX: Word Books, 1984], p. 8) reflects the general mood of many modern critical commentators when he writes: "...here and in the preface generally, 'we' may be interpreted to mean the Church in solidarity with eyewitnesses (so Dodd, 9-16). Without excluding the possibility that eyewitnesses were associated with John's testimony, and were thus able to support it, the writer is more likely to be taking the 'mantle of orthodoxy' (Houlden, 53), and speaking for *all* those, including members of the Johannine community, who were champions of the apostolic gospel." This idea is common among writers who reject, as Smalley does (*1,2,3 John,* p. xxii), the apostolic authorship of the epistles. Marianne Meye Thompson, of Fuller Seminary, pretty well straddles the issue in her 1992 volume in IVPNT (*1–3 John* [Downers Grove, IL: InterVarsity Press, 1992], pp. 20, 34-35).

[3] Raymond E. Brown, *The Epistles of John,* AB (Garden City, NY: Doubleday, 1982), pp. 175-76) states: "Speaking as a representative of the 'we,' the author addresses this proclamation of Jesus' ministry, this word of life, to an audience of Johannine Christians whom he wishes to bind in communion (*koinōnia*) with him; for he and the other tradition-bearers [not apostles, according to Brown] already have communion with the Father and the Son through the revelation of life they have received (verse 3). Communion among the Johannine Christians (which, as we shall see, is threatened) constitutes the author's goal in writing and will fill out his joy (verse 4)."

[4] Brown, (*Epistles,* p. 158): "...the most plausible meaning...[is] that 'What was from the beginning,' means the person, words, and deeds of Jesus as this complexus reflects his self-revelation (which is also the revelation of the Father) to his disciples after his baptism." Commentators often take *the beginning* in 1 John 1:1 as being equivalent to "the beginning" in John 1:1. But this equation is superficial and has little to commend it when we properly evaluate John's overriding concern in this epistle with *original* Christian truth, as over against the "new theology." If taken in the sense suggested in our Commentary (so also, J. L. Houlden, *A Commentary on the Johannine Epistles,* HNTC [New York: Harper & Row, 1973], p. 49; F. F. Bruce, *The Epistles of John: Introduction, Exposition and Notes* [Old Tappan, NJ: Fleming H. Revell, 1970], pp. 34-35; Thompson, *1–3 John,* p. 37), the phrase has essentially the same effect as it does in 2:7 (twice), 2:24 (twice), and 3:11. It is to be expected that in the Prologue the phrase will be used in a sense that is pivotal to the whole epistle. This observation is not lessened even if we take 2:13-14 as referring to the beginning of time (see Commentary there). For a full discussion see Brown, *Epistles,* pp. 155-58.

[5] Brown, *Epistles,* p. 164. The view taken in this commentary is also shared by Bruce, *Epistles,* p. 36; C. H. Dodd, *The Johannine Epistles,* MNTC (New York:

Harper & Row, 1946), pp. 3-5; Houlden, *Epistles* (but suggesting some ambiguity), pp. 50-52; and Thompson, *1–3 John,* p. 37.

[6] Bauer, Walter. *A Greek-English Lexicon of the New Testament and Other Early Christian Literature* (Chicago: University of Chicago Press, 1979), p. 393.

[7] See J. Shattenmann, "*koinōnia,*" *The New International Dictionary of New Testament Theology.* Colin Brown, gen. ed. 3 vols. (Grand Rapids: Zondervan Publishing House, 1975-78), 1: 641-44.

[8] James Hope Moulton and George Milligan, *The Vocabulary of the Greek Testament Illustrated from the Papyri and Other Non-literary Sources* (Grand Rapids: Wm. B. Eerdmans Publishing Co., 1960), p. 285.

[9] To the contrary, J. P. Louw, " Verbal Aspect in the First Letter of John," *Neot* 9 (1975): 101.

[10] NKJV reads *your* with many manuscripts. The Majority Text (hereafter *MajT*) reads *our*, which in the present state of our knowledge of the whole body of manuscripts appears to be the reading of the majority of them.

CHAPTER 2

Walking in God's Light

(1 John 1:5–2:2)

II. PREAMBLE: LIVING IN FELLOWSHIP WITH GOD (1:5–2:11)

Since the apostle's expressed concern is that his readers might have fellowship with the apostolic circle and thus also with the Father and the Son (1:3), it is reasonable to specify what this fellowship is really like. So, as an introductory section to his epistle, John discusses the nature of true fellowship with God.

A. Staying on the Path: Walking in God's Light (1:5-2:2)

⁵This is the message which we have heard from Him and declare to you, that God is light and in Him is no darkness at all.

The apostle John now wishes to set forth the grounds on which the readers can experience the fellowship with the Father and with His Son Jesus Christ, about which he has just spoken in the Prologue (cf. verse 3). This leads him into a moderately long introductory section that extends from 1:5 through 2:11. Since the Revisionists are a threat to the readers' ongoing fellowship with God, it is important to state the fundamental principles for such fellowship. Unless a Christian really knows *how* to have fellowship with God, he or she will be an easy target for Satan's efforts to undermine believers' harmony with the Father and the Son.

The apostle begins with a declaration about the character of God: **God is light**. This simple yet profound message[1] about God is crucial to all fellowship between Himself and His creatures. To begin with, God is free from every moral defect. His light is unsullied by any degree of moral impurity whatsoever, **and in Him is no darkness at all**.

This latter statement is so emphatic in Greek, "darkness is not in Him—none," that we might well guess that the Revisionists may have claimed that there *was* darkness in the Deity. Of course, in paganism, the mythology about the gods reflected their capriciousness and willingness to do harm. But if the Revisionists moved mainly within the realm of Jewish thought, they might have used a text like Isaiah 45:7 where God says: "I form the light and create darkness, I make peace and create calamity [Hebrew: *ra'* = evil]; I, the Lord, do all these things."

In the highly syncretistic religious atmosphere of the first century, pagan conceptions about the gods may have influenced heretical Jewish tendencies to produce an image of God that ran counter to true biblical revelation. The heretics may have thought of Him as having a nature that included both **light** and **darkness**.[2] If, indeed, the Revisionists did have such a view of God, they could easily argue that "evil," as well as "good," originated from the Creator and so moral distinctions were invalid. This could have led to a disregard for God's commandments, something which may possibly have characterized them (cf. 1 John 2:3-4; perhaps also here in verse 6). It was vital that the Christian readers of this epistle have no misunderstanding on this point. God is *completely* holy.

But in the second place, the statement that **God is light** points also to the revelatory aspect of His being and nature. God reveals Himself in and to His creation, but in doing so He also reveals the wickedness that is found in creation. Thus, it is in the very nature of what God is that man is inevitably exposed as falling far short of His moral glory (cf. Romans 3:23). Man thus tends to hide from One like this, as Adam and Eve did in the Garden of Eden (Genesis 3:8), and tries to avoid exposure of evil deeds by the light (John 3:20). To have fellowship with such a God, a Christian cannot hide from the light. To do so is to forfeit this fellowship, as the next verse plainly states.

> [6]**If we say that we have fellowship with Him, and walk in darkness, we lie and do not practice the truth.**

The words **if we say** show clearly that the apostle has his readers in mind. The **we** of this verse obviously links back to the "we" of verse 5, where it refers to the apostles. But in view of the "you" of that verse, it is natural to take the **we** here to include both the apostles *and* their Christian audience. Whether an apostle or a reader makes such a statement, the simple fact is that the statement is a lie.

In modern times a peculiar exegesis has arisen according to which the **we** of this verse really refers *neither* to the apostles *nor* to their Christian readers. Instead, it is taken as a statement made by the Revisionists, but impossible for any true Christian to make. In this view, the **we** is the functional equivalent of "someone."

This is a transparently erroneous exegesis. Since no one regards the "we" of verse 5 in this way, the radical change of reference in verse 6 is totally devoid of probability. Such a conclusion, in fact, is a form of *eisegesis,* a reading *into* the text something not found there, and is theologically motivated. There is absolutely nothing in the text to support it. Even if the Revisionists *did* make such statements—as they may well have done, still it is the readers who are warned here against making them. Brown's statement is on target:

> It is significant that the subject of these boasts in 1:6, 8, 10 is not a "they" but a "we." He thinks of those who remain within and form a "we" with him. But the use of conditions indicates the strong possibility that even those who are now with him may make such objectionable boasts.[3]

Let there be no mistake about it. Christians can indeed make such statements and, as the reference back to verse 6 attests, the apostles do not exclude even themselves from this significant danger. Had they felt themselves impervious to such a failure, they could easily have said, "If *you* say." But they did not. No doubt they were far less likely to fall into this spiritual trap than their less experienced readers, but the apostles remained fallible men, as a reading of Galatians 2:11-14 shows. Christians are always subject to the temptation to justify sin and to claim fellowship with God at the same time. This may be done to preserve their public image with fellow Christians, or it may be a way of rationalizing what they are doing, or both.

To say **we have fellowship with Him** is a false claim, if at the same time we are walking **in darkness**. Since "God is light" and totally free from darkness (verse 5), a person who walks **in darkness** is moving in a moral and spiritual sphere from which God is absent. He is moving in the realm of evil, while God remains in the realm of holiness. Thus, the believer who walks in sin has lost touch with a completely holy God. If he nevertheless claims **fellowship** with such a Person, he is telling a falsehood and acting inconsistently with the truth (**we lie and do not practice the truth**).

The phrase **practice the truth** is found elsewhere in John's writings only at John 3:21. It literally means "to do the truth" (**practice** overtranslates it), but the phrase is probably to be understood in both places in the sense of "to act consistently with the truth."[4] The idea here would then be that to claim **fellowship** with God while walking **in darkness** is to behave contrary to the truth about God, especially the truth about His holiness as stated in verse 5. It is to not act consistently with the reality of God's nature and character.

> [7]**But if we walk in the light as He is in the light, we have fellowship with one another, and the blood of Jesus Christ His Son cleanses us from all sin.**

There is an alternative to the perverse behavior described in verse 6. Instead of walking "in darkness," we should **walk in the light** and thus have **fellowship** with God. In so doing we will find an ongoing realization of the cleansing benefits of **the blood of Jesus Christ His Son.**

What does it mean to **walk in the light?** It certainly cannot mean that we **walk** *according to* **the light**, since to do so would require sinless perfection. **The light**, we have been told (verse 5), is totally free from any and all darkness. But as verse 8 makes emphatically clear, we Christians are not. To **walk *in* the light** means just what it says: we are to conduct ourselves **in** the sphere where God Himself is, **as He is in the light**, and thus to *share* **the light** with Him. Consequently, the basic reality which is "shared" in this **fellowship** is nothing less than **the light** itself.

All fellowship involves something that is shared between the parties. On the human level, one may share time or experiences or property. So too, those who are God's children can share many things with Him. But if **the light** is not shared, then nothing else can be shared with Him, since **the light** is where **He is** and the only sphere in which He operates. Thus sharing **the light** is the sine qua non of all **fellowship** with our Maker.

How do we do this? If I enter a lighted room and walk around in it, I am walking in the light; I am moving in a sphere which the light illuminates as it shines not only on me but upon everything around me. If I were to personalize the light, I could also say that I was walking *in the presence of* the light. Since according to this passage God not only *is* light (verse 5), but **He is** also *in* **the light**, to **walk in the light** must mean essentially to live in God's presence, exposed to what He has revealed about Himself. This, of course, is done through openness in prayer and through openness to the Word of God in which He is revealed.

By contrast, to "walk in darkness" (verse 6) is to hide from God and to refuse to acknowledge what we know about Him. The believer who wants fellowship with the Lord must maintain an openness to his Lord and a willingness to be honest in His presence about everything that God shows him. As in human life, so in our relationship with God, a refusal to be honest and open destroys true fellowship. This basic principle is reinforced in the verses that immediately follow this one.

The result of walking **in the light** is that **we have fellowship with one another**. That is to say, **we have fellowship with** God and He has **fellowship** with us. The words **one another** do not refer to Christians having fellowship with Christians, since that is not what the apostle is talking about. Instead, his point is that when believers **walk in the light**, since God Himself **is in the light**, they have something in common with God, namely, **the light**.

But we might still ask how a perfectly holy God can **have fellowship** with us, even **in the light**, since we remain sinful people. The answer is that while **we walk in the light** something else is happening at the same time: **the blood of Jesus Christ His Son cleanses us from all sin**. It is to be noted here that the apostle does *not* say "has cleansed" but **cleanses**, i.e., "is cleansing."

As the structure of John's sentence makes clear, when **we walk in the light** two things take place: (1) we experience **fellowship** with God and He with us, and (2) we are being cleansed **from all sin** by **the blood of Jesus Christ**. This simply means that as we maintain an open and honest relationship with God, the many sinful failures and habits that still cling to us do not prevent this **fellowship**, because God treats us as those who are clean by virtue of the Savior's shed blood.

It is true, of course, that all Christians have *already* been cleansed (cf. 1 Corinthians 6:11) and have a full forgiveness in Christ (cf. Ephesians 1:7). But as verse 9 makes clear, there is an ongoing forgiveness that occurs as part of the Father/child relationship. So, too, there is an ongoing cleansing based on Christ's **blood** which enables imperfect children like ourselves to have a genuine experience of sharing with a perfectly holy heavenly Father. Thus, every moment of **fellowship** with the living God is a moment bought for us by the precious **blood** of God's sacrificial Lamb.

> [8]**If we say that we have no sin, we deceive ourselves, and the truth is not in us.**

There is a danger here. When we are open before God and walking in true fellowship with the Father and the Son, we may not be conscious of the fact that we need continuous cleansing from "the blood of Jesus Christ." Therefore, we may be tempted to claim that we are free from all sin, at least for the moment. But the fact that we are not *conscious* of any sin does not mean that we do not have any. Our own deep-seated sinfulness guarantees that at no point in time—however long or short—may we rightly claim to **have no sin.**[5]

In fact, anyone who does make such a claim is a victim of self-deception: **we deceive ourselves.** The apostle is obviously thinking of those who really believe this claim about themselves, and not those who make the claim hypocritically.[6] Someone has humorously suggested that if a man makes this claim, he does not deceive his wife, his children, or his friends—but only himself!

A sincere claim to sinlessness, even if intended to cover only a brief period of our experience, betrays the fact that **the truth is not in us** in any effective or dynamic way. It would be a gratuitous mistake to think that the words **the truth is not in us** indicate that the person in question is not saved. The apostle continues to use first person pronouns, **we** and **us,** just as he has done from verse 5 on. The claims under consideration in verses 5-10 are ones that true Christians could make. Indeed, the claim made in this verse is precisely the type of claim a Christian *might* make if he was having the experience described in verse 7. We are warned, therefore, that even when we feel closest to God, we should remember that this closeness is not due to our being free of sin. Instead, as has been pointed out, only "the blood of Jesus Christ" makes such closeness possible, since we are never *at any time* free from the taint of wickedness.

If **the truth** has its proper effect upon us, if it is dynamically in control of our thinking, we will not fall into this trap. If we do fall into it, **the truth is not in us** as an active and controlling force that shapes our thoughts and attitudes. Bultmann was essentially correct to point out the practical equivalence of "we do not do the truth" (verse 6) with the words **the truth is not in us** here and to say that these words designate "the futility of such a mode of being."[7]

⁹If we confess our sins, He is faithful and just to forgive us *our* sins and to cleanse us from all unrighteousness.

Instead of denying our sinfulness, however sincerely, we should be prepared to acknowledge it. It is true that, as we walk in the light in fellowship with God, at any given time we may not be *conscious* of our sinfulness. But "the light" which shines forth from the God with whom we have fellowship has a revelatory role to play in our lives. As long as we walk in that light, we are in a position to *be shown* our failures; when that happens we should **confess** them.

It should be noted that the word *repentance* is not used here, nor anywhere in the epistle. The reason for this is simple. In John's usage, Christian repentance is appropriate when a pattern of sin is persisted in and needs to be changed (see Revelation 2:5, 16, 21, 22; 3:3, 19). In our text, John is talking about those who *discover* sin while in fellowship with God, not those who have wandered away from Him or have lost some previous spiritual attainment. That is a separate issue. The audience of First John is spiritually stable and has nothing to repent of (see 2:12-14, 21). Their task is to "abide," or "stay," in Christ and His truth (see 2:24, 28), not to "turn back" to Him.

(It is hardly worth refuting the incredible view sometimes advanced that 1 John 1:9 is meant for the unsaved. Nowhere in the Johannine literature is "confession of sin" given as a condition for having eternal life. Faith is the only condition John knows for this [cf. John 3:16; 5:24; 6:47; 1 John 5:1, 12, 13; and *passim*]. Moreover, this view of the verse flies in the face of the first person plural that controls verses 5 to 10. See the discussion of the first person plural under verse 6.)

The exposure of our sin by the light confronts us with a challenge to the fellowship in which we are walking with God. If we deny what the light shows us, we have ceased to be honest and open with God and fellowship ends. But **if we confess** (Greek: *homologeō*, "agree, admit, acknowledge") the **sins** that the light reveals, we can depend on God to **forgive** them and **to cleanse us from all unrighteousness**. If this happens, fellowship continues.

An analogy can be found in a man who has just put on a suit which he has superficially examined for dirt or spots. If he walks into a lighted room wearing that suit, he may be active in that room for some time before he actually notices a spot or two on the suit. At this point he can deny the truth of what he has seen in the light by saying, "No, that is not a spot of dirt but a part of the weave of the fabric." But if he does say this (to push the analogy further) the light in effect goes out and he is now in darkness.

In the same way, a Christian can maintain his fellowship in the light by promptly confessing what God's truth reveals to him. Failure to do so plunges him into darkness. Of course, a Christian can also deliberately step out of the light by deciding to do what he knows to be wrong. The Christian who deliberately chooses sin has also deliberately chosen to forfeit his openness and integrity before God. He has stepped into the darkness and can return to the light only by confession.

The importance of all this can hardly be overstated. King David, in his great psalm of confession after his sin with Bathsheba, gives expression to a simple yet profound truth. He says to God, "Behold, You desire truth in the inward parts" (Psalm 51:6). In another psalm we read, "If I regard iniquity in my heart, the Lord will not hear me" (Psalm 66:18). And in the Book of Proverbs we are told, "He who covers his sins will not prosper, but whoever confesses and forsakes them will have mercy" (Proverbs 28:13). Clearly, God values inner integrity, and the absence of this in our hearts is precisely what it means to "walk in darkness."

If then we are open and honest toward God so that we **confess** the **sins** that the light reveals to us, what is the result? The apostle states that in this case **He is faithful and just to forgive us *our* sins and to cleanse us from all unrighteousness.**

In extending forgiveness, God is **faithful**. He can be relied upon to **forgive** when we **confess our sin**. Often a believer feels very guilty about his failures and is tempted to wonder whether God's forgiveness will really be given. The apostle encourages us therefore to depend on His reliability in this matter, rather than on our feelings.

God is also **just** when He acts in forgiveness. The word **just** in Greek is *dikaios*, meaning "righteous." Because of the shed blood of Christ (verse 7), there is no compromise of God's righteousness when He forgives. We need not fear that God will refuse to forgive because it would not be "right" for Him to do so. The blood of Jesus Christ was sufficient for all the sins of *the whole world* (cf. 2:2), and thus for all of ours!

So when **we confess our sins**, God can be relied upon, and is completely **just**, not only **to forgive us *our* sins** but also to **cleanse us from all unrighteousness**. The NKJV places the word *our* in italics since there is nothing in the Greek that strictly corresponds to it. We could translate "to forgive us *the* sins," with the implication being "the sins *we confess*." No one but God can ever possibly know the full extent of our sinfulness, so that we can only actually confess the sins of which we are aware. God does not ask more of us than that.

But what about the sins of which we are *unaware*? These are covered by the words **and to cleanse us from *all* unrighteousness**. Therefore, whenever we make confession—honestly acknowledging what we know to be wrong, whatever other sin there may be in our hearts or lives is totally cleansed away. Nothing is left uncleansed, since *all* **unrighteousness** is as broad as possible. If there is any distinction here at all between **sins** and **unrighteousness**, then it would probably be that **unrighteousness** is broader and covers any latent attitude or outlook that is sinful in character, whether or not it has found expression in overt sin. The point of the verse, of course, is that when we honestly acknowledge whatever **sins** we are aware of, the cleansing that follows *covers everything* that needs cleansing.

> **[10]If we say that we have not sinned, we make Him a liar, and His word is not in us.**

But suppose that, instead of confessing as sin what the light has shown us, we say **that we have not sinned**, what then? In that case, **we make Him a liar**. We have denied the testimony of **His word** and thus, in effect, charged God with untruthfulness.

It is inappropriate here to take the words **we have not sinned** as a categorical denial that we have *ever* or *at any time* sinned.[8] Few Christians would be likely to make such a claim and, as previously stated, the passage is definitely for Christians. The sequence of thought in this passage shows us what is meant. Even while we are in fellowship with God, we are not free from the need for cleansing (verse 7); should we deny that truth, we are self-deceived (verse 8). If we confess whatever sins the light shows us, we are forgiven (verse 9). But, if we deny what the light shows us, we are making God (who is that Light: verse 5) **a liar. His word is not in us** as an effective, controlling influence. (See the discussion of "the truth is not in us" in verse 8.)

Suppose, for example, that I steal something—an act which God's **word** condemns. But suppose I also claim that *in this case,* or *under some special set of circumstances,* it was not really an act of theft at all—that I was somehow entitled to do it. If that is my response, then I am contradicting God's **word**, I am showing that His **word** is not a controlling force within me, and I am saying in effect that God is **a liar**, since He has called my act a theft and I have refused to do so.

Clearly then, the connecting thread that unites verses 5 to 10 is the idea of *truth* or its opposite, *falsehood* or *deception*. The man who claims fellowship while in darkness is lying and not doing "the truth" (verse 6). The man who thinks he has no sin is self-deceived and "the truth" is not effectively at work within him (verse 8). The man who will not acknowledge as sin whatever God calls sin is calling God **a liar**, by denying the *truth* of His word. By contrast, the person who walks in fellowship with God agrees with the light and confesses. For the believer, the essential essence of fellowship is our willingness to share the light with God and to agree with everything we can see in that light. When that is the case, God is pleased because He finds "truth in" our "inward parts" (Psalm 51:6). We can then enjoy His ongoing forgiveness and cleansing.

Despite the clear teaching of this passage, from time to time it has been claimed that since the born again believer is already forgiven for his sins, he does not need to ask for it even after he commits sin. Those who take this view are mixing apples and oranges.

It is true that there is a perfect and permanent forgiveness that we have "in Christ." Paul speaks of it in Ephesians 1:7 ("*In Him* we have...the forgiveness of sins"); Ephesians 4:32 ("even as God *in Christ* forgave you"); and Colossians 2:13 ("And you...He has made alive *together with Him*, having forgiven you all trespasses"). Colossians 1:14 might be added, depending on how the textual evidence is taken. But this is "status truth" (also called "positional truth"). Thus "in Christ" our *status* is that of people who have died with Him, been buried with Him, raised with Him, and seated with Him in heavenly places (cf. Galatians 2:20; Ephesians 2:5-6; Colossians 2:12). If this is our status before God, there can be no question about our having full forgiveness, since God sees us as alive and seated before Him in His Son.

The status just described is analogous to God's full acceptance of Israel, as expressed in Balaam's inspired utterance: "He has not observed iniquity in Jacob, nor has He seen wickedness in Israel" (Numbers 23:21). Yet, on a *practical* level, Israel was full of failures!

Although we are seated in Christ as fully accepted and forgiven people, we live down here on earth, and our ongoing sins must receive the forgiveness of our heavenly Father if we are to be in fellowship with Him. This is not hard to understand, since earthly parent/child relationships work exactly the same way. If a child has never told a parent, "I'm sorry," something is clearly wrong in the relationship, even though the child remains his parent's child. In the same way, as born again people we are permanently in the family of God; but when harmony with our Father is breached, He requires confession as a condition for restoring that harmony.

That is why our Lord taught His disciples to pray *daily*, "Give us *this day* our daily bread," and also, "Forgive us our debts" (Matthew 6:11-12). Forgiveness of sins is as urgent a daily spiritual need as daily bread is a physical need. To teach otherwise is contrary to Scripture.

FIRST JOHN 2

> ¹**My little children, these things I write to you, so that you may not sin. And if anyone sins, we have an Advocate with the Father, Jesus Christ the righteous.**

Before concluding this basic discussion on fellowship with God, the apostle wishes to enter a disclaimer. He has insisted so strongly on the sinfulness of all Christians that someone might draw the conclusion that he takes sin, or the inevitability of sin, for granted. Thus, his words could be wrongly perceived as discouraging the believer's resistance to sin.

But this is not his intent! Tenderly he addresses his readers as **my little children**. (That his readers are genuine Christians he never doubts anywhere in his letter: cf. 2:12-14). He does not want his spiritual **children** to misconstrue his intention in writing **these things** to them. "**These things**" (i.e., 1:5-10) are not written either to excuse or to encourage sin. Instead, they are written **so that you may not sin**.

A little reflection will show how this is so. In 1:5-10 John has stigmatized sin as something contrary to the very nature of God who is light. If a person takes a lenient view of sin, he can easily make the false claim to fellowship in 1:6. Or, he may not take seriously the need to receive cleansing from it, even as he walks in the light where God is (verse 7). Or, he may fall into the superficial view that since he is not *conscious* of sin, he therefore *has* none (verse 8). He may also take lightly his need for confession of sin (verse 9), or may rationalize his sin and deny it (verse 10). In fact, everything the apostle has just written is designed to treat sin as a serious issue between God and the believer. It is an issue on which God demands full openness and honesty from anyone who wishes to have fellowship with Him.

John's words are not in any sense an encouragement to sin nor an encouragement to cease resisting it strongly. On the contrary, those who read these words with true spiritual perception will redouble their efforts to avoid it.

But John does not lose his hold on reality. Though sin is to be vigorously shunned, it can and does occur in the lives of believers. So John adds, **And if anyone sins, we have an Advocate with the Father**. Though the Christian should seek, with God's help, not to sin, when he does sin he is not deserted. Instead, precisely at the moment of weakness and failure, the Christian is assured that he has an *Advocate* before God who will take up his case **with the Father**.

In the New Testament, the word translated **Advocate** (Greek: *paraklētos*) is used only five times, all by the apostle John (John 14:16, 26; 15:26; 16:7; and here). The four cases in the Gospel of John all refer to the Holy Spirit. Thus 1 John 2:1 is a unique reference in Scripture to our Lord Jesus Himself as an **Advocate**. The Greek word can have the sense of "lawyer," but this is rare. The more general use carries meanings like: "*one who appears in another's behalf, mediator, intercessor, helper.*"[9] Based on a thorough study of the word in nonbiblical Greek, Grayston suggests the words "sponsor" or "patron" for its occurrences in John's writings.[10] Given the sacrificial reference in 2:2, we might here prefer the word *Mediator*. However, the NKJV's **Advocate** is quite satisfactory for our purposes, although *Patron* or *Sponsor* also have real merit, due to their overtones of a person of high status.

We may ask what exactly the Lord **Jesus Christ** does as an **Advocate** for the sinning believer. We should certainly not think that He pleads with God to keep us "saved." The many promises made in John's Gospel that guarantee the security of the believer stand against such an idea. Since it is His Father's will that His Son should not lose any of those the Father has given Him (John 6:37-40), there is no need at all for the Son to plead with Him not to cast sinning believers away.

Additionally, the nature of the salvation experience argues power-fully against the kind of intercession we are talking about. The believer has been born into God's family (1 John 3:1; John 1:12-13). He has been given "living water," which prevents all future thirst, and "the bread of life," which prevents all future hunger (John 4:14; 6:35). He has also been justified by faith so that no charge can be laid against him (Romans 8:33). That God would even consider revoking all these saving acts, because of a believer's sin, is unthinkable. His own promises are involved and the sacrifice of Christ has already paid for the believer's eternal salvation. There is no danger that the believer will be lost, and to posit that the Son intercedes so that this won't happen is to suggest a kind of charade.

How then does our **Advocate** mediate for us when we sin? The clearest biblical suggestion is found in Luke 22:31-33. There as Peter's impending failure draws near, the Lord Jesus announces that He has *already* prayed for Peter. His prayer is not for Peter to remain saved, but rather that his "faith should not fail"—which is different. Though "the gifts and the calling of God are irrevocable" (Romans 11:29), the faith that appropriates those gifts is nevertheless subject to failure (cf. 2 Timo-thy 2:18); nor is our ability to go on trusting God in daily life beyond failing. A devastating failure such as Peter was about to experience could have had a crushing effect on his faith, but our Lord intercedes that this might not occur. Equally, His intercession anticipates Peter's restoration to fellowship with Him ("when you have returned to Me") and subse-quent effectiveness in service ("strengthen your brethren").

We can therefore conclude that the work of our Lord as He intercedes for His own is directed toward the maintenance of their faith, toward their spiritual recovery, and toward their future usefulness. But exactly in what form these matters are approached in His intercession, or whether all three are always considered in His prayers, is a mystery that rests ultimately upon His sovereign knowledge of each individual Christian.

Our **Advocate** is **with the Father**—He is in God's immediate presence. Therefore, He is ideally situated to mediate whenever we are overtaken by any failure.

Moreover, our **Advocate** is none other than **Jesus Christ the righteous**. The description of Him as **righteous** is pointedly appropriate. At the very time when we behave *unrighteously* (**if anyone sins**), our Patron before God is the One who is ever **righteous**. Thus, this **Advocate** is ideally *situated* (**with the Father**) and ideally *qualified* (**righteous**) to make our case with God.

> ²**And He Himself is the propitiation for our sins, and not for ours only but also for the whole world.**

In addition, our Advocate has another superb qualification as our Patron before God: **He Himself is the propitiation for our sins**. Undergirding all of our Lord's intercessory work for us is the foundational truth that He has personally made satisfaction to God **for our sins**.

The word **propitiation** (Greek: *hilasmos*) has been much discussed by modern theologians and commentators. What is at issue is whether the word implies the placating of an offended god ("to propitiate") or whether the focus is upon the removal of sin's guilt and contamination ("to expiate"). The linguistic points in this long-running discussion are well covered by C. Brown.[11] It is correct to conclude, as he does, that the idea of placating or satisfying God's displeasure with sin can hardly be eliminated from this word. Since in English the verb *to propitiate* means "to conciliate" or "to appease," it is appropriate to retain the familiar translation, **propitiation**, in this verse.

The apostle is here affirming that the Lord Jesus Christ Himself in His own person is **the propitiation for our sins**. Of course, His sacrificial death for sin is clearly in view. But it is significant for this context that it is not His *sacrifice* per se that is called a **propitiation**, but Christ **Himself**. Thus, our Advocate stands before God as One who is a visible and personal "satisfaction" for **our sins**. As the writer of Hebrews puts it: "When He had by Himself purged our sins, [He] sat down at the right hand of the Majesty on high" (Hebrews 1:3). And there in the very presence of God, the Father's eye can rest on the person of His Son with complete satisfaction. This is not only because of what He *is,* righteous, but also because of what He *has done* at the cross, the wounds of which are still visible in His resurrected body (John 20:25-27).

Clearly, the sinning believer's Advocate is perfect. God looks at Him with complete satisfaction—He is completely *propitiated* or appeased with regard to any sin we commit. He is thus fully disposed to respond to our Advocate's intercession for us, since no matter what our sin may be, Christ has made satisfaction for it. Indeed, as a **propitiation** for sin, He more than *just barely* "satisfies" God for **our** personal **sins**, or even for all the *sins* of all Christians everywhere. The astounding fact is that this **propitiation** covers the sins of all humanity, **not for ours only but also for the whole world**.

Needless to say, these words firmly contradict the ultra-Calvinist view that Christ died only for the elect. The tortured efforts made to defend that view in the face of this verse are futile. The contrast here is explicitly between the believers John is addressing and **the whole world** of mankind which John later says "lies under the sway of the wicked one" (1 John 5:19). Johannine thought and terminology leave absolutely no room for any such concept as "the world of the elect." Christ's death, therefore, covers the totality of human sin from the beginning of creation until the end of history when eternity begins. For the apostle John, Jesus Christ is "'the Lamb of God who takes away the sin of the world,'" just as John the Baptist announced Him at the beginning (John 1:29).

The argument that, if Christ paid for all human sin all would be saved, is a misconception. The removal of sin as a barrier to God's saving grace does not automatically bring regeneration and eternal life. While God's holy and just requirement that sin receive His judicial retribution is fulfilled at the cross, the sinner remains dead and "alienated from the life of God" (Ephesians 4:18). Faith is the prescribed way for this alienation to be bridged. At the final judgment of the lost (Revelation 20:11-15), sin *as sin* is not considered. Instead, men are "judged according to their works" (Revelation 20:12) to demonstrate to each that their "works" give them no claim on God's salvation.

Since so many have supposed that their "works" will win them God's acceptance in the final judgment, each person will "have his day in court," demonstrating that "by the deeds ("works") of the law no flesh will be justified in [God's] sight" (Romans 3:20). But even these "works" are not made the basis for the final judgment. Instead, people are condemned because they do not have God's life in them: "And anyone not found written in the Book of Life was cast into the lake of fire" (Revelation 20:15). Hell is the appropriate environment for all who cannot live forever with God. *Our Savior's universal sacrifice for sin makes eternal life available, but not automatic.* By the cross God is fully propitiated for *all* sin, so that He then might have mercy on any who believe. The worldwide extent of God's love is proved by the worldwide extent of this propitiation (John 3:16)!

The point of affirming universal atonement here is that it has a pastoral impact on those John is addressing. Since even in Christians, feelings of guilt often persist after confession is made, Satan can use such feelings to make believers wonder if their sin is somehow too serious to merit effective intercession from our Advocate with the Father. It is reassuring to be reminded of the universal sufficiency of our Lord's sacrificial work, so that God sees in Him a perfect **propitiation** for every human being who ever has or ever will live on earth. This includes, of course, the most depraved of sinners such as (in John's day) people like Nero, a matricide, or Caligula (of whom his biographer said: "So much for Caligula as emperor; we must now tell of his career as a monster"[12]). More modern names, like Hitler and Stalin, also come to mind. In the fullest possible sense, "Jesus paid it all!"

Thus, the universality of our Lord's atoning work on the cross is a testimony to the profound truth that "God so loved *the world* that He gave His only begotten Son" (John 3:16). But it is more than that. It is also a powerful reminder to the believer of the total sufficiency of our Advocate's work of **propitiation** for all sin. We cannot doubt, therefore, that when we sin, His intercession for us can obtain from the Father all of the mercy and grace which at such times we so greatly need.

ENDNOTES

[1]There is no good reason to understand **message** (Greek: *angelia*) as an equivalent to "gospel" (Greek: *euangelion*), as Raymond E. Brown (*The Epistles of John*, AB [Garden City, NY: Doubleday, 1982], p. 193) and others do. The content of **the message** is stated by the verse itself. The only other use of this word in the New Testament is in this epistle at 3:11, where it also does *not* refer to the gospel.

[2]Irenaeus (ca. 140-202) argues that the Gnostic doctrine of creation entailed the concept of "shadow" and "darkness" within the Pleroma, but he writes as if they would have been most reluctant to admit this: cf. *Adversus haereses* 2.4.2-3.

[3]Brown, *Epistles*, pp. 231-32.

[4]Thompson's note (*1–3 John*, IVPNT [Downers Grove, IL: InterVarsity Press, 1992], p. 41) is to the point: "The phrase *put the truth into practice* (Gk: *poiein tēn alētheian*) is found in the Old Testament (Neh 9:33) but is paralleled more closely in Jewish texts from 200 B.C. to A.D. 200, such as the Qumran Scrolls, the Testaments of the Twelve Patriarchs, and the apocryphal book of Tobit, where it has the meaning of living in accord with the truth. Doing things that are evil (see Jn 3:20) and doing what is sinful (see 1 Jn 3:4, 8-9) are its opposite."

[5]Numerous commentators have claimed a special sense for the words **we have no sin**, referring them to sin as a principle within us (Brooke Foss Westcott, *The Epistles of St John: The Greek Text with Notes* [Grand Rapids: Wm. B. Eerdmans Publishing Co., 1966], p. 22; A. E. Brooke, *A Critical and Exegetical Commentary on the Johannine Epistles*, ICC [Edinburgh: T & T Clark, 1912], p. 17) or taking them as "the equivalent of having a sinful character or disposition" (Stephen S. Smalley, *1,2,3 John*, WBC [Waco, TX: Word Books, 1984], p. 29). But this is clearly an overrefinement that goes against Johannine usage elsewhere. The Greek phrase *echein hamartian* occurs elsewhere in the New Testament only in John's Gospel (cf. 9:41; 15:22; 19:11). In all these places, the obvious meaning seems to be to bear present guilt for some particular sin. [According to the critical editions of the New Testament, the phrase also occurs in John 15:24 and, if read there, it would have the same meaning as in the other three instances in the Gospel.]

[6]Brown (*Epistles*, p. 205) correctly observes: "The statement, 'We do not have sin,' cannot be reduced to: 'We do not have concupiscence, or an affection for sin.' There is no indication that we should confine this 'sin' to original sin, or to sexual sin, or to minor sin, or to forgiven past sin, despite early church fathers who have understood it in one of these ways (Tertullian, Cyprian, Cyril of Jerusalem)." But he goes on to add: "Even granted the Hebrew distinction between conscious and unconscious sin, there is no evidence that the author is

talking about only unconscious sin (*pace* Hodges, "Fellowship" 55)." I think my point has escaped Brown. Of course, in so far as the words themselves are concerned, **we have no sin,** there is nothing to suggest only unconscious sin. But the phrase **we deceive ourselves** shows that the one making the claim in this verse *must be unconscious* of his sin, since if he were conscious of it there would be no self-deception. A false claim, knowingly made, perhaps deceives others, but not the claimant.

[7]Rudolf Bultmann, *The Johannine Epistles: A Commentary on the Johannine Epistles,* Herm (Philadelphia: Fortress Press, 1973), p. 21. Westcott's statement (*Epistles,* p. 23) is also good: "The Truth may therefore...be regarded as without us or within us: as something outwardly realized (*v. 6 do the truth*), or as something inwardly efficacious (*the truth is in us*)." Soteriological concerns are not present here, simply the effectiveness of the truth within us.

[8]The opinion that this is a claim to sinlessness, at least in the post-conversion experience, is widely held by the commentators (e.g., Brown, *Epistles,* pp. 211-12; C. H. Dodd, *The Johannine Epistles,* MNTC [New York: Harper & Row, 1946], p. 23; Smalley, *1,2,3 John,* pp. 32-33; Brooke, *Epistles,* p. 21; etc.). But it is unlikely that the first readers would construe this as a sweeping denial of *all* sin, without some additional word as in: **we have *not ever* sinned.** More naturally, it is to be taken as a denial that one has done wrong in doing such and such a thing, and therefore does not need to "confess" it (cf. verse 9). Thus, in context, the denial is the opposite of confession. It is the difference between saying to God, in a particular situation, "I have sinned," and "I have *not* sinned." The Greek perfect suggests the nuance: "and so am (am not) guilty."

[9]Bauer, Walter. *A Greek-English Lexicon of the New Testament and Other Early Christian Literature* (Chicago: University of Chicago Press, 1979), p. 618.

[10]Kenneth Grayston, "The Meaning of *PARAKLETOS,*" *JSNT* 13 (1981):67- 82.

[11]C. Brown, under "*hilaskōmai,*" NIDNTT, Colin Brown, gen. ed., 3 vols. (Grand Rapids: Zondervan Publishing House, 1975-78), 3: 151-57.

[12]Suetonius, *The Lives of the Caesars,* 4.22.

CHAPTER 3

Knowing the God of Light

(1 John 2:3-11)

The apostle has been discussing the basic principles underlying true fellowship with a God who is light and in whom there is no trace of the darkness of sin. At their core these principles involve walking openly before God in the light of His revelation of Himself and being prepared at all times to acknowledge any sin of which we become aware. When we fail, we are not to be overwhelmed by our failure, but to rely on the intercession of our Advocate with God the Father. That segment, which began at 1:5, ends with 2:2.

The section that follows, namely 2:3-11, is also part of the Preamble: "Living in Fellowship with God" (1:5–2:11). This new section carries the subject to a higher level. Here John focuses our attention on the result, or goal, toward which fellowship should always lead: namely, the knowledge of God.

B. Reaching the Goal: Knowing the God of Light (2:3-11)

³Now by this we know that we know Him, if we keep His commandments.

The most obvious goal of fellowship with "the Father and with His Son Jesus Christ" (1:3) is to get to **know** the One with whom we are having fellowship. But any claim that we have achieved a real and personal knowledge of God can be at once tested by whether **we keep His commandments.** The words **by this** are explained by the phrase **if we keep His commandments.** (See discussion under verse 5.) As often in this epistle, the word **Him** might refer either to God or Christ, or it may be intentionally vague, since for John they are One. A strict reference to the last Person named is not required, since a new sub-unit begins here.[1]

It is at precisely this point that much contemporary interpretation of the Epistle of First John jumps the track. This verse is often taken as a way of knowing whether or not we are really *saved*. But that view flies directly into the face of all Johannine theology, according to which we are saved by believing in Christ for eternal life (John 3:16; 5:24; 6:35 and *passim*; the references are numerous). The response often made is that although salvation is by faith, we cannot know whether our faith is real unless we **keep His commandments**.

The idea that a Christian can believe in Christ, without knowing whether he or she has *really* believed, is complete nonsense. Of course we can know whether or not we believe. That we can know this is both common sense and completely biblical. When Jesus framed His great statement about being the Resurrection and the Life and about guaranteeing eternal life to every believer, He asked Martha, "Do you believe this?" (John 11:25-26) Martha's reply was a strong affirmation, "Yes, Lord, I believe that you are the Christ, the Son of God, who is to come into the world" (John 11:27).

To the same effect is the story of the conversion of the man born blind. Jesus asks him, "Do you believe in the Son of God?" (John 9:35). When the man inquires, "Who is He, Lord, that I may believe in Him?" Jesus replies majestically, "You have both seen Him and it is He who is talking with you" (John 9:36-37). The blind man does not respond to this by saying, "I hope I believe" or "Whether I believe or not will be seen from my works!" Such responses would have been nonsense. Instead he says, *"Lord, I believe"* (John 9:38). The idea that a believer cannot really know he has believed is a theological construct without a shred of support from the Word of God.

First John 2:3 is not talking about the *saving* knowledge of Christ. It is true that all believers do know God and Christ at a fundamental level; they know God as "the only true God" and they know that Jesus Christ has been sent by Him (John 17:3). But at the level of communion and fellowship, a believer may *not* know his Lord.

This is shown in the Lord Jesus' exchange with Philip in John 14:7-9. After announcing that He is "the way, the truth, and the life," the Lord goes on to say to *all* the disciples, "If you [Greek, plural] had *known* Me [implication: but you didn't], you [Greek, plural] would have *known* [implication: but you don't] My Father also; and from now on you [Greek, plural] know Him and have seen Him."[2] When Philip asks to see the Father, Jesus again responds, "Have I been with you [Greek, plural] so long, and yet you [Greek, singular] have not *known* Me, Philip?" Clearly, there was a sense in which Philip and the other disciples *did not know* the One in whom they had believed.

Even in human relationships the word *know* is quite flexible. I may *know* persons in the sense that I recognize them or am acquainted with them; but at the same time I may *not* know them in the sense of intimate knowledge or real perception of their character or nature. "I thought I knew you, but I don't," is a perfectly comprehensible statement in English. So too, the Christian who does know God as the true and living God and who knows His Son as his Savior (John 17:3) may be very much a stranger to God in terms of intimate knowledge of His character and ways. All interpreters of the New Testament must keep in mind that, in both English and Greek, words for "knowing" are *polymorphous*, i.e., used in many ways.

Thus the test suggested by 1 John 2:3 is not of the *saving* knowledge of God or of Christ, but of the *experiential* knowledge of God and His Son. To get this wrong, as many commentators have, is to lay the groundwork for a complete misreading of the epistle! Such a misreading is indeed common in the commentaries today and may be traced back primarily to Robert Law's study on this epistle.[3]

At the level of the experiential knowledge of the Lord, it is certainly true that any claim to this is forfeited if we live heedless of **His commandments**. After all, the God we are claiming to **know** "is light and in Him is no darkness at all" (1:5). Just as a claim to fellowship with Him is false if we "walk in darkness," so too a disobedient lifestyle falsifies any claim to intimate knowledge of **Him**.

The English translation **we know that we know Him** unfortunately obscures a slight shift in the verb forms in Greek that involves a subtle, but important, distinction. We might translate the phrase: **we know** (present tense) **that we** *have come to* **know** (perfect tense) **Him**.[4] The Christian who has *come to know* the Lord (through fellowship and obedience to His commandments) can be assured that he has attained this knowledge. It is not a matter of guesswork or wishful thinking. A genuine knowledge of the Father and the Son does indeed flow into an obedient heart, and the longer one walks with God in this way, the richer and deeper this knowledge becomes. The experience thus obtained is anticipated in the words of Jesus to the disciples, "He who has My commandments and keeps them, it is he who loves Me. And he who loves Me will be loved by My Father, and I will love him and *manifest Myself* to him" (John 14:21; italics added). Clearly, this self-manifestation of the Savior to the hearts of obedient disciples is what *coming to know Him* is all about.

The Greek verb rendered **keep** ($\overline{te}re\overline{o}$) is used in this epistle six times with "commandments" as its object (here and in verse 4; in 3:22-24; and 5:2-3); once with "His word" as the object (verse 5); and in 5:18 with "himself" as the object. The verb fundamentally means to "*to keep watch over, guard*."[5] To keep a commandment simply means to "carry out a command." However, the Greek verb ($\overline{te}re\overline{o}$) carries an additional connotation of being "observant" or "careful" about the commandments. The English "to keep a commandment" does not suggest this additional idea found in the Greek. John is not thinking, therefore, about *mere performance* of the commands of God, but rather about that attitude of obedience which is marked by *concern for*, and *attentiveness to*, God's will. We are to "guard" His commands!

When God's commandments are kept with the carefulness of a diligent heart, the spiritual conditions are right for the Father and the Son to make themselves *known* to the obedient disciple. No other kind of person can rightly claim such knowledge.

⁴He who says, "I know Him," and does not keep His commandments, is a liar, and the truth is not in him.

But someone *might* claim such knowledge without the obedience that goes with it. In that case, the person making the claim **is a liar** and **the truth is not in him** as a dynamic, controlling force (see 1:8 and the discussion there).

There is no reason to think that the apostle has only the Revisionists in mind here, although they may well have made such a claim. Unlike 1:6, John does not say, "If *we* say" (thinking of his Christian audience), but rather "**he who says**," that is, *whoever* they may be, Christian or not. The change to this construction need not be viewed as merely "stylistic."[6] It is easy to believe that the Revisionists might want to promote their false doctrine with a claim like this. But equally, ordinary Christians are often tempted to make special claims to the knowledge of God, sometimes as a way to cover up, or compensate for, the failures that burden their consciences. But without obedience to God's commandments, no person can truthfully claim an intimate personal knowledge of the Father and the Son.

Here again, as in verse 3, the words **I know Him** could be translated *I have come to know Him*. On the lips of the Revisionists this claim would probably imply the attainment of a knowledge of God which the readers lacked and which the Revisionists offered to supply. John will shortly stress the spiritual sufficiency of his Christian readers (see 2:12-14).

> **⁵But whoever keeps His word, truly the love of God is perfected in him. By this we know that we are in Him.**

In contrast to the false claim discussed in verse 4, the apostle now observes that the person who guards, or **keeps**, **His word** has a special experience of **the love of God**.

The expression **His word** is, of course, a collective way of referring to "His commandments" (verse 4). It therefore implies a body of instruction that has been committed to Christians through the teaching of the church. In fact, in the Great Commission the apostles (including John) were instructed to teach future disciples "to observe [Greek: *tēreō*, as in 1 John 2:3; see discussion there] all things that I have commanded you" (Matthew 28:20). Evidently it was the custom of the apostles to do this after a person had come to saving faith in Christ (see Acts 2:41-42; 13:43).

In 1 John 2:3-11 the apostle is now discussing the experience of one to whom these commandments have been communicated; that is, the person who has received instruction inside the church. This fits with the observation that John makes in verse 3 of knowing that we *have come to know* God (see discussion there). Obviously a newly saved individual does not immediately possess the instruction in God's commandments that he needs. But when he has been taught these commands (i.e., **His word**) and puts them into practice, it is then that he acquires the knowledge of the Father and the Son that goes with this.

This is why the seminal verse in John 14:21 (mentioned under verse 3) sheds so much light on this passage in First John. There our Lord lays down *two* conditions for the self-manifestation of which He speaks. He says: "He who [1] *has My commandments* and [2] *keeps* [*tēreō* again] *them*, it is he who loves Me. And he who loves Me will be loved by My Father, and

I will love him and manifest Myself to him." Obviously a person must first *have* the Lord's commandments before he can *keep* them. When these two conditions are met, the self-manifestation of Christ brings true and intimate knowledge of God to the obedient disciple.

When one of the disciples asks Jesus about the statement He has just made (i.e., in John 14:21), our Lord repeats the statement in slightly altered form. He says, "If anyone loves Me, he will keep [guard] My word; and My Father will love him, and We will come to him and make Our home with him. He who does not love Me does not keep My words; and the word which you hear is not Mine but the Father's who sent Me" (John 14:23-24). It is to be noted that these statements are made only at the end of the three and one-half years of teaching that the disciples had received from God's Son. Now they *did* have His commands and were enjoined to show their love for Him by *keeping* them.

There is no reason to doubt that when John penned 1 John 2:3-5 he had in mind the statements of Jesus in John 14:21 and 23-24. Even the change from "commandments" (1 John 2:3) to **word** (this verse) is reflected in that passage in his Gospel, where we find "My commandments" in verse 21 and "My word" in verse 23. We are thus firmly stationed on what may be called discipleship truth, in contrast to truth about eternal salvation. Love for Christ and obedience to **His word** are in no way a test of saving faith, despite the repeated claim by many that they are. Instead, they are tests of genuine, heartfelt discipleship to the One who loved us and gave Himself for us (Galatians 2:20).

As the verses from John's Gospel make clear, obedience to His word is inseparably connected to the experience of "the love of God." This phrase could be taken either as "God's love for us" (subjective genitive) or as "our love for God" (objective genitive). The Greek permits either interpretation. In the light of John 14, it is quite possible that John has both ideas in mind in 1 John 2:5. According to John 14, obedience is an expression of love for Christ and disobedience is an expression of a lack of love for Him (John 14:23-24). But at the same time, the one who loves Christ will be the special object of the love of the Father and the Son (John 14:23).

So John tells us here that the obedient Christian disciple is a person in whom **truly the love of God is perfected**. The Greek word translated **is perfected** (*teteleiotai*) suggests ideas like "bring to completion," "bring to its goal," "bring to full measure."[7] God's love for the believer is wonderful at the point of salvation (see 1 John 3:1). But its goal is not reached until the believer returns that love by obedience, with the result that he knows the deeply personal love of the Father and Son as they "make [their] home with him" (John 14:23).

In view of all that has just been said about verse 5, it seems clear that 1 John 2:3-11 is concerned with one who has had some time in the faith, has learned what his Lord commands, and by obedience has come to know God and His love in a special way. This goes beyond the truth John deals with in 1:5–2:2. As described there, fellowship with God requires only openness to the light and a willingness to acknowledge whatever sin the light reveals. Even the believer who is a babe in Christ can live in harmonious fellowship with the Lord. But in time he will learn God's will and, if he does it, will enter the more advanced stage of fellowship in which he comes to know God and His love. In such a person **the love of God is perfected**. That is, it has reached its "goal" in him.

The next statement of the verse, **by this we know that we are in Him**, takes the discussion one step further. The words **by this** might refer either forward or backward. If forward, the reference is to verse 6. If backward, the reference is to the experience of having God's love perfected in us. However, since verse 6 has no grammatical tie to the previous statement, Johannine usage suggests a reference backward.[8] Thus the words **by this** refer to the experience of love just described: i.e., **by** means of **this** experience of God's love, we can **know that we are in Him**.

The expression **in Him** (Greek: *en autō*) must not be superficially read as an equivalent to Paul's concept of being "in Christ" (Greek: *en Christō*). Instead, the seedbed for John's idea is our Lord's teaching in John 13–17, especially 15:1-8. This well-known passage about the vine and its branches can rightly be understood as a metaphor for the relationship between a disciple and his Lord. This is made clear by the words that conclude the vine/branch discourse: "By this My Father is glorified, that you bear much fruit; *so you will be My disciples*" (John 15:8, italics added). Unlike the salvation relationship, the relationship of a disciple to his Teacher can be lost: "If anyone does not abide *in Me*, he is cast out as a branch" (John 15:6, emphasis added). The "anyone," of course, means "any disciple," since only a disciple can "abide" in Christ. As the whole discourse in John 15 makes clear, the disciple must *remain* in his Master, just as the branch must *abide* in the Vine (John 15:4). To be "cast out as a branch" means to lose the disciple/Teacher relationship, *not* to lose eternal life.

In using the words **in Him**, therefore, John is referring to the "abiding" Teacher/disciple relationship. This is made evident in the very next verse. The disciple's experience of **the love of God** being **perfected in him** is evidence that this disciple is indeed **in Him** in the sense of "abiding" in his Lord. Verse 6 elaborates this thought.

⁶He who says he abides in Him ought himself also to walk just as He walked.

If anyone claims that **he abides in** Christ, this claim can be verified only by a Christlike lifestyle. This is John's first use in the epistle of the term *abide*. The Greek word is *menō* ("to remain," "to dwell," "to live,") and is a favorite word which John uses to describe the life of discipleship to Jesus Christ (see John 15:4-7 and see the discussion above).[9]

The words of verse 5 about being "in Him" are functionally equivalent to the idea of "abiding" in Him. If we can "know that we are *in Him*" by keeping His commands and by experiencing the perfecting of God's love, the reverse side of the same coin is that we **ought...also to walk** (live) **just as He walked**. This, of course, is also discipleship truth. The goal of a disciple is to be *like* his Teacher (see Matthew 10:24-25). An un-Christlike believer is not living the true Christian life. He is not walking as a disciple of His Lord should walk.

As we have already seen, 1 John 2:3-5 deals with Christian living that has gone beyond the stage of spiritual babyhood and involves both learning and doing the Lord's commands. In the same way, the "abiding" relationship is possible only when there has been sufficient advance in Christian experience. It was after Jesus and His disciples emerged from the Upper Room, at the very conclusion of His three and one-half years of instructing them, that the Lord introduced them to the concept of "abiding" in Him (John 15:1-8). Shortly afterward He also reminded them of the completeness of their spiritual education by telling them, "All things that I have heard from My Father I have made known to you" (John 15:15).

A Christlike walk, the highest attainment open to a disciple, is *not* reached the moment one is born again. It requires time for instruction so that one's heart is prepared to act on what he has learned. This heightened experience is marked by obedience to the Lord's commandments (verses 3-4), by the experience of knowing Him (verses 3-4), and by the experience of God's perfected love (verse 5). Such a disciple **abides in Him**. That is, he *lives*, or *dwells*, in his Lord, just as a branch lives, or dwells, in a vine. So long as this connection is maintained, the experience of "abiding" in Christ continues.

The "abider" is a believer who has learned to live like the Lord Jesus Christ. But how did Christ live? What makes us Christlike? The next few verses deal with this issue.

> **⁷Brethren, I write no new commandment to you, but an old commandment which you have had from the beginning. The old commandment is the word which you heard from the beginning.**

In speaking of God's commandments and of a Christlike walk, the apostle is not teaching his readers something **new**. Rather he is dealing with an **old commandment which** they **had from the beginning** of their Christian experience.

The summing up of all God's commandments into a single **commandment** is characteristic of John. See John 15:10, 12; 1 John 3:22-23; 2 John 6. As these texts show, the commandment to love one another summarizes all of the Savior's commandments. (Similarly, Paul could summarize the law under the commandment to love one's neighbor: Romans 13:8-10.) In the light of verses 8 to 11, the old commandment is nothing less than the one spoken years before by our Lord, "A new commandment I give to you, that you love one another; as I have loved you, that you also love one another" (John 13:34). Thus, to "walk just as He walked" (verse 6) is to walk in love toward one's fellow Christians.

This memorable "new" **commandment** was now **old** for John's readership (although he would shortly also call it "new," verse 8). But it was **old** for them precisely because they had received it **from the beginning**, that is, in the very earliest period of their Christian lives. This is the only reasonable sense for the phrase **from the beginning**. Thus it does not quite mean the same thing here as the phrase *from the beginning* in 1 John 1:1 (see discussion there). At the same time, however, there is an implicit connection between 1:1 and 2:7, since John is concerned in this letter with the original truth of Christianity in contrast to the spurious "new truth" evidently taught by the Revisionists. Thus the commandment which John's readers had **from the beginning** was indeed part of what John had heard "from the beginning" (verse 1).

The statement about **the old commandment** being **the word which you heard from the beginning** is not a mere redundancy. By switching to the expression, **the word which you heard**, John makes an additional point. Not only was there not a new *responsibility* (commandment) to be given to his readers, there was no new *content* to that responsibility. It was the same **word** (Greek: *logos*, i.e., message, communication, etc.) which they had originally **heard**.

Down through the centuries of Christian theology, "progressives" have employed two techniques in their efforts to "update" traditional beliefs and doctrines. One method is to add new ideas to the old established teaching. Another is to give new meaning to old formulations. For example, in Christian groups committed to precise doctrinal formulations, the "progressives" often seek to reinterpret the meaning of these formulations in a way more congenial to the "new" theology. In 1 John 2:7 the apostle shuts the door on both of these operations in regard to the Christian truth he is communicating.

Perhaps the Revisionists of John's day, like most others of their stripe, reinterpreted the meaning of the commandment to love one another. This John would not allow. **The old commandment** still had the same content as before. It was the same **word** that the readers had previously comprehended. They did not need any new information.

> [8]**Again, a new commandment I write to you, which thing is true in Him and in you, because the darkness is passing away, and the true light is already shining.**

From another point of view (**Again**), the commandment John spoke about in verse 7 as being "old" can equally well be called **a new commandment**. This is because it belongs to the new age that is in the process of dawning.

The Lord Jesus had called His command to love one another "new" because He was just then speaking it for the first time (John 13:34). Its newness for John here is something different, even though he probably has our Lord's terminology in mind (and may even be drawing out its further implications). For the readers, this is an "old commandment" because they had heard it from the very first. But they should also consider it as **new**, since it does not partake of the character of the old, transient spiritual **darkness** but takes its character from **the true light** of the new age to come.

That this is John's meaning is signaled by the words **is passing away** and **already**. The Greek word rendered **is passing away** is *parago* and occurs in First John only here and in verse 17 where we are told that "the world is passing away" (see also its use in the same sense in 1 Corinthians 7:31, "the form of this world is passing away"). Since the world is morally at odds with God the Father (2:15-17), it is clear that darkness is a way of describing its moral condition. Thus the apostle is stating that the "old" moral situation of the world is temporary and destined to pass from the scene. The "new" reality that will replace it, **the true light**, is already shining. Clearly John is talking in terms of eschatology, the teaching about "last things."

With this in mind, we can more readily understand the words **which thing is true in Him and in you.**[10] As we have seen, the new commandment calls upon disciples to love one another as Christ has loved them. There is to be a correspondence between the Giver of the command and the recipients of the command. Here the word **true** is best understood in connection with the words **the true light**. The point is this: that as Christ's disciples carry out the command to love one another, this command has the *character of truth,* both in them as they do it and in Him who gave and exemplified it. Such obedience reflects the realities of the age to come, **the true light** of which already shines.

Stated another way, Christian love is *truth manifested* both in the Teacher who modeled it and in us who obey it as we "walk just as He walked." The love thus expressed partakes of none of the falseness and deceit that characterizes **the darkness** around us, where "love" is often feigned or selfish.

On the contrary, the love that is expressed among Christians belongs to **the true light** that **is already shining**. Christian eschatology looks forward to a day when the moral **darkness** of the present age will disappear entirely, and when the reality of all that God is will shine forth in unhindered brilliance (2 Peter 3:13). But that **true light** has already had a manifestation in the Person of the Incarnate Son of God, who perfectly revealed the nature of God His Father in the love He had for the world (John 3:16) and for His own (John 13:1). Therefore, when the Christian carries out the command to love after the model of the Savior's love, the *truth* that is thereby manifested is nothing less than a manifestation of the spiritual reality of the age to come. The dark age of hatred is soon to be gone. The new age of love has already dawned.

It follows, therefore, that others can see the **light** of the new age shining in us as we exemplify Christ's own love by loving one another. As Jesus Himself said, "By this all will know that you are My disciples, if you have love for one another" (John 13:35).

> **⁹He who says he is in the light, and hates his brother, is in darkness until now.**

It follows from what John has just said that hatred among Christians is completely contrary to the light of the new age that is "already" shining.

Many expositors, however, are unwilling to face the sad reality that hatred can and does exist among truly born again believers. The claim that this verse can only refer to "professing" believers is without a shred of evidence in the text. If John was thinking of an unsaved (but professing) Christian person hating a true Christian, he would not have written: **He who says he is in the light, and hates his brother**... The word **his** is completely unnecessary, and even misleading, if a non-Christian is hating a Christian. The correct way to say that would be, "He who...hates *a* brother" (i.e., someone who hates a Christian).

Furthermore, as we have seen, in this context the subject matter is our Lord's command to "love one another" (John 13:34). This is also true throughout the epistle where the command to love is in view. It is the love of Christian toward Christian that John has in mind (cf. especially, 4:20–5:1). The term **brother** must therefore be understood in the Christian sense.

The claim that a Christian could not ever hate another Christian would be ludicrous, were it not also so tragically misleading. Every honest believer knows perfectly well that he or she must often struggle against feelings of hostility and animosity toward other believers. All pastors know that such problems exist in their congregations. If the Bible taught that feelings of hatred were a sure sign of an unsaved condition, then virtually no one in the whole church would be saved! But the Bible does not teach this.

The apostle here acknowledges the sad reality, but wants the Christian who hates to be quite sure that his moral condition is deplorable. In fact, a claim by such a person that **he is in the light** is falsified by his hatred of his fellow Christian. The claim and the hatred taken together simply prove that the hostile Christian **is in darkness until now**.

This does not mean the person is unsaved. The context clearly determines the parameters of this statement. From verse 3 on, we have been talking about the more advanced Christian (who both *has* and *keeps* his Lord's commandments) and who thus has come to *know* God in an intimate sense. Since the command to love one another belongs not to the passing "darkness" but to "the true light" of the new age which "is already shining," the obedient, loving believer clearly lives **in the light** of the age to come. But just as clearly, the unloving believer does not. Indeed, such a believer has never really experienced that light and thus **is in darkness until now**. That is, this believer lives in the spirit and ethos of the darkness that "is passing away" (see verse 8).

In this context, therefore, the claim to be **in the light** is the functional equivalent of the earlier false claim to "know Him" (verse 4). Both claims are falsified by disobedience —in verse 4 to "His commandments" and here to the all-embracing command to love one another. Thus, the Christian who *claims* to be **in the light** while hating **his brother** has *never* attained this level of experience. He has *never* learned to live in the spirit of the age to come, or to reflect "the true light" of that age. Thus, such a person **is in darkness until now**.

Hatred of a fellow Christian, combined with a claim to be **in the light** that heralds the new age, shows only too plainly a profound ignorance of that **light**.

> **[10]He who loves his brother abides in the light, and there is no cause for stumbling in him.**

By contrast with the false claimant of verse 9, the Christian **who loves his brother** is not only **in the light** but also abides there.

As already stated above, this unit of the epistle (2:3-11) is concerned with the experience of Christian living that should follow spiritual infancy. There is no need for the "infant" stage of Christianity to be unduly prolonged, as it was for the Corinthians (see 1 Corinthians 3:1-4). But the development of the newly saved Christian into a "spiritual" Christian (see 1 Corinthians 2:13–3:4) will depend on the quality of the instruction he receives in the church and on his own willingness to apply that instruction in his personal life. It seems evident that the kind of person Paul describes as "he who is spiritual" and who "judges all things" (1 Corinthians 2:15) is exactly the person John designates as one who has come to know God and is "abiding" in Christ (see verse 6 and the discussion there).

For John, then, the "abiding" life is one that is lived **in the light** of the new age—a **light** that "already shines" due to the manifestation of God's Son. The person who walks in love is abiding in Christ and in this **light**. By loving as Christ loved, he is walking "as He walked" (verse 6).

The one who lives this way is also a person in whom **there is no cause for stumbling**. The words **no cause for stumbling** translate a Greek word (*skandalon*) which basically means a trap or a snare of some kind, and came in Christian usage to mean whatever ensnares a person in sin. In the person **who loves his brother** there is no such trap. Although the reference here could be to something that causes *others* to stumble, in view of verse 11 (which is the opposite) and of the phrase **in him**, the reference is most likely to something that might ensnare the individual himself. No trap is laid *within* himself.[11]

This does not mean, of course, that this person is sinless (see 1:8), but rather that in so walking (as Christ walked) he lays no trap for himself; that is, he does not create an inner spiritual condition by which he can be trapped and ensnared in sin. This suggests that the one who hates his brother sets up the inward spiritual conditions which make entrapment by sin extremely likely.

Christian experience bears this out. When hostility to a brother rules a Christian's heart, it leads him readily and rapidly into sinful words and behavior. The spirit of hate toward a brother is a spiritual trap that the hater lays for himself.

[11]But he who hates his brother is in darkness and walks in darkness, and does not know where he is going, because the darkness has blinded his eyes.

Hatred of a fellow Christian betrays a terrible disorientation on the part of the one doing the hating. Not only is he in spiritual darkness, but that is where he *lives* (**walks**). Nor does he know where his chosen path may take him because **the darkness has blinded his eyes**.

No course of life is more fraught with spiritual and temporal danger for a Christian than one that includes an attitude of hatred toward another Christian. The Christian who hates has lost touch with "the true light" (verse 8) which displays God's loving nature. And he has also embraced "the darkness" which "is passing away" (verse 8), with all its hostility to God and Christ and all who belong to Christ. He easily becomes a tool in the hands of Satan, as so many have in Christian churches, resulting in serious divisions and church splits. The person himself cannot anticipate the damage he may do, nor can he anticipate the seriousness of the divine discipline that may fall on him (see Hebrews 12:3-11; Romans 16:17-18; 1 Timothy 1:19-20; and similar texts). As John says, he **does not know where he is going**.

And it is with this solemn thought that John concludes this unit of his epistle. Over the span of 1:5–2:11, he has reviewed for his readers basic truths which they have already been taught. Simple fellowship with God takes place when the Christian walks with an open and honest heart in the light of what God is (1:5). More advanced fellowship occurs when the commandments of our Lord are learned and kept so that we *abide* or *dwell* in Him, walking as He walked in love. The one who so lives *knows* God.[12] The opposite lifestyle, marked by hatred toward one's brother, is a pathway to spiritual disaster, even though the disobedient Christian can never be lost by his Lord (John 6:35-40).

To live **in darkness** and hate is to make the Savior a stranger in one's experience on earth. Though saved, such a Christian has forfeited the vital, intimate knowledge of his God.

ENDNOTES

[1]Cf. Also Raymond E. Brown, *The Epistles of John,* AB (Garden City, NY: Doubleday, 1982), p. 249.

[2]The Greek text underlying John 14:7 has been disputed. The most widely used Greek New Testaments (the United Bible Societies' edition [4th] and the Nestle/Aland edition [27th]) print a Greek text of 14:7 which may be literally rendered: "If you have known Me, you will know My Father also." But the probability that this reading is original is extremely low. Not only are the vast majority of extant manuscripts against it, but even Codex Vaticanus (B), highly favored by many textual critics, agrees with the *MajT* reading (although using a different verb for "know" in the second clause). The choice found in the critical editions is defended in Bruce Metzger's *A Textual Commentary on the Greek New Testament: A Companion Volume to the United Bible Societies' Greek New Testament.* 2nd ed. (Stuttgart, Germany: Deutsche Bibelgesellschaft and United Bible Societies, 1994), p. 207. In a dissenting note, Kurt Aland writes: "The purpose of the Evangelist as well as the laws of textual development have been misunderstood. If a negative and a positive statement about the apostles stand side by side in the textual tradition, the positive is usually the later." Furthermore, the reading adopted by UBS and Nestle/Aland coheres poorly with verse 9 where the Greek form of our Lord's question ("…and you have not known Me, Philip?") implies the answer, "No, I haven't." We may safely reject the critical reading.

[3]Robert Law, *The Tests of Life: A Study of the First Epistle of St. John,* 3rd ed. (Edinburgh: T. & T. Clark, 1914 [reprint ed., Grand Rapids: Baker Book House, 1968]).

[4]It is well to be reminded that the perfect tense "is not a past tense but a present one, indicating not the past action as such but the present 'state of affairs' resulting from the past action" (Maximilian Zerwick, *Biblical Greek: Illustrated by Examples* [Rome: Scripta Pontificii Instituti Biblici, 1963], p. 96). The translation suggested in our Commentary ("we have come to know") fits the grammar almost perfectly, although with other English verbs than "to know" it is not always easy to convey the nuance of the perfect tense without inappropriate amplification.

[5]Bauer, Walter. *A Greek-English Lexicon of the New Testament and Other Early Christian Literature* (Chicago: University of Chicago Press, 1979), p. 814.

[6]Marianne Meye Thompson, *1–3 John,* IVPNT (Downers Grove, IL: InterVarsity Press, 1992), p. 53.

[7]Cf. BGD, pp. 809-810.

[8]In a significant study by John and Joy Anderson ("Cataphora in 1 John," *NoT* 7 [1993]: 41-46) the *en touto* (by this) in 1 John 2:5 is taken as an example of *cataphora* (reference forward). But close examination of their list of examples for 1 John suggests that the Andersons have failed to note that both in 3:10a and in 4:2 the *en touto* clause is followed by an *asyndetic* sentence (i.e., one with no connective word) and not by an explanatory subordinate construction. (In 2:5 the words **that we are in Him** give the content of the knowledge and are not explanatory of *en touto*.) In these three cases the reference can easily be backward (see our Commentary). In all other cases listed by them on pp. 42-43 of their article, a subordinate, explanatory structure of some kind follows the *en touto* clause. This pattern holds for John's use of *en touto* in the Fourth Gospel as well. There the instances are: (1) *cataphora*, 9:30; 13:35; 15:8; and (2) *anaphora* (reference back), 4:37 (the *hoti* explains the "saying" and *not* the *en touto*); 16:30. It is highly probable, therefore, that the constructions at 2:5, 3:10b, and 4:2 should be regarded as displaying a structural signal that *cataphora* is not involved in the *en touto* found in these places. Another way of stating this principle is that John never employs a following *asyndetic construction* to explain the content of *en touto*. Brown (*Epistles,* pp. 248-49) has a very helpful discussion of the problem of reference in John's *en touto*, but I think my approach is cleaner and a more consistent account of John's usage. We can thus correct Brown with respect to 4:2 which he takes as cataphoric and 4:17 which he takes as anaphoric (see our Commentary on these verses); and in John 4:37 and 1 John 2:5 which he thinks refer "to both what precedes and follows" (p. 249). In John 4:37, the *en touto* is adequately explained by the preceding statements in verse 36, although verse 38 elaborates with the additional thought of Jesus as the author of this kind of experience. But other than the differences specified here, I find myself in agreement with Brown on all of the other references in the Gospel and the epistle (the phrase is not found in Second or Third John).

[9]According to Brown (*Epistles,* p. 259) John's use of *meno* represents "55% of the total New Testament usage; 40 times in GJohn" and "24 times in I John, 3 in II John." The figures are the same for the Hodges/Farstad edition of the *MajT*, although the verb was omitted at the end of 1 John 4:16 by the edition of the Textus Receptus from which the KJV was made, and does not appear in the NKJV either.

[10]The words **which thing** refer to the *subject matter* of the commandment, i.e., "the matter of love." These words render a neuter relative pronoun in Greek (*ho*) which does not have strict grammatical concord with its natural antecedent, "a new commandment" (which is feminine in Greek). But the neuter is easily explained as a reference, not to the formal commandment per se, but to the *content of the commandment* viewed as "something to be done." Grammarians

The First Epistle of John

call this *ad sensum* agreement and the use is similar to the impersonal *ho* employed three times in 1 John 1:1 and again in 1:3. Cf. also the phrase "that…which [*ho*] you heard from the beginning" and "what [*ho*] you heard from the beginning" (2:24). The commentators have tended to strain plausibility in discussing the construction here: cf. Stephen S. Smalley, *1,2,3 John,* WBC (Waco, TX: Word Books, 1984), p. 56: "the allusion here is…to the newness (the new *quality*) of the law of love." See also, to the same effect, A. E. Brooke, *A Critical and Exegetical Commentary on the Johannine Epistles,* ICC (Edinburgh: T. & T. Clark, 1912), p. 36; and see the labored explanations of Brooke Foss Westcott, *The Epistles of St John: The Greek Text with Notes* (Grand Rapids: Wm. B. Eerdmans Publishing Co., 1966), p. 53, and Law, *Tests,* p. 376. At the same time, it is surely less than clear to simply say: "It is better, then, to take the phrase [with *ho*] as modifying the whole preceding idea" (Thompson, *1–3 John,* p. 59).

[11]It would also be possible to translate the words rendered "in him" (Greek: *en autō*) as "in it" and refer them to **the light**. But Thompson (*1–3 John,* p. 60) is no doubt right to say that "it would be self-evident to say that there is nothing in the light that can make a person stumble." A reference to the state of the person's inner life is much more appropriate here.

[12]With John's concept of knowing a God of love one might compare Jeremiah 9:24:

"But let him who glories glory in this,
That he *understands and knows* Me,
That I am the Lord, exercising lovingkindness, judgment,
and righteousness in the earth.
For in these I delight," says the Lord
(italics added).

CHAPTER 4

Warning the Well-Prepared

(1 John 2:12-27)

In the section of First John we have just concluded (1:5–2:11), the apostle has given his readers an extended review of the fundamental truths about fellowship with God. Fellowship, after all, is the theme of the epistle (1:3). If John is to prevent the loss of this fellowship, endangered as it is by the heresies of the Revisionists, he must call his Christian audience back to first principles. If they hold to these firmly, they will continue to enjoy fellowship with the circle and, above all, with God the Father and His Son Jesus Christ (1:3).

But John has not yet stated in so many words what exactly occasions this epistle. It is true that some of his statements hint that false ideas are afloat, but their nature and those who circulate them are not clearly mentioned. For this reason, the effort made by some commentators to find heretical affirmations in the previous section is doomed to failure. Christian people who are out of touch with God can perfectly well make all of the false statements referred to in 1:5–2:11. That the Revisionists may also have made some of these statements is not unlikely, but it is impossible for us to know which, if any, of them these heretics actually employed.

In this section, however, John refers to the Revisionists directly. In so doing he makes clear the overall purpose of the epistle. The appearance of these "antichrists" on the scene is what has occasioned this letter. Appropriately, the apostle's concern is with the threat they constitute to the readers' continuing fellowship with God (cf. 1:3). Of course, no matter how much the readership might be misled, there was no danger to their eternal salvation; although, as we shall see, there *was* a threat to their *assurance* of salvation.

But before directly referring to the Revisionists, John first asserts the spiritual competence of his Christian readers.

III. PURPOSE: THE READERS MUST RESIST THE ANTICHRISTS (2:12-27)

A. By Recognizing Their Spiritual Assets (2:12-14)

In a series of tightly constructed statements, the apostle John reminds his Christian readership of their spiritual assets. This was necessary since the Revisionists apparently called these into question. Only by casting doubt on the sufficiency of the readers' religious experience could the Revisionists hope to gain a hearing for their doctrines.

Commentators have debated just how the titles, "little children," "fathers," and "young men" apply to the readership. If the underlying rationale of the titles is to distinguish different levels of spiritual development or competence, then the sequence is strange. Instead of little children, fathers, and young men, we should expect the sequence: little children, young men, and fathers. Moreover, elsewhere in the letter the whole readership is addressed as "little children" (2:1, 18, 28; 3:7, 18; 4:4; 5:21). For these reasons it seems quite unlikely that different levels of spiritual growth are indicated by the three titles.[1]

The writer's own usage gives us the answer: all the titles refer to the entire readership from various points of view. This seems confirmed by the fact that the second designation of the readers as "little children" (2:13) employs the Greek word *paidion*, which is immediately reused for the second and last time in the letter in reference to *all the readers* (2:18). The following exposition will seek to show that taking the two sets of titles as references to all the readers produces an understanding of the text that discloses it as a very carefully constructed passage.[2]

> [12]I write to you, little children,
>   Because your sins are forgiven you
>   for His name's sake.

In view of all the warnings the apostle has given in the previous section (1:5–2:11), the readers may wonder why he is writing to them. Is it because he finds them spiritually deficient? Is it even because he wonders if they are truly saved?[3]

The answer to both questions is an emphatic No! Once we have looked closely at verses 12-14, it will seem absurd that John could be thought to regard his readers as possible "false professors" of the Christian faith. Despite the fact that so many expositors have read First John that way, nothing could be further from the intention of the writer than to question his readers' eternal salvation. On the contrary, he emphatically affirms it. The use of this epistle as a series of "tests" to determine the genuineness of a person's salvation is a grotesque misreading. Those who make this egregious error have no one but themselves to blame, since in the verses under consideration the writer is perfectly clear about his view of the spiritual status of the readers.

To begin with, the readers have experienced the forgiveness of **sins**. This fact immediately marks them as the **little children** of their heavenly Father (cf. verse 13). This forgiveness has been granted **for His name's sake** (literally, "on account of His name"). That is, their forgiveness is predicated on the effectiveness and efficacy of Christ's name. Although the reference to **His name** could be to God the Father, elsewhere in the epistle the reference of the word *name* is to Jesus Christ (cf. 3:23; 5:13) and is likely to be the same here, in view of the Savior's propitiatory work on the cross (cf. 2:2). Saving faith is belief in **His name** (cf. 5:13; John 1:12; 3:18).

In the phrase **your sins**, the NKJV translators have supplied the word **your**. The Greek literally says "the sins." While the definite article used here (*hai*) can sometimes carry the possessive idea, it seems likely that the phrase ought to be translated without a possessive word in order to emphasize the character of their experience. The word **your** perhaps inappropriately suggests they have no more need of forgiveness. But as 1:9 indicates, the forgiveness of sins is an ongoing need in the believer's life—not to retain salvation, but to maintain fellowship with God. Thus, we should read the text in a slightly different fashion: "Because sins have been forgiven [Greek perfect tense] you for His name's sake." They *have* had the experience of forgiveness.

As we shall see in verses 25-26, the Revisionists seem to have called the readers' entire salvation experience into question and probably asserted that the readers have never experienced true forgiveness. But, says John, they *have*.

> [13a]I write to you, fathers,
>   Because you have known Him
>   *who is* from the beginning.
> [13b]I write to you, young men,
>   Because you have overcome
>   the wicked one.

It is noteworthy that in addressing the readers as "little children" (verse 12), the subject matter of 1:5–2:2 (the forgiveness...of sins) is referred to by John. Here, in addressing them as **fathers**, it is the subject matter of 2:3-11 that John has in mind, i.e., the idea of knowing God.

This tie is further confirmed by the fact that John uses the Greek perfect tense for the kind of knowledge he is speaking of both here and in 2:3-4. So here also we could translate: **Because you have *come to know* Him *who is* from the beginning**. In view of the statements found in 2:3-4, the assertion that the readership "has come to know" God implies that they have reached the stage where they both *have* and *keep* their Lord's commandments (see discussion on 2:3-4). This is the first of numerous statements implying that the readers constitute a relatively mature group of believers. As suggested in the Introduction under Audience, this may be due to the fact that this epistle was directed to the elders of one or more churches as a means of reaffirming their qualifications to lead and teach their congregations. When the letter was read aloud in a congregation, it would fortify the authority of the local leaders as over against the Revisionists, who no doubt challenged them for the ear of the congregation.

The words **Him *who is* from the beginning** could be a reference either to God or to Christ, both of whom are **from the beginning**. This is the third use of the phrase in the epistle, the two previous ones being 1:1 and 2:7. However, this use is different from 1:1, which refers to the beginning of the Christian revelation in the Person of Christ, and from 2:7, which refers to the readers' initial experience of the Christian faith. Instead, here the words **from the beginning** are most naturally taken as a reference to the eternality of the One whom the readership knows. It is as if the readers, viewed as **fathers**, had a spiritual experience that stretched back to the very **beginning**, since they knew the One who began all things. Though they were not possessed of exceptional chronological age, their spiritual contact with the Eternal One put them in contact with reality as it was **from the beginning** of everything. The term **fathers**, therefore, carries with it an overtone of seasoned experience with the Eternal God.

But the readers are also **young men** who **have overcome the wicked one**, i.e., Satan. Although under the designations "little children" and **fathers**, John has previous material in mind (see discussion earlier in this verse), that is not the case here. There has been no prior mention of the wicked one in this epistle, but the antichrists who are discussed in verses 18-27 are obviously agents of Satan (cf. 4:1-6). Thus it is now evident why the designation "**young men**" follows, rather than precedes, that of "**fathers**." It is precisely the readership's invaluable experience as "little children" (the forgiveness of sins) and as **fathers** (the knowledge of God) that renders them vigorous **young men** prepared to do battle with **the wicked one**.

In fact, these **young men** have already **overcome** Satan. The Greek verb (perfect tense, *nenikēkate*) suggests a past victory, the fruits of which still somehow remain. It is probable that John is here thinking of the readers' faith in Jesus as the Christ, since this truth was denied by the satanically inspired antichrists (see below, verse 22) and since such faith is a victory over the world (5:4-5) which lies in "the wicked one" (5:19). It should be stressed that every case of new birth, in which a person believes in Christ for eternal life, is very definitely a victory over **the wicked one**. As Paul informs us in Second Corinthians, Satan is actively engaged in blinding men's minds for the very purpose of preventing faith in the gospel of God's Son. When God breaks through that blindness and a lost sinner believes, then Satan is directly defeated (2 Corinthians 4:3-6). And since the effects of new birth can never be reversed by Satan, this defeat is decisive and permanent (Luke 8:12). At a minimum, the readers, viewed as **young men**, have experienced this victory and so can be truly said to **have overcome the wicked one** (5:4).

> **[13c]I write to you, little children,**
> **Because you have known the Father.**

Here the apostle clearly begins a new sequence, repeating the order of "**little children**," "fathers," and "young men." Strikingly, he attributes the *knowledge of God* to them as **little children**.

The English translation necessarily conceals the fact that the writer has chosen a new word for **little children** (Greek: *paidion*, instead of *teknion*). Thus the entire statement has been recast, as over against verse 12, even down to the point of choosing a different word of address. That this is deliberate is clear when the statements made to "fathers" and "young men" in verse 14 are compared to the previous ones earlier in this verse. What we discover is this: (1) the statement made to "little children" in verse 12 is *entirely changed* here; (2) the statement made to "fathers" earlier in this verse is *entirely the same* in verse 14; and (3) the statement made to "young men" earlier in this verse is *partly changed and partly the same* in verse 14. Such structuring is far from accidental.

What does it mean? It may be suggested that in two of these categories, statements made in the first set reflect what might be called *minimum experience* in each category, while the second set in the same two categories expresses *more advanced experience* in the category in question. The obvious exception to this is the category of "fathers" who "have known Him who is from the beginning" (verses 13-14; see discussion under verse 14).

As **little children**, therefore, the readership has gone well beyond the minimal experience of the forgiveness of sins (verse 12). All believers in Christ have experienced forgiveness as part of their salvation experience (see Acts 10:43). Even in their earliest days as "little children" in God's family, they experience "family forgiveness" as they confess their sins to God their heavenly Father (see 1 John 1:9). But obviously with time they can "come to know" **the Father** with whom they are having fellowship. Just as a baby cannot be said to do much more than recognize his parents, so it is in the spiritual realm. Coming to know **the Father** requires time in the faith and spiritual growth.

As we have seen, for the concept of "coming to know" God, John prefers the Greek perfect tense, no doubt because it readily conveys the idea of a state or a situation that results from what has been accomplished in the past. The author has used this tense in 2:3-4 in connection with obedience, and uses it of "fathers" earlier in this verse and again of the same category in verse 14. Here he uses it when he writes, **you have known the Father**. In every case where he employs this tense, an appropriate translation would be *to come to know.* The concept expresses a Christian attainment. (See the discussion under 2:3-4.)

No doubt the statement made to "fathers" about knowing "Him who is from the beginning" (this verse and verse 14) and the one made to **little children** about knowing **the Father** are not sharply distinct. Yet a subtle shading of the knowledge of God is probably implied. On the one hand, the **little children** know God in His role as *Father;* that is, they know His fatherly concern, compassion, love, etc. On the other hand, the fathers also know Him as the Eternal God whose qualities (love, fidelity, long-suffering, etc.) are eternally manifested in all that He has ever done or will do. Of course, both of these aspects of God are part of the fundamental knowledge of Him, and separating them runs the risk of making artificial distinctions. Still it is a fact that He who can be called the Everlasting Father (Isaiah 9:6) combines eternality with fatherhood in such a way that both aspects are truly enriched.

But it is clear that, in this second reference to **little children**, advancement beyond mere infancy is implied.

> [14]**I have written to you, fathers,**
>   **Because you have known Him**
>   *who is* **from the beginning.**
> **I have written to you, young men,**
>   **Because you are strong, and**
>   **the word of God abides in you,**
>   **And you have overcome the wicked one.**

The writer now changes from the present tense, "I write" (verses 12-13), to the past, **I have written**. This is no doubt due to the fact already observed that, while verse 13c is entirely different from the other address to "little children" in verse 12, here there is a clear element of repetition. The past tense calls attention to this fact, especially in the case of the **fathers**.[4]

To the readers viewed as **fathers** he chooses to say no more than he has already said. For what could mark an advance on the knowledge of **Him** *who is* **from the beginning?** The only possible advance is a greater *depth* to such knowledge. The writer thus assures them, by means of this repetition, that their knowledge of God is fully sufficient. No doubt the Revisionists thought otherwise.

Of particular interest are John's comments to the readers viewed as **young men**. Here he repeats the claim that they **have overcome the wicked one**. But significantly, he adds to this the words, **you are strong, and the word of God abides in you**. Clearly this adds a dimension to the experience of his audience as young men which is not suggested in the statement of verse 13. They are still viewed as those who have conquered Satan; they are not at all weakened by their conflict but instead they possess strength and God's word is vitally alive (**abides**, cf. verse 6 above) in them.

As a close reading of John 15:1-8 shows, the "abiding" relationship is one of reciprocal interaction between Christ and His disciples. They are commanded, "Abide in Me," but this is immediately followed by the guarantee, "and I in you" (John 15:4). The same relationship pertains to His **word**: "If you abide in Me, and *My words abide in you*, you will ask what you desire, and it shall be done for you" (John 15:7; italics added). Thus, as **young men** in whom **the word of God abides**, John's audience is strategically prepared for battle, since the resource of answered prayer is open to them (see 1 John 3:22; 5:14-15).

Stepping back from the details of this intricate passage (verses 12-14), it is important to assess its total impact. That it is very reassuring goes almost without saying. The doubling produced by the repetition of the triad of titles has a reinforcing effect that was not lost upon all who first heard the epistle read aloud. (See Genesis 41:32 and the doubling of Pharaoh's dream to communicate that the prophecy was "established by God.") The stress on knowledge attained and victory achieved creates the strong impression that the apostle regards his readers as well equipped to confront the spiritual dangers about which he is going to warn them (verses 15-27).

Finally, the deliberate retention of the title **young men** to the end of each triad of titles is significant. Although we might have expected the term **fathers** to climax each series, this is not what the writer does. The reason is apparent. They are confronting (1) the allurements of a world which "lies under the sway of the wicked one" (verses 15-17; cf. 5:19), and (2) the false teaching of the antichrists, the agents of the wicked one (verses 18-27; cf. 4:1-6). It is important for them to think of themselves as spiritually strong **young men** who have already experienced victory over **the wicked one**. As the cumulative effect of the verses suggests, there is no reason why this victory should not be theirs.

B. By Recognizing Their Spiritual Adversaries (2:15-27)

Having fortified the readership with strong assurances that their spiritual status is highly satisfactory, even exceptional, the apostle now turns to the enemies they must contend with. There are two of them: (1) the world system which is hostile to God; and (2) the antichrists who are hostile to Jesus Christ. The two enemies are intrinsically connected, since behind both of them stands their archenemy, the wicked one, Satan himself.

1. Resisting the World (2:15-17)

It is with good reason that the apostle speaks first of the world before speaking about the antichrists. As he will later say, "They are of the world. Therefore they speak as of the world, and the world hears them" (4:5). If the readers effectively resist the world, they may be expected also to resist the antichrists.

> **15Do not love the world or the things in the world. If anyone loves the world, the love of the Father is not in him.**

John is not so sanguine as to believe that his readers do not need to be warned against "loving" **the world**. Even though he has just praised their spiritual attainments (verses 12-14), this warning is necessary. **The world**, conceived of as a moral and spiritual system designed to draw humanity away from the living God, is profoundly seductive (see verse 16) and no Christian, however advanced, is fully immune to its allurements. If Christians think that they are impervious to its blandishments, they do not understand the intrinsic sinfulness of their own hearts. By their overconfidence they invite the very failure to which they feel they are immune: "Therefore let him who thinks he stands take heed lest he fall" (1 Corinthians 10:12).

So the Christian must not **love the world** as a whole, neither should he love any of its sinful components, **the things in the world.** A Christian can easily delude himself into thinking that he does not **love the world** at all when, in fact, he is deeply attracted to one or another of its sinful aspects. For example, he may deplore the world's immorality and moral depravity while maintaining a deep drive to acquire material things. John's words in the following verse will help us to see this more clearly.

If, however, the Christian does **love the world or the things in** it, he does *not* love God, his heavenly **Father.** This is surely what John means by the statement that **the love of the Father is not in him.** Although the words **the love of the Father** could theoretically mean "the Father's love for" the person who loves the world, there is no good reason to take them that way. Even Jesus Himself warned that "no servant can serve two masters; for either he will hate the one and love the other, or else he will be loyal to the one and despise the other" (Luke 16:13). Similarly, James warned, "Whoever therefore wants to be a friend of the world makes himself an enemy of God" (James 4:4).

Our attitude toward the world is a touchstone of our love for God or of our lack of love for Him. It is impossible to love both the world and God at the same time. Christians are often eager to deny this impossibility and are tempted to compartmentalize their affections and to claim still to love God while obviously loving some sinful aspect of the world system. But the apostle denies this as a possibility.

> **¹⁶For all that is in the world—the lust of the flesh, the lust of the eyes, and the pride of life—is not of the Father but is of the world.**

What then are the components of the world we are not to love? What are its fundamental elements? The *entirety* of its constituent elements (**all that is in the world**) can be summarized under three categories that the apostle here names. Taken together they skillfully sum up the totality of the allurements this godless system has to offer.

The first is **the lust of the flesh.** Under this category of desire may be subsumed every illicit physical activity that appeals to the sinful hearts of men. Immorality in all its forms is surely to be located here, but so is physical excess as represented, for example, by drunkenness or gluttony.

It should be mentioned that the phrase **the lust of the flesh** (like the two following phrases) is best taken as a metonymy of the adjunct. This is a figure of speech in which a "desire is put for the person or thing desired."[5] So, in this instance, **the lust of the flesh** stands for those things that the flesh craves, such as illicit sexual pleasure or the gratification of addictive drugs.

The second element of the world is **the lust of the eyes**. Whatever is visually appealing but not properly ours to desire or obtain is included in this category. The object before **the eyes** might be a person or thing, but the sinful desire to have it is what is often signified elsewhere by the word *covetousness*. As a metonymy of the subject (where *eyes* stands for the object[s] they see), **the lust of the eyes** refers to anything which, when seen, is wrongly desired.

By **the pride of life** the apostle suggests something like "the vain display of earthly life." The Greek word rendered "pride" is *alazoneia* and signifies arrogance or pretentiousness, such as one sees in a person who boasts about self, possessions, or accomplishments.[6] The word translated "life" (*bios*) does not so much suggest intrinsic life (as does the word $\overline{zoe}$, which John always uses when he refers to *eternal* life), but rather "life" in its outward features and manifestations. The two Greek words taken together combine to suggest the idea of boastful pretension in earthly matters.[7]

A little reflection will show that the three core elements of the world system are not totally distinct but have many areas of overlap. For example, the breaking of the tenth commandment ("You shall not covet your neighbor's…wife" Exodus 20:17) might involve both her visual appeal to your eyes (**the lust of the eyes**) and the physical attraction which you feel for her (**the lust of the flesh**). If after committing the act of adultery, the man then brags about his sexual conquest, this would involve **the pride of life**.

None of these three seductive elements has its source in God **the Father**, but in **the world**. They are **not of the Father but of the world**. In making this statement, John comes very close to the words of James, "Let no one say when he is tempted, 'I am tempted by God'; for God cannot be tempted by evil, nor does He Himself tempt anyone" (James 1:13). Although we cannot be certain about it, it may be that the Revisionists (of whom John will shortly speak) maintained that one could freely participate in the activities of **the world**. They may have argued that since God was its Maker, one was simply using what the Creator had made available in the material realm of creation. But although the physical world is "of God" who created it, **the world** as a moral system **is not**.

If, as some have thought, the Revisionists were Docetists who denied the reality of our Lord's physical body (see 1:1-4 and Introduction), they may well have regarded the material world either as an illusion or morally indifferent, or both. In that case, one could indulge physical desires without restraint, and all Christian commandments to the contrary could be safely ignored.

In any case, John wants his readers to understand that, despite any specious argument they may have heard, **all that is in the world** bears the taint of wickedness with which God **the Father** has nothing to do (cf. 1:5).

> **¹⁷And the world is passing away, and the lust of it; but he who does the will of God abides forever.**

But not only is **the world** morally at odds with God, it is also transient. So the apostle reminds his readership that **the world is passing away**. That is to say, **the world** has only a brief existence within time and is destined to disappear when God's purposes are realized on earth. This statement recalls verse 8 where John states that "the darkness is passing away, and the true light is already shining." The Christian is to realize that the present state of affairs, whether described as **the world** or as "the darkness," is so temporary as to be an utterly unworthy object of our longings and desires.

Naturally, when **the world** no longer exists as an entity morally and spiritually opposed to God, none of its illicit experiences will continue to exist either. **The lust of it**, that is, the world's sinful gratification, is every bit as transient as the system it reflects. Indeed, it often happens that after indulging some particular worldly lust, the participant discovers that its gratification is short-lived and must be renewed again and again in ever more intensive forms. Thus the "addicted" sinner (cf. John 8:34), is reminded of the highly temporary nature of all that **the world** contains.

By contrast, **he who does the will of God abides forever**. We might have expected this to be stated in an impersonal way to contrast it with **the world** and **the lust of it**, by some such statement as "obedience to God's will lasts forever." But this is not what the author does. Instead, he stresses that *the obedient person himself* **abides forever**. This clearly suggests that it is by obedience that we establish an eternal identity that outlasts the present world system. If I am a laborer on earth, an architect, a musician, a scientist, a teacher—however skilled I may be at any of these activities—none of these designations will survive the present age. But there is an eternal permanence to the character and activity of a person who can be identified as one **who does the will of God**.

It may be said of such a person that he **abides forever**. The Greek words *menei eis ton aiōna* need mean no more than that he *will remain forever*. But the "abiding" life has already been referred to (verse 6) and is a prominent theme in the epistle (see 2:28 and discussion), so that it is likely that there is a reference here to that *kind* of life. We have already been told that the "abider" walks as Christ walked (again, verse 6), so that the permanence of the one **who does the will of God** is inseparable from the Christ-likeness which such a person has achieved. As we shall see, likeness to Christ can give us boldness at the Judgment Seat of Christ (1 John 4:17), where the eternal worth of our earthly Christian lives will be assessed (1 Corinthians 3:11-15; 2 Corinthians 5:10). Spiritual recognition at the Judgment Seat is an obvious component in the enduring recognition of the obedient Christian throughout eternity.

Just as Abraham through obedience to God obtained the title "the friend of God" (cf. James 2:21-23), by which he is known today in three world religions and will be known forever, so too the obedient Christian can attain this same identity by obedience (John 15:14-15). Likewise, it would be reasonable to conclude that the Christian's identity in eternity will be determined by obedience to God in time. And since all lives of obedience are unique in their particulars, each eternal "identity" will be as unique as the snowflakes that fall from heaven.

Thus the concept of the obedient Christian "abiding" **forever** is heavily freighted with significance by virtue of its connection to the whole theme of "abiding in Christ." The famous motto, "Only one life, 'twill soon be past; only what's done for Christ will last," might be modified to fit our epistle thus:

The wicked world and all its lusts,
   will someday be forever past.
The abiding one, he alone,
   is someone who forever lasts.

2. Resisting the Antichrists (2:18-27)

Since "the world is passing away" (verse 17), it would hardly be surprising if there were signs of this passing. As John's readers evidently knew, an eschatological figure identified as the Antichrist was destined to appear on the world stage hardly more than three and one-half years before the establishment of God's kingdom upon earth. It was an evident demonstration of the approaching consummation of the age that there were precursors of this Antichrist already on the scene. John now discusses this sobering fact with his readership.

[18]Little children, it is the last hour; and as you have heard that the Antichrist is coming, even now many antichrists have come, by which we know that it is the last hour.

Not only is "the world passing away," according to the apostle, but what is more, the apostle and his readers are living in **the last hour.**[8]

Needless to say, this claim has been derided by unbelievers and taken as yet another proof that, though the early Christians expected the Second Advent in *their own lifetime*, history now shows that they were wrong. In expressing this opinion, of course, such people fulfill the prophecy of the apostle Peter who predicted that "scoffers will come in the last days...saying, 'Where is the promise of His coming? For since the fathers fell asleep, all things continue as they were from the beginning of creation'" (2 Peter 3:3-4; see also Matthew 24:48ff). Peter's answer to this charge is simply that God experiences time differently than man does, since "with the Lord one day is as a thousand years, and a thousand years as one day" (2 Peter 3:8).

Peter's statement takes on a fresh appearance in the light of contemporary physics. The transformation of modern physics through Einstein's theory of *special relativity* (supplemented later by *general relativity*) has produced a new perspective on time. Time, we now understand, is a fourth dimension which, along with the three dimensions of space, constitutes our *spacetime* universe. Under *special relativity* we have learned that the speed at which time "passes" is relative to the speed at which an object moves through space. The faster the movement through space, the slower the passage of time, and vice versa. But since nothing can pass through *spacetime* faster than the speed of light (670 million miles per hour), a photon (or, particle) of light experiences *no time,* i.e., it *does not age.* Thus, for a photon of light, one day and one thousand years are both timeless and thus identical to the photon![9]

Inasmuch as God is light (certainly at the spiritual level, cf. 1:5!) it is not a stretch to say that His experience of time is like that of physical light. Hence, there is no difference to God between one day and a thousand years, as Peter states. Moreover, even *we* would find the passage of a thousand years to be very brief if we could sufficiently accelerate our motion through space (as no doubt the angels can). Thus critics of the Bible who find fault with the Lord's statement, "I am coming quickly" (Revelation 22:12), are arguing from the now outdated notion that time passes at a fixed rate of speed in our universe. We now know this assumption is false. The "speed" of time is relative to the observer and depends on the speed of his motion through space. Second Peter 3:8 amazingly foreshadows the insights of modern physics, and his subsequent remark that "the Lord is not slack concerning his promise, *as some count slackness* (3:9) can now be seen to imply "relativity" in one's estimate of time! For "slow moving" earth people, time *seems* to go slowly!

This is relevant to John's text. In his Gospel, John uses the word **hour** in both the literal sense of a portion of the day (e.g., John 1:39; 4:6; 11:9) and also of a time period of undetermined length that has special qualities (e.g., John 2:4; 4:21, 23; 5:25, 28; 16:25; and many other places). Thus we may understand the phrase **the last hour** in the latter sense as a period during which human history will climax with the rise (and overthrow) of Satan's final great deception, of which the **Antichrist** is the primary human agent. The term **hour**, in accord with Johannine usage, does not signal a fixed period of time, so much as a *unique* period of time after which the world system, of verses 15-17, will indeed pass away.

We may say, therefore, that **the last hour** of which John speaks is constituted as such not by its *duration* (which in any case is relative!), but by the fact that it is the last era of this present age and will be followed by the establishment of the kingdom of God on earth. As experienced by humanity it is a long period in duration, now more than two thousand years. But, as just mentioned, it is experienced differently by God.

The readers had already received teaching about the end times and had **heard that the Antichrist is coming**. Many interpreters take the term **Antichrist** as a reference to the "man of sin" who claims godhood in the Jewish temple (2 Thessalonians 2:3-4) and who will rule the world (Revelation 13:5-8). But John is the only New Testament writer to use this term, and it is clear from 4:1-3 that the **many antichrists** of this verse are essentially the same as the "many false prophets" of 4:1. This strongly suggests that *the* **Antichrist** is none other than *the* False Prophet of Revelation 13:11-17; 16:13; 19:20; 20:10 who will assist the man of sin.

John is saying here that the teachers of error are precursors of the supreme human deceiver, the False Prophet or **Antichrist**. Like miniature replicas of this arch-deceiver, these **many antichrists** make it plain that **the last hour** has dawned. They bring with them the great lie of **the** ultimate **Antichrist** himself: the denial that Jesus is the Christ (see verse 22).

> [19]**They went out from us, but they were not of us; for if they had been of us, they would have continued with us; but** *they went out* **that they might be made manifest, that none of them were of us.**

The special deceptiveness of the "many antichrists" was that **they** had once been part of the same fellowship to which the apostles themselves belonged: **they went out from us**. No other meaning than this one is really suitable in this context. The **us** which is repeated four times in this verse obviously is in contrast to the "you" of the following verse, which is emphatic in Greek. Here we meet for the first time the "we"—"you"—"us" contrast which we also meet in a similar context in 4:4-6.[10]

It completely distorts the text to treat the **us** of verse 19 as though it meant simply "us Christians." The antichrists had most definitely *not* left the church or churches to whom John writes, for if they had they would no longer have been a problem! On the contrary, the apostle is clearly concerned about the exposure his readers have had, or will have, to these men. One of the claims they must have made, which gave them a false aura of authority, was that they had originated in the same sphere where the apostles themselves operated, in all probability a reference to the Jerusalem church.

It is remarkable how similar this sounds to the situation we meet in Acts 15 where the church struggles with legalists. There we are told that "certain men came down from Judea and taught the brethren" (Acts 15:1). In their letter to the Christians on the Gentile mission fields, the apostles and elders of Jerusalem wrote, "Since we have heard that some who *went out from us* have troubled you with words, unsettling your souls, saying, 'You must be circumcised and keep the law'—to whom we gave no such commandment" (Acts 15:24; italics added). The words *went out from us* in Acts involve exactly the same Greek expression as here: **they went out from us**. This striking parallel with Acts has been generally ignored by the commentary literature dealing with 1 John 2:19, perhaps due at least in part to the widespread view that the apostle John is not the author of this epistle.

But given apostolic authorship and the Acts parallel, we may hypothesize that the bearers of this error had once been in the Jerusalem fellowship. The Revisionists, or antichrists, therefore, had a prestigious point of origin, but the apostle disclaims them here as emphatically as the leaders of the Jerusalem church had disclaimed the legalists of Acts 15. Indeed, the very fact of their departure from the apostolic fellowship was an indication that they did not really "belong" to it in the first place. If they had, why would they have left?

The apostle's argument here clearly implies a schism of some kind between the antichrists and the apostolic circle. No doubt this had to do with the doctrine taught by them (see discussion under verse 22). It is likely that John thinks of these men as individuals who concealed their true views for some time. Though outwardly in apparent agreement with apostolic doctrine, they **were** in fact **not of us** in the sense that this outward harmony was a façade. When the break came and *they went out*, they were then flying their true colors, and John sees this break as having as its purpose **that they might be made manifest, that none of them were of us**. Had they really been in harmony with apostolic perspectives (i.e., **if they had been of us**), there would have been no reason for the schism (i.e., **they would have continued with us**).

The question may be asked whether John thought of these men as unsaved. He may very well have thought of them that way. Even Paul in

Galatians 2:4 spoke of the fact that, in the Jerusalem church, there were "false brethren secretly brought in (who came in by stealth to spy out our liberty which we have in Christ Jesus, that they might bring us into bondage)." It should not surprise us if, given the dynamic movement that early Christianity was in Israel, there should be legalistic zealots and fanatics who came into the church with their own agendas, while only pretending to believe in Christ. It seems Paul realized that this had in fact happened.

So John might well have thought that these Revisionists had only professed a belief which they did not really have. But this is far from certain. In his second epistle he states: "Whoever transgresses and does not abide in the doctrine of Christ does not have God" (2 John 9). This statement, which certainly sounds like apostasy from a doctrine once held, follows very shortly after a reference to "deceivers" who can be called antichrists (2 John 7). So we must leave open the possibility that John may have viewed the antichrists as dangerous apostates from the Christian faith who now denied the truth they had once believed.

Of course, if they had once believed it, they had eternal salvation, even as Paul reminds us, "If we are faithless, He remains faithful; He cannot deny Himself" (2 Timothy 2:13). The Greek verb translated "we are faithless" is *apistoumen* and may mean either "to disbelieve" or "to be unfaithful" and probably covers both ideas, since 2 Timothy 2:11-13 is a poetic, proverbial type of saying. Even the blasphemers named Hymenaeus and Alexander, who "concerning the faith" had "suffered shipwreck," were subjected to discipline so "that they may learn [Greek = be child-trained] not to blaspheme" (1 Timothy 1:20). It is likely enough that this Hymenaeus was the same as the Hymenaeus mentioned in Second Timothy and charged with teaching "that the resurrection is already past" (2 Timothy 2:17-18). The early church wrestled with genuine converts who went doctrinally astray just as the modern church does, and any view of the New Testament that denies this reality is conspicuous for its lack of realism.

Whether or not they were ever saved, it is at least clear that the antichrists of whom John speaks had long since ceased to be a true part of the apostolic fellowship. Their departure from it was not only to be expected, but was also a powerful indictment of their former pretense to being a part of it.

²⁰But you have an anointing from the Holy One, and you know all things.

Despite the fact that "many antichrists" have now appeared on the scene, and despite their prestigious origin somewhere within the apostolic circle, the readers have no need of the teachings that they bring. In fact, the readers **know all things**.

This assertion that the readers **know all things** does not, of course, suggest anything like omniscience! Neither does it suggest a total grasp of what is sometimes called "secular" learning. Instead, it suggests a completely adequate knowledge of Christian truth. The precedent for John's statement is found in his Gospel where he reports that Jesus told His disciples, "'But the Helper, the Holy Spirit, whom the Father will send in My name, He will teach you *all things...*'" (John 14:26; italics added). Later the Lord states, "'However, when He, the Spirit of truth, has come, He will guide you into *all truth*'" (John 16:13; italics added). Clearly there was a body of doctrine, or truth, which the disciples were to learn in its completeness through the teaching ministry of the Holy Spirit.

By the term **anointing** the apostle no doubt means the Holy Spirit. The other major suggestion, that he means the word, or gospel, of God, is much less likely.[11] In the New Testament, the word of God is never directly connected with the idea of anointing, while the Holy Spirit clearly is. In fact, Jesus was anointed as the Christ by the Holy Spirit (cf. Luke 4:18; Acts 4:27; 10:38). Since the antichrists are marked by denying that Jesus is the Christ (verse 22), it is fitting that the readership, which confesses this truth, should be identified as "anointed ones" even as Jesus is *the* Anointed One (the Christ). The fact that the readers' *anointing* has a teaching role, which is a personal function (verse 27), is additional confirmation that this *anointing* is the Holy Spirit.

The readership, therefore, possesses knowledge about the whole body of truth that the Lord had promised the apostles that the Holy Spirit would teach them.

Once again we have reason to believe that the recipients of this epistle were spiritually advanced Christians (see discussion under verses 13-14). As suggested in the Introduction, this readership may well consist of the spiritual leadership (or, elders) in the churches to which John is sending his letter. If so, when the letter was read aloud in the public meetings, it would reinforce the spiritual authority of the leadership. With this under-standing, since the leaders **know all things**, there is nothing the Christians in these churches need to learn from the Revisionists. The leaders themselves are competent to teach the whole body of Christian truth.

> **[21] I have not written to you because you do not know the truth, but because you know it, and that no lie is of the truth.**

This verse reiterates what John has just said. In no sense has he **written to** them because they are ignorant of the truth. On the contrary, he writes precisely because they **know it**.

It is clear how far from reality is the popular view that John is writing to *test* whether the readership is genuinely saved or not. In the face of verses 12-14, as well as of this verse, such a view reflects a stubborn blindness to the statements of the epistle itself. If they **know the truth**, they have obviously believed it.

John knew, even if contemporary interpreters do not, that the assurance that we possess **the truth** is the key to resisting false teaching. The professing Christian church today has lost sight of this fact and has fallen prey to innumerable doctrinal deviations.

In addition to knowing **the truth**, John's readers also know **that no lie is of the truth**. This is a significant addition to John's thought. Doctrinal error is not to be treated as simply a flawed conception of **the truth** from which we can possibly learn something. On the contrary, a **lie** is just that, a **lie**. It is contrary to **the truth** and thus does not have its source in, nor is it **of the truth**. John would have been most impatient with Christian academics who always manage to praise a false idea as somehow "insightful," no matter how far it is from **the truth**.

> **[22] Who is a liar but he who denies that Jesus is the Christ? He is antichrist who denies the Father and the Son.**

The lie that John particularly has in mind is the denial **that Jesus is the Christ**. For John, of course, the belief **that Jesus is the Christ** is *saving* belief (see 1 John 5:1 and discussion there; cf. John 20:30-31). The person **who denies** this truth **is a liar** who subverts the very basis upon which anyone is eternally saved.

In Johannine theology it is necessary to understand that—on John's terms—**the Christ** is the One who guarantees to every believer both resurrection and eternal life. This is made clear in our Lord's famous exchange with Martha in John 11:25-27. When Martha responds to Jesus' question, "'Do you believe this?'" she states: "'Yes, Lord, I believe that you are the Christ, the Son of God, who is to come into the world.'" Thus Martha gives a full-fledged Johannine statement of faith (cf. John 20:30-31). This faith includes the truth that Jesus stated, that He imparts eternal life and promises resurrection to everyone who believes in Him (John 11:25-26).[12]

One obvious effect of the lie John has in mind is that it involved the denial that John's readers had eternal life (see verse 25 and discussion). If **Jesus** was not **the Christ,** then the readers' assurance that they possessed this life by faith in Him was a mirage. If their assurance collapsed, so would their fellowship with God that was based on that assurance. The results would have been diametrically opposite of the author's wishes for them, as expressed in the Prologue (1:1-4).

The matter was serious. So serious, in fact, that any purveyor of this "lie" was clearly an **antichrist** whose denial of Jesus Christ was also a denial of both **the Father and the Son.**

> **[23]Whoever denies the Son does not have the Father either; he who acknowledges the Son has the Father also.[13]**

John now supports the claim made in the previous verse that to deny that Jesus is the Christ is to deny *both* **the Father** and **the Son.** In the Fourth Gospel, Jesus makes the statement, "He who believes in Me, believes not in Me but in Him who sent Me. And he who sees Me sees Him who sent Me'" (John 12:44-45). So perfectly reflective of His Father was Jesus, that both His words and works were those of the Father (cf. John 14:10-11). To deny **the Son** was to automatically deny **the Father** (cf. verse 22). Therefore, it could be said that the one who **denies the Son does not have the Father either.** That is to say, he **does not have** either **the Son** or **the Father.**

Such a statement is often taken to mean that the antichrists were unsaved, which they may well have been. But it is hazardous to press the language used here too far. The verb translated **have** in English (Greek: *echō*) is an extremely common one in Greek and is used by John in various senses. It can, of course, mean "to possess" and John uses it of the *possession* of the Son or of eternal life (cf. 5:12-13). But it can also mean "to have at hand, to have at one's disposal" (e.g., John 4:11; 5:7; 1 John 2:1). Moreover, expressions like "to *have* fellowship" (to *experience* fellowship: 1 John 1:3, 7), "to *have* a commandment" (*to be under* a responsibility to: 1 John 2:7; 4:21), or even "fear *has* torment" (fear *involves* torment: 1 John 4:18) show the extremely flexible use this author makes of the verb *to have*.

It is quite likely in light of 2 John 9 (see discussion there) that the claim that the denier of **the Son does not have the Father either** is meant to assert that such people are operating totally bereft of any divine involvement or cooperation. Neither **the Son** nor **the Father** has anything to do with their activities. This would be true whether the person in question was unregenerate or a believer who had "departed" from the faith (cf. 1 Timothy 4:1).

> [24]**Therefore let that abide in you which you heard from the beginning. If what you heard from the beginning abides in you, you also will abide in the Son and in the Father.**

The **Son** and **the Father,** who have nothing to do with the heretical Revisionists (cf. previous verse), are the very ones in whom the readers should **abide.** But to do that they must allow the truth they had **heard from the beginning** of their Christian experience (cf. 2:7) to **abide in** them.

This is the second time in the epistle that we meet the idea of God's word or His truth *abiding* in the readership. The first instance occurred at the very conclusion of the series of positive affirmations that the author makes about the readers in 2:12-14. There they are addressed for the final time, once again under the designation "young men," and are assured of their competence to resist "the wicked one." Here it is the way that the readers will in fact triumph over the wicked one's agents, the antichrists. They are simply to let God's word continue to **abide in** them in the form in which they heard it **from the beginning.** They are to accept no "revisions" or "substitutes" for the truth as originally heard by them. This original truth should be allowed to make its enduring home in them.

The result of allowing the original Christian truth to **abide in** them will be that they **will abide in the Son and in the Father**. As pointed out earlier (see verses 5-6, 14 and the discussions there), the "abiding life" is the life lived by a disciple who both has and keeps his Lord's commandments; and it is also a Christlike life marked by love for the brethren. Such a life will continue to be the experience of this relatively mature readership so long as they do not abandon the truth as it was taught to them **from the beginning**. They should, therefore, totally reject the lies brought by the Revisionists.

25And this is the promise that He has promised us— eternal life.

That this statement should occur here is in no way surprising. The antichrists, we have been told, deny "that Jesus is the Christ" (verse 22). But it is only by *believing* this truth that a person obtains **eternal life** (1 John 5:1; John 20:30-31). Thus God has made a **promise** of **eternal life** to any person who believes that Jesus is the Christ. Every verse that offers this life to a believer is a divine guarantee that he or she *has* it (cf. John 3:16; 5:24; 6:35, 47 and *passim*). It was nothing less than this God-given **promise** that was called into question by the doctrine of the antichrists. Here John strongly reassures his readers that this **promise** remains valid. The pronoun **He** could refer to God or to Christ Himself, since **the promise** can be said to come from either or both.

It should be further noted, however, that the insertion of the statement about **eternal life** in the middle of a discussion about the Revisionists is a clear signal that John is *directly* confronting the false ideas of these heretics. The next verse confirms this.

26These *things* I have written to you concerning those who *try to* deceive you.

Verse 25 was not a mere throwaway line for John, (nor was it only remotely tangential to what the antichrists actually taught). On the contrary, the apostle was actually thinking of **those who *try to* deceive you**.

This reference to "deceivers," immediately following verse 25, shows that the Revisionists brought with them a doctrine of salvation quite different from the one the readers had "heard from the beginning" (cf. verse 24). They denied that Jesus was the Christ (verse 22), and apparently also denied that "eternal life" was available through Him, or through Him alone (in light of verse 25). They may even have claimed some special relationship to "the Father" based on their new knowledge, however, John denied that they had any such relationship (verses 22-23).

In the English translation, **those who *try to* deceive you**, there are no words that precisely correspond to *try to*, but the translators are probably correct to add them. The Greek verb tense used for **deceive** is capable of this nuance, provided the context supports it. In view of verses 12-14 and verses 20-21, the nuance seems justified, since there has already been exposure to the antichrists. The readers have not as yet been taken in by these people, but John's letter shows his concern with this danger. In particular, if the letter is to the leadership of a church or churches, John is fortifying the authority of the leaders as they resist these false teachers. He is calling the Revisionists deceivers.

> [27]**But the anointing which you have received from Him abides in you, and you do not need that anyone teach you; but as the same anointing teaches you concerning all things, and is true, and is not a lie, and just as it has taught you, you will abide in Him.**

This verse is the climax of the purpose section of the epistle which extends from 2:12 to here. It fittingly summarizes the contents of this section as we have followed them through John's text. His readers are highly competent in the truth and need only to hold fast to what they already know to enjoy the full benefits of the "abiding life," which is discipleship to Jesus Christ.

We find again here, as in verse 20, a reference to an **anointing** which **teaches** them **concerning all things**. The reference can hardly be to anyone other than the Holy Spirit. The Spirit's designation as **the anointing which you have received from Him** is of special interest, since Jesus Himself is said to have been "anointed" by God "with the Holy Spirit and with power" (Acts 10:38). That took place when the Holy Spirit descended upon Jesus at His baptism (Matthew 3:16-17; and parallels). In fact, the Greek word "Christ" (Messiah) means "the Anointed One."

John is probably suggesting here that the readers are "anointed ones" by means of the Spirit who came to them from the "Anointed One" (although, again, the **Him** could refer to either the Father or the Son, or to both without differentiation). Their **anointing** was nothing less than the Spirit of the "Anointed One," that is, the Spirit of Christ. The readers' **anointing**, therefore, teaches them to reject the **lie** about the "Anointed One."

The word translated **anointing** (Greek: *chrisma*) is used only in this passage in the New Testament (1 John 2:20, 27 [twice]). As pointed out by Vorster,[14] there is no need to see John's use of the term as a reflection of Gnostic ideas or as a Gnostic term that he appropriated for Christian use. Still, only one New Testament passage seems to speak of a general anointing for Christians: 2 Corinthians 1:21, "Now He who establishes us with you in Christ and has anointed us is God." Yet even in this passage it is possible that the "us" refers to Paul and to his special ministry to the Corinthians. In the Old Testament it was the custom for prophets, priests, and kings to be anointed. It is not at all unlikely that the statement here about **the anointing which you have received from Him** refers to the elders or leaders, men raised up and enabled by the Holy Spirit to guide their congregation(s). Paul certainly viewed elders as raised up by the Spirit (Acts 20:28). No doubt the apostle John had the same view and, all things considered, this seems to be the best way to read the passage.[15]

The elders therefore are those in whom this **anointing...abides.** As a result they need no teaching from any source (**you do not need that anyone teach you**). The fact that they need no human teacher is, of course, a mark of their maturity (see Hebrews 5:12) and this maturity has already been implied elsewhere in this section (cf. verses 13b–14, 20). Naturally the elders do not need the teaching brought by the antichrists, although these deceivers in all probability claimed that they did. It is not hard to imagine that the Revisionists, coming as they did out of the bosom of the apostolic circle (cf. verse 19), made much of their own superior knowledge and denigrated the local leaders as insufficiently well taught or instructed. Given the charismatic personality which false teachers often possess, such claims might well have made an impact on the congregations. The highly commendatory words of the apostle here would certainly be a powerful antidote to the scornful treatment the antichrists probably exhibited toward the local leaders who resisted them.

Moreover, **the same anointing** that John has just said **abides in** these leaders, and leaves them without any need of human teachers, continues to teach them **concerning all things**. No doubt the sense of **all things** is somewhat different than the "all things" of verse 20. The reference in verse 20 was to a complete body of Christian truth which the leaders "know" (see discussion there). But here the reference seems to be to the *ongoing* ministry (note the *as*) of the Holy Spirit to this leadership. In the course of guiding their congregations the leaders needed to know how to evaluate various situations and/or problems that the congregation encountered. Their anointing continued to give them the ability to do this by applying the truth that they already knew to any issue at hand. This is surely included in Paul's statement that "he who is spiritual judges all things" (1 Corinthians 2:15). Thus the leaders were perfectly capable of correctly evaluating the doctrine of the Revisionists and rejecting it as false. As John had already said of them, they "know...that no lie is of the truth" (verse 21).

As John's letter was read out in the congregation(s), such words again fortified the authority of the leadership as Spirit-taught men who could correctly evaluate the false teaching brought by the antichrists. What this **same anointing** taught them in its ongoing ministry to them was **true and...not a lie**, in contrast to the doctrine of the antichrists which *was* a lie.

John's total statement, beginning with **but as the same anointing teaches you**, is of special interest. The two parallel statements are (1) **as [it] teaches you concerning all things** and (2) **and just as it has taught you**. This shows that the ongoing teaching ministry of the Holy Spirit is always consistent with what the Spirit has *already* taught, i.e., **as [it] teaches...and just as it has taught**. That is, whatever the Spirit has previously taught will not be negated or denied by anything He continues to teach. So whatever "revisions" to previous Christian teaching the antichrists may have brought could be rejected as not the teaching of the leaders' **anointing**.

In our present age, we have a great many claims to new insight into truth (cf. the "health and wealth" preachers or the "spiritual warfare" teachers of the '90s). We can always test them by previous teaching (i.e., by the Bible), and where they contradict the Spirit's biblical teaching we must categorically reject them.

The leaders are thus assured of the sufficiency of the ongoing teaching of their **anointing** and of the consistency of this teaching with His previous teaching, so that by taking heed to both things, John is sure that they **will abide in Him**. Of course, what John predicates of these mature leaders is what he also wants of the believers who make up their congregations. They should imitate their leaders and allow the Spirit to teach them **concerning all things** through these godly men. At the same time they should hold fast to the truth **just as** the Spirit **has** already **taught** them, so that they too, like their leaders, **will abide in Him**.

This is still good advice for Christians today. We should remember, however, that Christians who are not yet mature *need* human teachers (cf. Hebrews 5:13). Even mature Christians (like the addressees of First John) *can profit* from the ministry of other teachers who communicate in the power of the Spirit. The fact that the mature do not *need* them, does not mean they should be ignored or lightly esteemed. A mature believer will surely value them highly.

ENDNOTES

[1] It has also been suggested that the categories of "fathers" and "young men" represent a subdividing of the audience after each reference to the whole congregation as "little children." Under this view, they are "children" in relation to the writer, but "fathers" and "young men" in relation to their actual age. This seems forced and unnatural, in the face of the prima facie impression that a double triad of categories is involved. In the absence of any real hint in the text that such a subdividing of the categories is taking place, this view should be rejected. The subdivision of "children" into "fathers" and "young men" reflects an awkward and unnatural correlation between these terms. Still, this view is often found among the commentators: e.g., Raymond E. Brown, *The Epistles of John*, AB (Garden City, NY: Doubleday, 1982), pp. 297-300 (as usual, a very helpful survey of the problem); A. E. Brooke, *A Critical and Exegetical Commentary on the Johannine Epistles*, ICC (Edinburgh: T. & T. Clark, 1912), p. 43; Brooke Foss Westcott, *The Epistles of St John: The Greek Text with Notes* (Grand Rapids: Wm. B. Eerdmans Publishing Co., 1966), pp. 57-58; Rudolf Bultmann, *The Johannine Epistles: A Commentary on the Johannine Epistles*, Herm (Philadelphia: Fortress Press, 1973), p. 31; Marianne Meye Thompson, *1-3 John*, IVPNTC (Downers Grove, IL: InterVarsity Press, 1992), pp. 62-63.

[2] Though holding the view mentioned in note 1, Brown feels the force of our observation about John's use of the words for children: "Indeed, it is almost impossible that suddenly here, and here alone, *teknia* and *paidia* could refer only to one group constituting one-third of the audience" (*Epistles*, p. 298). The view

of the text defended in our Commentary (that the three categories are *not* subdivisions of the audience) goes back as far as Augustine and in modern times has been favored by C. H. Dodd, *The Johannine Epistles,* MNTC (New York: Harper & Row, 1946), pp. 37-39; and I. Howard Marshall, *The Epistles of John,* NICNT (Grand Rapids: Wm. B. Eerdmans Publishing Co., 1978), pp. 139-41. Stephen S. Smalley, *1,2,3 John,* WBC (Waco, TX: Word Books, 1984), pp. 69-71, is ambivalent.

[3] The Greek word *hoti,* here rendered **because** (as it is throughout verses 12-14), could be handled as "declarative" in the sense of "that," given the content of the writing. But the statements in the *hoti* clauses do not seem naturally to convey the content of the epistle. On the contrary, the statements of verses 12-14 appear to be quite parallel to the statements in verse 21 where the causal sense of the first two uses of *hoti* seems by far the most natural rendering. Despite the opinion of a number of writers that *hoti* is also declarative in verse 21, it is odd to think of John saying, "I have not written to you that you do not know the truth" —which quite patently he had not! The translations are surely on target to take *hoti* in verse 20 as causal (cf. KJV, NKJV, NIV, NASB, JB, NACE, NRSV, etc.). But the substantial difference in meaning between the two possibilities is not very great. In either case, the readers have these attainments.

[4] Needless to say some scribe or editor felt that the tense should be consistent throughout the second triad, so that the final *graphō* (before "children" in verse 13) was changed to *egrapsa* to agree with the two uses of this form found in verse 14. This produces a balanced use of the tenses, with *graphō* introducing the first triad in verses 12, 13a, b; and *egrapsa* introducing the second triad in verses 13c and 14a, b. But this misses the much more subtle reason for John's variation in tenses. As pointed out above, the second reference to "children" is totally different from the first and hence is entirely new. John switches to the past tense in verses 14a and b because only here is there repetition of something said earlier. The critical editions of the Greek New Testament follow the scribal harmonization and read *egrapsa* in verse 13c, following the favored Egyptian manuscripts against the *MajT*, which reads *graphō* there.

[5] E. W. Bullinger, *Figures of Speech Used in the Bible: Explained and Illustrated* (London: Messrs. Eyre and Spottiswoode, 1898 [reprint ed., Grand Rapids: Baker Book House, 1968]), p. 601.

[6] See the treatment of E Güting and C. Brown, "*hyperēphanos,* NIDNTT, Colin Brown, gen. ed. (Grand Rapids: Zondervan Publishing House, 1975-78), 3:28-32; cf. James 4:16.

[7] After quoting an amusing segment from Theophrastus's *Characters* about the self-important, boastful *Alazon* (same root as John's *alazoneia*), Dodd skillfully summarizes as follows: "The vulgar 'climber' of this light-hearted but

pungent caricature came to the front in the irresponsible, acquisitive, individu-alistic society of the Hellenistic world. Our author [of 1 John], looking upon contemporary society from a Christian standpoint, and judging it with a deeper seriousness, sees it as the very incarnation of this pretentious, self-glorifying spirit" (*Epistles*, p. 42). One could easily substitute "Western society" here for Dodd's "Hellenistic world"! The transience of human pride was caught unfor-gettably by Benjamin Franklin (*Poor Richard's Almanac*, 1732-57) with these words: "Pride breakfasted with Plenty, dined with Poverty, and supped with Infamy."

[8] The Greek phrase for **the last hour** (*eschatē hōra*) has no definite article. But this need not lead to the translation proposed by some (e.g., Westcott, *Epistles*, pp. 68-69): **a last hour**. There are various reasons why a definite Greek noun may lack an article, among which is the so-called Colwell's rule that definite predicate nouns which precede the "to be" verb are normally anarthrous (i.e., without an article), which could be applied here. But Brown may be right in saying (*Epistles*, p. 330): "More plausibly the absence of the article flows from the author's treating 'last' as if it were an ordinal number—GJohn never uses the article with 'hour' modified by an ordinal (BFD 256; John 1:39; 4:6; 19:4)."

[9] For a stimulating and comprehensible treatment of the state of contem-porary physics, see Brian Greene's excellent work, *The Elegant Universe: Superstrings, Hidden Dimensions, and the Quest for the Ultimate Theory* (New York: W. W. Norton & Company, 1999).

[10] For a fuller defense, cf. Edward M. Curtis, "The First Person Plural in 1 John 2:18-27," *EJ* 10 (1992): 27-36.

[11] Cf. Brown, *Epistles*, pp. 345-47.

[12] For a fuller discussion of the issues involved here, see Zane C. Hodges, "Assurance: Of the Essence of Saving Faith," *Journal of the Grace Evangelical Society* 10 (Spring 1997): 3-17.

[13] The words **he who acknowledges the Son has the Father also**, while found in the NKJV, are not found in a majority of the surviving manuscripts of First John. W. L. Richards in his invaluable study of the Greek text of John's letters (*The Classification of the Greek Manuscripts of the Johannine Epistles*. No. 35: Society of Biblical Literature Dissertation Series [Missoula, MT: Scholars Press, 1977]) has subjected 81 of the approximately 600 manuscripts containing the Epistles of John to careful analysis. Of these 81, 79 offer testimony on the words in question. Richards found that the words are omitted by 59 of them (counting also the TR, 72 percent) and included in 21 (25.6 percent), while $\mathbf{P}^{74}$ and one other (2.4 percent) are not extant here. If the percentages held throughout the total extant copies of this passage, we could expect perhaps 400 or more favoring omission, while we could expect close to 150 favoring inclusion. This is not quite as wide a margin as the *MajT* usually shows for a reading. It remains

a possibility that the words in brackets could have been omitted by a common scribal accident called *homoioteleuton* in some very early copy of First John (leaving many descendants) or even omitted more than once by the copyists. The immediately preceding words end with the verb *echei* as does the bracketed phrase itself. A copyist's eye could easily have skipped from the first *echei* to the second, omitting the intervening material. Until the manuscript tradition of First John has been submitted to rigorous genealogical analysis, the text must remain somewhat uncertain here. In the Commentary we elect to follow the Majority reading and not to comment on the second statement of 2:23.

[14]W. S. Vorster, "Heterodoxy in 1 John," *Neot* 9 (1975): 93-94.

[15]Commentators debate whether the Greek word *chrisma* here refers to "ointment" or to an "anointing," since both meanings are possible for the word. Linguistically, Brown appeals to contemporary Jewish usage to support the meaning "anointing" (*Epistles*, pp. 342-43). But if "ointment" were the meaning, it would not change our understanding of the passage very much since, in our view, verse 27 requires the idea to be a metaphor for the Holy Spirit Himself. The search for a specific occasion for such an "anointing" (e.g., at the baptism of the Christian convert) is an exercise in guesswork. If elders are referred to, as we suggest in the Commentary, we cannot really say whether at this date there was an installation service of some kind involving the use of literal "ointment." John's text is adequately understood as a declaration that the readers addressed (the elders?) have the spiritual enablement that they need and can learn nothing from the new theology of the Revisionists.

CHAPTER 5

Learning to See God's Children

(1 John 2:28–3:10a)

The warning against the antichrists or, as we have called them, the Revisionists, is now finished. The apostle's burden has been to affirm the high spiritual caliber of his readership and to urge them to continue to live the "abiding" life, which they are currently doing. In the face of the false teaching of the Revisionists, they are to cling to the truth they have heard from the beginning and to allow that truth to shape them inwardly. To go the direction of the antichrists is to forfeit all the rich experience which abiding in the Son and in the Father makes possible.

But what exactly is the abiding experience like? Although John has already pointed out that it involves a Christlike walk (2:6), he has said little about its exact character. Yet it is already clear that it involves obedience to the command to love one another (cf. 2:7-11). Beginning at this point in the epistle, love becomes a controlling and overriding theme.

With the material now before us, from 2:28 through 4:19, we come to what may be called the body of the epistle—that is to say, its major unit of exhortation. This unit is marked off by a literary device known as an *inclusio*. Ancient authors employed this device at *the end of a literary unit* by mentioning a word, phrase, or idea given at the *beginning of the unit* and thus alerting the reader or hearer that the unit was complete.[1] In the case of the unit covered by 2:28–4:19, the *inclusio* occurs with the mention of "boldness [Greek: *parrēsian*] in the day of judgment" in 4:17 which resurfaces the idea first raised in 2:28 of "confidence [Greek: *parrēsian*]…before Him at His coming." Obviously, both texts refer to essentially the same thing, i.e., the coming of our Lord which brings also the Judgment Seat of Christ, where the Christian should earnestly desire to have "boldness."

John will maintain in this unit that it is the "abiding" life which alone can prepare the believer to stand before Christ at His Judgment Seat with boldness rather than shame (cf. 2:28). The apostle uses this major unit of his letter to elevate the significance of abiding in the Son and in the Father to the highest degree of spiritual significance, except for eternal salvation itself. As we have seen, his readers *do* have salvation based on the promise of God (cf. verse 25) and can never lose it (cf. e.g., John 6:35-40). But the "abiding life" is far from automatic. It will actually be forfeited if any believers deviate from the truth they already have, in order to embrace the errors of the antichrists.

Thus, John begins what turns out to be a startling exposition of the significance of abiding in Christ within the local Christian church. It must be said, however, that for the most part, the discussion into which he now leads us has been largely misunderstood in the Christian church as a whole, and many of John's statements have been woefully distorted in the interests of certain forms of theology. With the Lord's help, we need to view the entire unit in a way substantially different from what is common in the commentary literature as a whole.

It is not too much to say that the major stumbling block for students of this unit of the epistle has been the general surrender to the idea that the epistle has no defined progression of thought, and that the author simply meanders around several of his favorite themes. This demeaning approach to the epistle—as though it were the work of an "old man" who just talked out loud—is a sad comment on the lack of diligent study of this "old man's" actual text. Whatever John's age, he has suffered no loss of mental or spiritual acuity. In fact, *no writer of the New Testament deploys his verbiage with more precision than this one.* The failure to recognize this fact reflects poorly on the church's interpretive tradition from which the Epistle of First John has indeed "suffered many things!"

IV. BODY OF THE EPISTLE: THE LIFE THAT LEADS TO BOLDNESS BEFORE CHRIST'S JUDGMENT SEAT (2:28–4:19)

A. The Theme Verse: Abide to be Bold (2:28)

28And now, little children, abide in Him, that when He appears, we may have confidence and not be ashamed before Him at His coming.

John gives here what may be called a thematic statement for the unit of material which follows (i.e., 2:29–4:19). Not surprisingly, it calls on the readers to **abide in Him**. The previous unit has stressed the idea of "abiding." The Greek word *menō* is found no less than seven times in verses 12-27. It is even used once of the antichrists who did not *continue* with the apostolic circle (verse 19). The readers must allow the truth to "abide" in them and thus they will be able to "abide" in the Son and in the Father (verses 24-27). Once more, the **Him** might refer to either the Father or the Son—or to both in their oneness—but the following statement about His appearing shows that the focus is on the Son. So the exhortation of verse 28 is precisely the outworking of the concern for abiding revealed in 2:12-27.[2]

But here, for the first time in the epistle, the writer speaks of the coming of Jesus Christ and the need to be ready to stand **before Him** with **confidence, and not be ashamed**. Even though it is obvious that the readership is saved (cf. discussion under verses 12-14), it is still possible for them to feel shame in the presence of Christ, and particularly at His Judgment Seat.

There is nothing strange about this. Even though eternal salvation is an entirely free gift which can never be lost, the New Testament makes plain that the believer must give an account of his or her Christian life in the presence of Christ (cf. 2 Corinthians 5:10; Romans 14:10-12). As is shown by the texts just cited, as well as by 1 Corinthians 3:11-15, this judgment is not merely a review of our good deeds, but a comprehensive review that embraces both "good and bad" (2 Corinthians 5:10). Therefore, shame is decidedly possible at the Judgment Seat. This is all the more true since Christians at that time will have their eternal bodies. Thus sin will no longer inhibit appropriate regret and embarrassment about those things in one's earthly life that did not please the Lord.

Instead of shame, the writer suggests that his readers can have **confidence...before Him at His coming**. **Confidence** translates a Greek word (*parrēsia*) that may also mean "*boldness*," as well as "*outspokenness, frankness.*"[3] Thus it reflects exactly the opposite of an experience of shame. A confident, outspoken man does not feel shame. Such an experience in the presence of our Lord at His review of our lives is an experience to be earnestly desired.

It is stated here that this experience depends on "abiding." But exactly how the experience is attained becomes completely clear only when we reach the final paragraph of the body of the epistle, that is, 4:17-19.

B. By Learning to See God's Children (2:29–3:10a)

The body of the epistle follows the theme verse (verse 28) and serves to develop in detail the thought that lies behind the thematic statement. It is to be noted that there is no connective word like "since," "then," or "therefore," connecting verses 28 and 29. This lack of a connective is technically known in Greek grammar as *asyndeton,* and it can be used to commence a new train of thought. That is the role it plays here in verse 29.

> **[29]If you know that He is righteous, you know that everyone who practices righteousness is born of Him.**

The apostle begins his new line of thought with a conditional sentence. The words **if you know that He is righteous** embody a Greek "present general" condition[4] that leaves open the opposite possibility. John does not use the form which expresses an assumption which (at least for purposes of argument) takes for granted the reality of the conditional clause. In other words, he does not take it for granted that his readers necessarily know **that He is righteous.**

It would be a mistake to deduce from the condition that perhaps they did *not* **know** this. That would be pressing the conditional form too far. (Even the conditional form that *assumes* the reality of the conditional statement may be used to express ideas known to be false: e.g., Luke 11:19.) In the light of all that has been said by the apostle about these readers, it could have been assumed that they *did* **know** this. It is more likely that the conditional element is introduced because the readership was well aware that there were those who denied this truth about the nature of God.

It was suggested in the discussion of 1:5 that it is quite possible that the Revisionists maintained that the nature of God contained both light *and* darkness. On this understanding, God by His very nature had experience with both good and evil. It would have been an obvious deduction from this that His children could do the same. There could be no true recognition of the children of God if someone held such a false view of God. Thus the conditional sentence probably carried the nuance: **if** in contrast to some others, **you** do **know that He is righteous**...then **you** also **know** the following.

One who knew that God was **righteous** could also **know that everyone who practices** (Greek: does) **righteousness is born of Him**. This is the first reference in the epistle to new birth. These words indicate that the born again person can be recognized as such if he manifests Christian **righteousness**. Of course, John is not talking here about anything like humanistic, or secular, righteousness. John's concept of **righteousness** is totally formed by Christian standards. As he will state in 3:23, the "commandments" of Christ (cf. the plural in 3:22) can be summarized under the heading of a single commandment, "And this is His commandment: that we should believe on the name of His Son Jesus Christ and love one another, as He gave us commandment" (3:23). Thus true **righteousness** is impossible apart from faith in Christ and love for one's fellow Christians.

We must not make this verse say more than it does. John certainly does *not* say, "Whoever does *not* do righteousness is *not* born of Him." That would be an inference in no way justified by John's statement. He is not talking here about how we can decide if a person is saved. If we know that a person *believes* (cf. 1 John 5:1 and discussion there), we can know he is saved. But here, John is clearly concerned with the deduction which we can make **if** we **know that** God **is righteous**. If *that* is known, it follows that one who to any extent reproduces His **righteous** nature is actually *manifesting* that nature and can rightly be *perceived* as **born of Him**.

To draw more than this out of the apostle's statement is unwarranted. It also fails to recognize that he is moving into a section where the correct perception of God's children is critical to his overall theme of "confidence...before Him at His coming" (see verse 28).

1 JOHN 3

[1]**Behold what manner of love the Father has bestowed on us, that we should be called children of God! Therefore the world does not know us, because it did not know Him.**

The chapter break in our Bibles is unfortunate. This verse clearly flows directly out of 2:29. The mention of new birth (2:29) draws forth from John an exclamation of wonder. How truly magnificent is the **love** of **the Father** that makes **us** His **children**! The Greek word translated **what manner of** (*potapos*) sometimes carries a sense of intensification, like "*how great*," "*how wonderful*," and the standard Greek lexicon suggests for this place the words "how glorious."[5] Clearly the **love** that privileges us to **be called** the **children of God** is of a high order indeed.

The apostle's exclamation of wonder, however, is introduced by the word **Behold**. Here John does not use the stereotyped form, *idou*, but rather issues a real call (Greek: *idete* [a true plural]) to actually see this reality. (By contrast *idou* often does not signify actual sight.)[6] It is as though John were saying to his readers, "Take a look at this love." As will be evident later, the visibility of God's **love** in the church is a crux consideration in the unit covered by 2:29–4:19. But obviously there must be something *visible* to see. As verse 29 has demonstrated, the performance of Christian righteousness makes the child of God *visible*, or recognizable in his actions.

If we see a child of God acting in Christian righteousness, we can look at him as a person who is the recipient of God's glorious **love**. By making himself visible, he makes God's **love** for him visible, too.

Yet this perception of the child of God, of which John is speaking, is not available to **the world**. In fact, **the world** is as ignorant of us as it was of **Him**, the Lord Jesus Christ. Even when the believer is acting in righteousness (cf. 2:29), in imitation of His Lord (cf. 2:6), the world can no more perceive this as a manifestation of divine life than it perceived Jesus, in His incarnation, as the revelation of "that eternal life which was with the Father and was manifested" among men (cf. 1:2). Thus the "beholding" urged here by the apostle is a uniquely Christian experience. Its importance will be developed as this section of the epistle progresses.

> [2]**Beloved, now we are children of God; and it has not yet been revealed what we shall be, but we know that when He is revealed, we shall be like Him, for we shall see Him as He is.**

Appropriately John now addresses his readers as **Beloved**. The word **Beloved** picks up the thought of the previous verse that we are the objects of the love of the Father, who regards us as His **children**. This is true right here and **now** (the Greek word for **now** is emphatic in this sentence). But even though this basic fact is true **now**, it **has not yet**

been revealed what we shall be like when we are transformed into our Savior's glorious likeness.

Even though the child of God can be manifested as such by doing righteousness (verse 29), the "visibility" he thus achieves does not consist of any physical aspect or characteristic. The physical transformation which all the children of God will have **when He** [the Lord] **is revealed** will become evident at that time—and at that time only. (Thus the world sees nothing to mark us out as God's children at the present time: cf. verse 1.) Still, one thing is known about that transformation: **we shall be like Him**. Just as doing righteousness makes manifest a likeness to the righteous One, so also our future destiny involves the same principle: manifest likeness to Christ physically as well as spiritually (cf. Romans 8:29; Philippians 3:20-21).

The NKJV translation of this verse conceals the fact that the word rendered twice here as **revealed**, is in fact the same Greek word rendered "appears" in 2:28 (i.e., *phanerōthē*). (The KJV renders the word "appear" in all three cases). This change of translation in the NKJV tends to make the connection between this verse and 2:28 less obvious. When Christ "appears" **what we shall be** will "appear" too, and since **we shall be like Him** then, we do not want to "be ashamed before Him" because we have been *unlike* Him *until* then (cf. 4:17-19).

The apostle gives as the reason why **we shall be like Him** the fact that at His coming **we shall see Him as He is**. The clear implication of this statement is that the sight of our Lord Jesus Christ in His glory will be automatically transforming for each child of God. This agrees with Paul's teaching that, even now, our spiritual transformation takes place as we behold our Lord's glory in the mirror of the Scriptures (cf. 2 Corinthians 3:18). Christians, therefore, have a marvelous expectation for the future— the glorious transforming sight of their Savior—and this should energize them to Christlikeness here and now. Or, in John's terms, it should inspire them to "abide in Him" (2:28).

> **³And everyone who has this hope in Him purifies himself, just as He is pure.**

The wonderful certitude that we will one day be completely like our Lord Jesus (i.e., both physically and spiritually) is a **hope** that fully purifies the believer.

Of course, as is usual in the New Testament, **hope** does not refer to something about which we are unsure. Rather, it refers to an unfulfilled expectation which we appropriate by faith (cf. Hebrews 11:1; Colossians 1:5, 23, 27; etc.). That is quite clear here, since **this hope** refers to something which, according to verse 2, "we *know*"!

The statement that the person possessing this expectation **purifies himself** is often taken as a reference to the experiential effect that the anticipation of the Lord's return can have on the believer. No doubt His anticipated return *can have* strongly positive spiritual effects. But this is not what John is likely to mean in this context.

John will very shortly talk about a "sinless" experience (cf. verses 6, 9-10) and the words **just as He is pure** strongly suggest that the same idea is latent here. As we shall see, the born again person does not sin *at all* because he has in him the sinless seed of God's nature and he *cannot* sin (see verse 9 and discussion). Thus, at the inward level of his redeemed nature, the believer is every bit as **pure** as his Savior is. That purity will be totally realized at the coming of the Lord (verse 2), but is ours now at the core of our being.

Thus the phrase **everyone who has this hope in Him** is an equivalent to John's familiar expression "whoever believes in Him [in His name, etc.]." (In Greek, the grammatical structures are the same: *pas ho* followed by the participle [here: *echōn*; elsewhere, *pisteuōn*: e.g., 1 John 5:1; John 3:15-16; 6:40]). The individual who has the *sure **hope*** of being like the Savior is one who has *believed* in Him. Like Abraham, his hope is founded on faith (Romans 4:18) so that he knows that his eternal future is guaranteed by his Lord (cf. John 11:25-26). It is this faith which results in the new birth (cf. 1 John 5:1) with the consequent inward purification which new birth produces (cf. verse 9; Titus 3:5-6).

The phrase **purifies himself** should be noted. It points to the causality of the believer's faith in Christ. When a person responds to the gospel message by believing it, he can be said to cause the purification which automatically follows as part and parcel of "the washing [Greek: *loutron*, 'bath'] of regeneration" (Titus 3:5). A rough analogy would be the turning on of water in a shower. The water does the actual cleansing, but the person could be said to "shower himself clean."

Under the influence of the extreme passivity taught in many Calvinist circles, the believer is often viewed as totally inactive in the experience of regeneration. This leads often to the extreme view that regeneration is the *cause* of faith, rather than the reverse (see discussion under 1 John 5:1). The Bible does not countenance such a perspective.

For example, Abraham was "fully convinced that what He [God] had promised He was also able to perform. And *therefore* 'it was accounted to him for righteousness'" (Romans 4:21-22, italics added). The *therefore* is significant. God's imputation of righteousness to Abraham was God's *response* to his faith. Obviously, Abraham was not first accounted righteousness and "therefore" he believed! To the same effect it is stated, "But to him who does not work but believes on Him who justifies the ungodly, *his faith is accounted* for righteousness" (Romans 4:5; italics added). Here we see that *faith itself* is reckoned as righteousness to the believer. The causal role of faith in justification is beyond question.

This does not mean that faith is temporally prior to salvation, since saving faith brings instantaneous regeneration and justification. But Scripture makes plain the cause/effect relationship between faith and eternal salvation. "Believe on the Lord Jesus Christ, and you will be saved" (Acts 16:31) cannot be reversed into "Be saved and you will believe in the Lord Jesus Christ"!

By believing, therefore, the Christian can be said to purify himself precisely because his faith is causally related to his perfect inward purification. (The meaning is the same, essentially, as that of 1 John 5:18; see discussion there). As we have just seen, this is not really different from the doctrine of justification. When an individual believes in Christ, God counts the exercise of that faith as "righteousness," not because faith *merits* it but because God imputes righteousness *only on that basis*. Here, too, a man **purifies himself**, not because of any intrinsic power in his faith, but because the exercise of this faith is the basis on which God cleanses him inwardly.

> **⁴Whoever commits sin also commits lawlessness, and sin is lawlessness.**

Sin is the antithesis of the purity that belongs to Christ, and to everyone who has the hope of being like Him.

In fact, in the English text we are told that to commit **sin** is to commit **lawlessness**, and also that **sin *is* lawlessness**. The translation **"lawlessness"** (Greek: *anomia*) is a clear improvement over the KJV's "transgresses...the law" and "transgression of the law." However, contemporary translators appear not to be able to resist the temptation to include a reference to disregard for law, or for *the* law, in their renderings. (E.g., NASB: "Every one who practices sin also practices lawlessness; and sin is lawlessness"; NIV: "Everyone who sins breaks the law; in fact, sin is lawlessness"; JB: "Anyone who sins at all breaks the law, because sin is to break the law.") But such translations are doubtful. This is most likely an example of what is called the root fallacy, i.e., making etymology, rather than usage, the key to a word's meaning.[7]

The usage of the word *anomia* in biblical Greek (both in the New Testament and the Greek Old Testament) argues strongly that normally no such specific meaning as **lawlessness** was attached to this word. In the Septuagint translation of the Old Testament, we find *anomia* used to translate no less than twenty-four different Hebrew words. The most frequent one is the Hebrew *'awon*, for which English words like "wickedness," or "iniquity," are good equivalents. We should thus prefer the translation of this verse by the Confraternity Version (imprim. 1961): "Everyone who commits sin, commits iniquity also; and sin is iniquity." The apostle's statement is intended to stigmatize sin as "evil," "wicked," "iniquitous."

Making light of sin, or at least of some sins, is far from unknown in the Christian church and a general reminder of sin's iniquitous character is always appropriate. But if the Revisionists argued that light and darkness, sin and righteousness, were all a part of the divine experience, then of course they would downplay the "wickedness" of such behavior and perhaps pass it off as morally neutral. If in fact they did something like this, John's words in this verse score a direct hit. One cannot soften the nature or character of sin without distorting reality. Sin is intrinsically evil.

It follows, therefore, that the commission of sin in no way expresses or manifests the purity of which John spoke in verse 3.

> **⁵And you know that He was manifested to take away our sins, and in Him there is no sin.**

For those who have inwardly purified themselves through the new birth (cf. verse 3), sin is not unsuitable only because it is evil (verse 4), but also because it stands in opposition and contrast to the person and work of Christ.

The apostle John agrees with Paul that sin has no place in the life of a Christian (cf. Romans 6:1-4). Of course, he has acknowledged its reality (cf. 1:8), but this does not mean it should be tolerated, much less endorsed in any way (cf. 2:1). On the contrary, as his readers know, **He** (i.e., Christ) **was manifested to take** it **away.**

The phrase **was manifested** employs for the fourth time in this immediate context the Greek verb *phaneroo* (to appear; to be manifested) which the author also used in 2:28 and 3:2 (twice). (See discussion under verse 2.) John is exploiting the ramifications of the concept of "manifestation" as it applies to the believer and to Jesus Christ. He *will be* manifested at His Second Advent, at which time the transformation of the believer (which is *not yet* manifested) *will also be* manifested. Yet, one can also say that Christ **was manifested** at His *First* Advent.

The purpose of His manifestation at His First Advent was **to take away our sins.** This declaration easily recalls the exclamation of John the Baptist, "Behold! The Lamb of God who *takes away* the sin of the world" (John 1:29). In both statements the same Greek verb (*airo*) is used. It seems likely that the sacrificial work of Christ, at His First Advent, is very much in John's mind. But both in John 1:29 and here, the reference may be broader than that and may include the thought that, because of His sacrificial death, ultimately the world's sin will be removed from human experience. That is to say, no one in God's eternal kingdom (after the final rebellion in the millennium: Revelation 20:7-10) will ever sin again. In this light the thought in our verse is not only that Christ died for our sins but that His ultimate goal is our total freedom from sin forever. In fact, the statements of verse 2 have already referred implicitly to this climax.

Our repudiation of sin, therefore, should be based not only on its iniquitous character, but also on the realization that the goal of our Savior who redeemed us, is to completely remove it from our lives. Moreover His own personal purity, already referred to in verse 3, offers further incentive to reject sin in all its forms. For He is entirely without it: **in Him there is no sin.** Thus Christ's sacrificial work for us, plus His own personal and absolute holiness, make sin utterly unsuitable for the born again believer. No matter what rationalizations the readers might have heard for sin, whether from the Revisionists or others, they should reject them categorically.

⁶Whoever abides in Him does not sin. Whoever sins has neither seen Him nor known Him.

In view of all that John has said thus far, since urging his readers to "abide in Him" (2:28), it clearly follows that the experience of abiding *in* a sinless Person means that such an experience is totally free from sin.

Many efforts have been made, both here and in verse 9, to soften this apparently absolute assertion. One popular way in recent times has been to appeal to the present tense (used here in the phrase **does not sin**) and to make the present tense mean, "does not *continue to* sin." But this explanation is untenable and will be discussed more fully under verse 9. Another view is that John is speaking of an ideal which is not fully realized in present experience.

All such explanations fly in the face of the context, especially the immediately preceding verse. The statement of verse 5 that "in Him is no sin" is clearly absolute and cannot be qualified at all. But if this is so, one who **abides in** the Sinless One cannot be said to be only "a little bit" sinful! If there can be "no sin" in Christ at all, one cannot take even a little bit of sin into an experience which is specifically said to be *in* Him. The failure to recognize the logical connection between verses 5 and 6 is the reason that verse 6 has been so often misunderstood. As a result, this misunderstanding carries over into verse 9.

To be sure, no Christian can ever claim (in this life) to be experientially completely free from sin, as 1:8 makes emphatically clear. But at the same time we can say that the experience of "abiding in Him" is in and of itself a sinless experience. Thus it is not "contaminated" by the presence of sin in other aspects of our experience. As we have seen, the "abiding life" is marked by obedience to Christ's commands (cf. 2:3-6 and discussion). The fact is that, if I obey the command to love my brother, that obedience is not tainted in God's sight by some different sort of failure in the life like unwatchfulness in prayer (cf. Ephesians 6:18).

It is also true that, when we are walking in fellowship with God and seeking to guard His commands, God is able to look past all our failures and sin and see the actual obedience that is there. We have already been told this! For in 1:7 we are informed that even while walking in the light, there is cleansing going on by virtue of the blood of Christ (see discussion under that verse). Thus as we walk in the light and do what He commands us, God sees us as people who are totally cleansed from whatever faults we may have and who live before God without any charge of unrighteousness.

Thus, when we **abide in Him**, the positive *obedience* is what God takes account of and recognizes. The sin which still remains in us is not *in any sense* sourced in the abiding life, and that sin is cleansed away in accordance with 1:7. The experience of "abiding" is therefore the equivalent of our experience of *obedience*. Obedience and sin are opposites.

Thus, sin is no part of the abiding experience at all. In fact, sin reflects both ignorance and blindness toward God and Christ. It follows that **Whoever sins has neither seen Him nor known Him**. Once again the statements are absolute and should be taken at face value. They apply to *anyone at all* who (**Whoever**) commits sin.

Most commentators have not been able to accept this conclusion, but it is unavoidable. The apostle is saying that sin, whenever and by whomever it is done, lies so completely outside of the "abiding life" that the one who does it **has neither seen nor known Him**. Once again it is illegitimate to resort to the present tense of the verb **sins**, as though it meant "continues to sin," (see discussion under verse 9). The flow of thought requires us to see an absolute antithesis between sin and Christ, and sin and abiding. Every interpretative attempt to accommodate "a little bit of sin" or "an occasional sin" in John's statements completely nullifies the definitive contrasts the apostle is drawing.

It should be noted that the statement that **Whoever sins has neither seen Him nor known Him** employs Greek verbs for "see" and "know" that are here found in the Greek perfect tense (*heōraken* and *egnōken*). More than any other Greek tense, the perfect tense is often very difficult to render precisely into English. In its normal function the tense suggests a present state or situation resulting from a past action or event. In Galatians 2:20, for example, the KJV translation, "I am crucified with Christ," is the best English rendering, since it clearly suggests a state resulting from a past occurrence. (By contrast, the rendering, "I have been crucified" fails to do this!) Thus the English present perfect, when passive, will often catch the nuance of the perfect tense in Greek.

In this verse, however, neither the verb for "see" or "know" is passive and the translation into English is more difficult. We must probably resort to paraphrase. It is helpful to keep Louw's statement in mind, "The perfect tense in Greek signifies a state of affairs. It is not concerned with the past occurrence of the event but with its reality, its existence."[8] Thus we might paraphrase as follows, *Whoever sins is in a not-seeing and not-knowing condition with reference to God.* That is, the commission of sin shows that the sinner has been overtaken by blindness and ignorance of God. The perfect tense here is not intended to categorize a person as either saved or unsaved, since even believers sin (1:8). Instead, the statement is intended to stigmatize all sin as the product, not only of not abiding, but also of ignorance and blindness toward God.

As translated in the NKJV, the phrases **has neither seen Him nor known Him** are what we call English present perfects (i.e., the present tense of the verb "to have" combined with a past participle). Used in the negative as they are here (cf. "neither," "nor"), the present perfect does *not* imply a "never" unless the context requires it. So I may say, "I have not finished my homework," implying the homework for that particular day. There is no implication that I have *never at any time* completed my homework! I may in fact have completed it regularly on other days. We should therefore not read **has neither seen Him nor known Him** as though these words implied a *never*. They do not. John simply means that when a person **sins,** at that point in time he has acted in blindness and ignorance of God.

As the writer of Hebrews puts it, we must beware of "the deceitfulness of sin" (Hebrews 3:13). Every sin in some way deceives us, and flows out of a darkening of the heart toward God. Not to recognize that John's statement is true of *all* sin is to miss his point completely. If the Revisionists rationalized sin, or even promoted their own participation in it as somehow "enlightened," they were wrong. People do not sin when they fully face the truth. They sin only when in some way they are blind to, and ignorant of, the true and living God.

> **⁷Little children, let no one deceive you. He who practices righteousness is righteous, just as He is righteous.**

Tenderly, John addresses his readers as **Little children** (Greek: *teknia*). If, as we have suggested, the epistle is actually addressed to leaders in a Christian church (or, churches), it remains true that they are but **Little children** to this aging apostle of Christ. His experience was measurably more profound than theirs. But John may also be alluding in these words to this aspect of their relationship to God (cf. 2:12-14), and in view of his use of the word "children" in 3:1-2 (Greek: *teknia*), this may be the main point. If so, his intent is no doubt to encourage them to take a simple, childlike view of this matter by remembering the true character of their heavenly Father who **is righteous.**

Simplicity of mind and spirit is often the best hedge for the Christian against heresies that purport to have more "profound" knowledge to share. It is clear that in the preceding material, especially verses 4-6, John has had the Revisionists in mind. The readership is not to allow these antichrists to **deceive** them. In some way these heretics denied the basic ideas discussed in verses 4-6. Most likely, as we have already noted, they thought they could commit sin and still claim to be in touch with God in doing so. This claim may have been based on the notion that God Himself could experience good and evil and so those who knew God could do so as well.

The rationalizing of sin is an old habit of sinful humanity and it has taken many forms over the centuries. Some of this tendency seems to be reflected in the letters to the churches of Asia Minor that John records in Revelation 2 and 3. There we hear about those who held "the doctrine of Balaam, who taught Balak to put a stumbling block before the children of Israel, to eat things sacrificed to idols, and to commit sexual immorality" (Revelation 2:14). Immediately afterwards there is a reference to "the doctrine of the Nicolaitans" (Revelation 2:15). In the letter that follows, we hear about a prophetess who taught people "to commit sexual immorality and to eat things sacrificed to idols" (Revelation 2:20). That such teachings as these may be in the apostle's mind is suggested by the epistle's closing exhortation to "keep yourselves from idols" (1 John 5:21).

If, as has often been thought, this epistle went to churches situated in Asia Minor, perhaps even to the same set of churches as those mentioned in Revelation 2 and 3, then the passages just cited could well be very relevant for First John. Christians struggled with the prevalence of idolatry in the general life of the Greco-Roman world, and the various guilds for artisans and craftsmen would be expected to hold gatherings in the temple of their patron god. Such temple feasts featured meat offered sacrificially to these gods as well as general immoral behavior, often involving temple prostitutes. Refusal by a Christian craftsman to participate in such gatherings could be viewed by his fellow craftsmen as antisocial and disloyal. The Christian might thus endanger his standing in the guild and risk his livelihood by refusing to take part in these affairs.

It goes without saying that some Christians might be eager for a way in which to rationalize their participation in these things. If the Revisionists taught that such experiences were morally neutral, or even enlightened, they were making an appeal to the self-interest of some of their Christian audience, and this would enhance their potential capacity to **deceive**. Surrendering one's livelihood for Christ's sake is never an easy choice, and Christians might well give way to sophisticated arguments that they did not need to do so.

Since a date before A.D. 70 can be plausibly maintained for both this epistle *and* the Book of Revelation, it is tempting to wonder whether the antichrists of First John are the immediate precursors of the Nicolaitans (cf. Revelation 2:6, 15). Irenaeus, a second century Christian writer, claimed that the sect was founded by Nicolaus, the proselyte from Antioch who was one of the seven chosen to serve the widows in the early church (Acts 6:5). Although it may be doubted that this godly man actually founded such a sect, the Revisionists may have had past associations with him and claimed his authority for their teaching. It seems plain that they did at least claim connections with the "mother church" at Jerusalem (cf. 2:19 and discussion there). By stressing roots like these, they could make their doctrines sound less heterodox. But an apostolic rebuttal, such as this epistle offers, was precisely what they could least afford in their deceptive approach.

In order not to be deceived, therefore, the readers must keep in mind the simple fact that **he who practices righteousness is righteous, just as He is righteous**. It was needless for the NKJV to change the KJV's "doeth righteousness" to **practices righteousness**, since the Greek verb is the common one for *to do* (*poieō*) and carries no special overtones here like "makes a habit of" or something similar. (Still less is **practices** justified by the use of the Greek present tense here: see discussion under verse 9.) The idea that John is expressing is the same one we have met from 2:29 on. The person who performs righteousness is born of God (2:29). The person who possesses the certitude of future likeness to Christ has already experienced a perfect inward purification and so is pure, "just as He [God or Christ] is pure" (3:3). The one who "abides in Him does

138

not sin" (3:6). Here John's point is that **righteousness** (rather than sin) is what indicates that a person has a perfect, inward righteousness—i.e., that person is **righteous just as He is righteous** (for the significance of **righteousness** to John, see the discussion under 2:29).

If the Revisionists taught that they could express their participation in the very nature of God through doing *either* good *or* evil, they were sadly mistaken. Only **righteousness** arises from the inner nature of one who is already **righteous** as God **is righteous**, for "in Him there is no darkness *at all*" (1 John 1:5; italics express the emphasis in the Greek statement). That is to say, sin has no part or role to play in displaying the nature of the **righteous** Father of believers. John now goes on to stress this truth as strongly as possible.

> **⁸He who sins is of the devil, for the devil has sinned from the beginning. For this purpose the Son of God was manifested, that He might destroy the works of the devil.**

Just as light and darkness are mutually exclusive, so are *righteousness* and *sin*. John does not admit any mixture of the two. As he has just said (verse 7), the one who does "righteousness *is* righteous"—completely so: i.e., "just as He is righteous." It follows that sin has no connection with God at all, but is totally connected with **the devil**. Thus it must be said that **he who sins is of the devil**.

Those interpreters who take a statement like this as the equivalent of saying that someone is unsaved totally miss the point. Since even John acknowledges that Christians sin (see 1:7-10), if **he who sins** is unsaved, *everyone* is unsaved! Of course, that is why the appeal is so often made to the present tense and the meaning is held to be, "he who continues to sin." But as we shall see under verse 9, this is an invalid appeal to grammar that is now widely abandoned. The phrase **of the devil** (Greek: *ek tou diabolou*) needs to mean no more than that a sinner's actions are *sourced in* **the devil**. This seems clearly to be John's meaning since he follows with the statement, **for the devil has sinned from the beginning**. That is to say, **the devil** is the source of all sin and his sinful career dates from **the beginning**. (**The beginning** does not refer here to eternity past, since the devil is a created being and not eternal. The reference will then be to the original state of creation as it was when Satan introduced sin into it by his own proud self-exaltation: cf. Isaiah 14:12-15; Ezekiel 28:11-15.) Thus, in this context, to be **of the devil** means "to be doing the devil's work" (for this kind of construction, see further under 3:10b).

One might readily think here of our Lord's words to Peter, "'Get behind Me, Satan! You are an offense to Me, for you are not mindful of the things of God, but the things of men'" (Matthew 16:23). At this point in time, Peter could be said to be **of the devil**!

Just as all genuine *righteousness* is sourced in the One who is righteous, so all *sin* is sourced in the one who **has sinned from the beginning**. It follows that a man cannot sin and then say that his actions are sourced in God, or in the knowledge of God. Instead, all sinful actions can be traced back to the originator of sin, **the devil** himself.

Not only that, but participation in sin is participation in the very thing that Jesus came to destroy, because **the Son of God was manifested** in order **that He might destroy the works of the devil**. (The words **For this purpose** refer forward to the goal of destroying sin). Just as our Lord "was manifested to take away our sins" (cf. verse 5 and discussion), so also He **was manifested** to **destroy the works of the devil**. The final termination of *all* sin is the ultimate aim of our Lord's First Advent.

Thus, if anyone sins, his action can be condemned as a work **of the devil**; this runs counter to the very purpose for which **the Son of God was manifested**.

> **⁹Whoever has been born of God does not sin, for His seed remains in him; and he cannot sin, because he has been born of God.**

Although this statement has seemed puzzling to many, its meaning is transparent on its face. The person who **has been born of God** has God's **seed** within **him** and so is not capable of sin (**he cannot sin**) by virtue of his birth from **God**. This assertion is as absolute as possible and draws obviously on the principle that "like begets like." The entire thrust of the claim is destroyed by a temporizing interpretation like, "The child of a sinless Parent can only sin *a little*." Such a view makes nonsense of John's logic. As Kubo states, "...the habitual view actually plays havoc with the author's intention and argument."[9]

Naturally, many have wondered how this claim can be squared with reality since Christians *do* sin, as even John acknowledges (cf. 1:8). But the answer lies near at hand. In 1:8, John warns: "If *we* say that *we* have no sin, we deceive ourselves." But here he says, **whoever has been born of God does not sin**. As a total person, we do sin and can never claim to be free of it, but our "inward self" that is regenerated does not sin.

This truth can be found elsewhere in the New Testament. For example, in describing his great struggle with sin in Romans 7, Paul reaches the realization that two diverse impulses are at work. So he can say, "For I delight in the law of God according to *the inward man*. But I see another law in my members, warring against the law of my mind, and bringing me into captivity to the law of sin which is in my members" (Romans 7:22-23; italics added). He had just previous to this concluded, "Now if I do what I will not to do, it is *no longer I that do it*, but sin that dwells in me" (Romans 7:20; italics added). His conclusion, then, is simple, "So then, with the mind I myself serve the law of God, but with the flesh the law of sin" (Romans 7:25). There is a clear sense, therefore, in which Paul could acknowledge that at the core of his being (i.e., in his *inward man*) he does not and cannot sin. Indeed, in the phrase *I myself serve the law of God*, the word *serve* is the Greek verb for slave-service (*douleuō*). The inward man (the "regenerate self") is therefore absolutely impervious to sin, fully enslaved to God's will, and as such he **cannot sin, because he has been born of God**. If sin occurs, it is not the inward man who performs it.

The same principle is clearly at work in Galatians 2:20. There Paul writes: "I have been crucified with Christ; it is no longer I who live, but *Christ lives in me*; and the life which I now live in the flesh I live by faith in the Son of God" (italics added). But if, in terms of the Christian life, *only Christ lives*, what is the quality of the life that He lives? The answer: A *sinless* one. We can say that any and all sin in a Christian is in no way a part of the "Christ-life" that is being lived through us. Sin *does* exist in the Christian, but it is foreign and extraneous to his regenerated inner self, where Christ dwells in perfect holiness. Put into Johannine terms, since Christ *is* eternal life (1 John 5:20), the one who possesses that life **cannot sin because he is born of God**. The divine **seed** (Greek: *sperma*) of that life **remains** (or, "abides," "stays" [Greek: *menō*]) **in him** who is born again, making sin an impossibility at the level of his regenerate inward self.

It is not likely that the word **seed** refers to the child of God or that **in**

him should be read as *in Him,* that is, "in God." John does not elsewhere use **seed** of the believer himself, and the flow of thought calls for a reference to what God has imparted to the child of God that makes the regenerate person incapable of sin. The idea is substantially the same as in 1 Peter 1:23 where the "seed" (Greek: *spora*) refers to the life-begetting word of God.[10]

One may also understand the **seed** here as another way of referring to the "living water" which, in John 4, becomes the inward source of eternal life: "but the water that I shall give him *will become* in him a *fountain* of water springing up into everlasting life" (John 4:14; italics added). That "living water" is the life-bearing truth that "Jesus is the Christ" (John 20:31; cf. John 4:25-26; 1 John 5:1). Thus, the life-producing word that *enters* the believer and *regenerates* him can be compared to a "drink of water" (John 4:14), to a "seed" sown in the heart like grain seed in a field (Luke 8:11; 1 Peter 1:23), or to a divine "sperm" which creates a sinless life in the one born of God (here). Brown's statement is worth quoting: "But in the long run the exact identification [of 'seed'] is not so important, so long as we recognize that the author is talking about a divine agency for begetting God's children, which not only brings us into being but also remains and keeps us His children."[11]

The understanding of 3:9 just given is consistent with the flow of thought as we have seen it from 2:29–3:8. Absolute contrasts are, of course, a familiar part of Johannine discourse. Most prominent among these are the light/darkness and the death/life antitheses. But to these we must add the sin/righteousness polarity that has appeared prominently in this unit of John's text. The failure to recognize this Johannine polarity has led to much confusion in the discussion of our present verse.

The view we have discussed makes unnecessary any attempt to extract the meaning from some grammatical nicety or nuance supposedly found in the Greek verbs. The opinion was widely popular for a number of decades that the key to understanding 1 John 3:9 is to be found in the present tense of the verb *to sin.* In this view the verse should be read, "Whoever has been born of God does not *continue to sin;* for His seed remains in him; and he cannot *continue to sin,* because he has been born of God." (Compare the similar rendering in NIV.) The meaning of this is supposed to be that prolonged continuation in sin does not occur if one is born again.

But this raises more questions than it answers. Do not all Christians *continue to sin* until the day of their death? Furthermore, do not all Christians sin *daily?* Isn't daily sin a continuation in doing it? What could the proposed translation possibly mean? Or, how can anyone claim *not* to be continuing to sin? Does the born again person come to some point at which he ceases to sin? The proposed translation solves nothing.[12]

There is no doubt that in an appropriate context the Greek present tense can have a present progressive force like "he is sinning." But the introduction of ideas like "continue to" or "to go on doing" require more than the Greek tense to make them intelligible. For this purpose there were Greek words available which are actually used in the New Testament. For example, *diapantos* occurs in Luke 24:53: "...and [they] were *continually* in the temple praising and blessing God." The same word occurs in Hebrews 13:15: "Therefore by Him let us *continually* offer the sacrifice of praise to God." (See also: Mark 5:5; Acts 10:2; 24:16; Romans 11:10; Hebrews 9:6). The Greek phrase *eis to dienekes* could have the same meaning (cf. Hebrews 7:3; 10:1). The Greek present tense did not by itself convey such ideas as is made clear by Louw.[13]

It is highly probable that if John had meant something similar to the NIV-type of translation of 1 John 3:9, he would have used the *available Greek words* to make his point. No first century Greek reader or hearer was likely to get a meaning such as the one that the NIV imports into this text, without the necessary additional words. As Louw has very acutely observed: "...expository discourse of which the First Letter of John is an example, employs the present predominantly for it is *a zero tense of factual actuality*"[14] (italics added). That is to say, it simply states the action without any kind of elaboration or description.

In addition, this appeal to the Greek tense, if used elsewhere in the epistle, would lead to havoc. For example, as C. H. Dodd pointed out, if we translate 1 John 1:8 as "if we say that *we do not continually have sin*, we deceive ourselves," the result is a contradiction of 3:9 translated the same way.[15] If someone who is born of God *does not continually sin*, why should he not say, *"I do not continually have sin"*? But if he does say this, he "deceives" himself according to 1:8. Thus the proposed translation of 3:9 will not work in 1:8. If applied there it produces a contradiction with 3:9.

It is small wonder that the "tense solution" in 1 John 3:9 is in the process of imploding in the current literature. It was shrewdly questioned by C. H. Dodd in his commentary in 1946 and dealt a major blow by S. Kubo in an article entitled, "1 John 3:9: Absolute or Habitual?" published in 1969.[16] It has since been given up by the three major critical commentaries published since Kubo's article; namely, I. Howard Marshall (1978), Raymond E. Brown (1982); and Stephen S. Smalley (1984). It seems quite clear that the "tense solution" as applied to 1 John 3:9 is an idea whose time has come—and gone![17]

The regenerate person can express himself only through righteousness (cf. 2:29 and discussion) and can never express himself through sin, because **he cannot sin**.

> [10a]**In this the children of God and the children of the devil are manifest:**

A unit of material concludes with this initial part of verse 10. Although the NKJV takes the statement as a reference to what follows it (note the colon in its translation), it is preferable to take the last half of the verse as the beginning of a new unit.

The words **In this** refer backward rather than forward in this context.[18] The use of the word **manifest** in verse 10a links the statement with what has preceded. As we have noted, the concept of *manifestation* is an overriding theme in 2:29–3:9. The Greek verb for this idea (*phaneroō*) appeared in the thematic statement of 2:28 and then occurs four more times in the brief space of 2:28–3:9. Prior to 2:28 it has been used only three times, twice in the prologue (cf. 1:2 [twice]) and in 2:19. After verse 10a it occurs *only once* in the rest of the epistle (4:9). The adjective used here in verse 10a (*phaneros*) is used only here in the entire epistle. For this reason verse 10a is best taken as a conclusion that draws on the preceding discussion about "manifestation."

The children of God...are manifest by the doing of righteousness. This is in no way to be regarded as some kind of test of salvation. The apostle John's one and only test of salvation is faith (cf. 1 John 5:1 and 5:9-13). Instead, this is simply a statement about *how* God's children do manifest themselves. It is totally gratuitous to read into the text the idea that *if they are not manifested this way* then they are not really His children! The text neither states this nor implies it. To make this claim is to read a preconceived theology into the text.

As was noted earlier, the First Epistle of John has been woefully misconceived as a handbook for deciding who is saved and who is not. Those who use it this way misuse it grievously. The section we are looking at is advancing the theme stated in 2:28 where boldness in the presence of the Lord is offered to those who abide in Him (2:28). In doing this, i.e., by abiding in Him, believers can and do manifest themselves as children of God. But those who do not abide do not so manifest themselves. The reality of their regenerate inward man remains hidden.

The same principle applies to **the children of the devil**. There is no good reason to take this phrase as a reference to unsaved people generally. The concept of the devil's **children** appears elsewhere in the New Testament in Matthew 13:38 ("the sons of the wicked one"), John 8:44 ("you are of your father the devil"), and Acts 13:10 ("you son of the devil"). In the latter two passages the terms are used in reference to outspoken opponents of Jesus (John 8:44) or of the gospel (Elymas, Acts 13:8-11). Thus the term **children of the devil** is fundamentally descriptive in nature. It does not designate a person as unregenerate but as a vocal opponent of the truth, just as is the devil himself.

The question might be raised whether a truly regenerate person could, in the sense we are discussing, ever be called a "child of the devil." In the light of 2 John 9 (see the discussion there), the answer must be Yes. A Christian who has deviated from sound doctrine about the Person and work of Jesus Christ, and who vigorously opposes the truth, could be so described. This is no more strange than that the Lord Jesus could address His own disciple Peter as "Satan" (Matthew 16:23; see discussion above under 3:8). This "child of the devil" is anyone who does the devil's work by opposing the truth.

Perhaps the most significant reference for our text is the parable of the wheat and the tares (see Matthew 13:24-30, and the interpretation in 13:36-43). John, of course, would have been familiar with this parable from his days with Jesus. It was not apparent at first that there were tares in the field; only later did they become evident. This would agree with 1 John 2:19 where it appears that the antichrists were originally a part of the Jerusalem (or Judean) church (see discussion there) and only later were *made manifest* (Greek: *phaneroō*) as opponents of apostolic doctrine.

The statement of 2:19 clearly anticipates the statement here in 10a.

In view of all this, it is best to conclude that **children of the devil** refers to people like the antichrists, or Revisionists, who are revealed as such by their opposition to Jesus Christ (cf. 1 John 2:22-23). Whereas the child of God manifests himself by the doing of the righteousness which Jesus commanded (cf. 2:29 and 3:7), **the children of the devil** are manifest because they oppose this righteousness—first and foremost by their opposition to faith in Jesus as the Christ (cf. 2:22). They thus fit the description that Paul gave of the vigorously hostile Elymas, who sought "to turn the proconsul [Sergius Paulus] from the faith." Paul says to this man, "O full of all deceit and all fraud, you *son of the devil,* you *enemy of all righteousness,* will you not cease perverting the straight ways of the Lord?" (Acts 13:10; italics added).

The apostle John could have said all this about **the children of the devil** whom he is confronting in this epistle. In effect, he does say all this over the course of his letter. These heretics have been clearly *manifested* and he wants the readers to see them for who they really are.

Brown's translation of this part of the verse is apt, "That is how God's children and the devil's children are revealed."[19]

ENDNOTES

[1] George A. Kennedy, *New Testament Interpretation through Rhetorical Criticism* (Chapel Hill, NC: University of North Carolina Press, 1984), pp. 33-34.

[2] Marianne Meye Thompson's note here (*1–3 John,* IVPNT [Downers Grove, IL: InterVarsity Press, 1992], p. 84) is succinct and helpful. After observing that commentators "differ on whether a new unit of thought begins with verse 28, 29 or 3:1," she aligns herself "with the NIV and most commentators" in suggesting that "a new subsection begins with verse 28; compare Brown (1982: 417-20); Bruce (1970: 77); Bultmann (1973: 43); Houlden (1973: 84); Marshall (1978: 164-65); Schnackenburg (1963: 162); Stott (1988: 120)." She adds: "The transitional phrase *kai nun,* the address to *dear children* (compare v. 18) and the introduction of new subject matter suggest that a new unit of thought begins with 2:28."

[3] Bauer, Walter. *A Greek-English Lexicon of the New Testament and Other Early Christian Literature* (Chicago; University of Chicago Press, 1979), p. 630.

[4] David L. Washburn, "Third Class Conditions in First John," *GTJ* 11 (1990): 225.

[5] BGD, p. 695.

[6] Brooke Foss Westcott (*The Epistles of St John: The Greek Text with Notes* [Grand Rapids: Wm. B. Eerdmans Publishing Co., 1966], p. 95) expresses surprise at the use of *idete*: "The use of the plural is remarkable, and elsewhere it is used only of something actually visible..." This, of course, is the point. Brown, commenting on Westcott's remark, says: "However, visibility may be the nuance intended. While not yet here, the parousia of Christ (2:28) is near; and the love that one can already see bestowed in the first coming guarantees the loving quality of the second coming" (Raymond E. Brown, *The Epistles of John,* AB [Garden City, NY: Doubleday, 1982], p. 387). Brown here misses the connection with John's argument about "seeing" God's born again children.

[7] Much contemporary New Testament lexicography seems to have gone astray here. An examination of the use of this word (Greek: *anomia*) by the Septuagint and other Greek Old Testament translations clearly shows that by the time of the translators, *anomia* was a rather broad word signifying "sin," "iniquity," "transgression," etc. See the list of Hebrew words for which it is used in Edwin Hatch and Henry A. Redpath, *A Concordance to the Septuagint and the other Greek Versions of the Old Testament (Including the Apocryphal Books)*, 2 vols. (Graz, Austria: Akademische Druck-U. Verlagsanstalt, 1954), 1:106-107. Those commentators who rely upon the root meaning fail to take adequate account of this lexical data: cf., e.g., A. E. Brooke, *A Critical and Exegetical Commentary on the Johannine Epistles,* ICC (Edinburgh: T. & T. Clark, 1912), pp. 84-85; Alfred Plummer, *The Epistles of St. John* (Cambridge: University Press, 1886 [reprint ed., Grand Rapids: Baker Book House, 1980]), p. 75; F. F. Bruce, *The Epistles of John: Introduction, Exposition and Notes* (Old Tappan, NJ: Fleming H. Revell, 1970), p. 89; C. H. Dodd, *The Johannine Epistles,* MNTC (New York: Harper & Row, 1946), pp. 72-73; Rudolf Bultmann, *The Johannine Epistles: A Commentary on the Johannine Epistles,* Herm (Philadelphia: Fortress Press, 1973), pp. 49-50; J. L. Houlden, *A Commentary on the Johannine Epistles,* HNTC (New York: Harper & Row, 1973), p. 92; Stephen S. Smalley, *1,2,3 John,* WBC (Waco, TX: Word Books, 1984), pp. 153-55; and John R. W. Stott, *The Letters of John: An Introduction and Commentary,* rev. ed., TNTC (Grand Rapids: Wm. B. Eerdmans Publishing Co., 1988), pp. 126-27. Brown, however, appropriately points out that "nowhere in I and II John does the author ever accuse his adversaries of statements against the Law. Nor is there evidence of libertine behavior by the secessionists... If the opponents were permissive about lawlessness, one would

have expected the author to say, 'Lawlessness is sin,' not 'Sin is lawlessness'" (*Epistles*, p. 399). Brown's solution, however, is to take *anomia* here "to mean apocalyptic iniquity," that is to say, "Sin is being identified as *the* Iniquity which is the expected state of hostility at the end of the world" and he links this with the eschatological statement of 2:18 where the opponents are "identified as the manifestation of the expected Antichrist" (*Epistles*, p. 399). But Brown's overall linguistic support for this view is thin (cf. pp. 399-400), and one may wonder whether the author would really define sin generally as "apocalyptic iniquity." Though the view seems forced, it is partially adopted by some of the commentators above who retain the root meaning of "lawlessness." It is fully adopted by Thompson (*1–3 John*, p. 92), who correctly notes that "in the Septuagint *anomia* lacks the specific connotations of 'breaking the law' that some try to deduce from its etymology." But surely the solution is much simpler than the one favored by Brown and Thompson. By the time of the Septuagint, *anomia* had apparently become a general word for sin with harsher overtones than *hamartia*, just as our words *wickedness* and *iniquity* are harsher than our word *sin*, which in usage is sometimes even trivial (cf., "this is sinfully delicious" or "it's a sin to feel so happy"). If anyone (the Revisionists?) was inclined to make light of sin, John wished them to know that they were talking about *iniquity*, something genuinely wicked and evil.

[8] J. P. Louw, "Verbal Aspect in the First Letter of John," *Neot* 9 (1975): 101.

[9] Sakae Kubo, "1 John 3:9: Absolute or Habitual?" *AUSS* 7 (1969): 56.

[10] A similar, though not identical, conclusion is reached by J. du Preez in a helpful survey of the problem ("'Sperma Autou' in 1 John 3:9," *Neot* 9 [1975]: 105-12), despite the adoption of the durative sense for the present tense in that verse. Cf. also Dodd's discussion of the Hellenistic background here (*Epistles*, pp. 75-78) where he takes the "seed" to be "the Gospel, as the Word of God, [which] is the immanent divine principle producing in men the regenerate nature which does not sin" (*Epistles*, p. 78). This is nicely stated.

[11] Brown, *Epistles*, p. 411.

[12] The NIV rendering, referred to in the discussion of 3:9, also shows the inevitable ambiguity into which this approach leads its proponents. The rendering is: "No one who is born of God will continue to sin, because God's seed remains in him; he cannot go on sinning because he has been born of God." This is easily read in English as meaning: *he will stop sinning*, which is not at all what the translators intended. Or, if they had, they would be contradicting 1:8! Must it not be said that all Christians *continue to sin* and *go on sinning* as long as they are in their earthly bodies? *The NIV Study Bible* note states: "Not a complete cessation from sin, but a life that is not characterized by sin." But since when does the Greek negative present mean "not to be characterized by" rather than "not to

continue to" sin? The note is a completely gratuitous leap to a new meaning. It is a futile effort to salvage a hopeless situation.

[13] Louw, *Neot:* 99-101.

[14] Ibid., 103.

[15] Dodd, *Epistles*, p. 79.

[16] Kubo, *AUSS:* 7:47-56.

[17] I am mystified by the fact that Marianne Meye Thompson, writing in her commentary of 1992, simply accepts without discussion the NIV rendering of 1 John 3:9. As is evident everywhere in her commentary, Thompson knows the literature well and is surely aware of the stringent criticism that has been directed toward the "present-tense solution." Yet to adopt it quietly, as if the literature as a whole did so, and to say nothing to her readers about its manifest problems, is an abdication of responsible commentary. It may also be a tacit admission that the position is scarcely capable of defense. Likewise Gary M. Burge, *The Letters of John,* NIV Application Commentary (Grand Rapids: Zondervan Publishing House, 1996), pp. 149-50, 155-57, 216-17, embraces the tense solution, but apparently with some diffidence. On the other hand, there is no trace of the "tense solution" in Rudolf Schnackenburg's treatment of 3:6 and 9 (*Die Johannesbriefe,* 2nd ed. [Freiburg, Germany: Herder, 1963], pp. 188-89, 190-92). For Schnackenburg, however, the present tense of "does not sin" (in 3:6) did not express either a factual claim or a "disguised" imperative, but instead a standard of conduct. Compare p. 188: "*Oux hamartanei* ist weder eine apodiktische Aussage ('kann nicht sündigen') noch ein verkappter Imperativ ('darf nicht sündigen'); vielmehr will dieses kategorische Präsens eine Beobachtung und Regel angeben." A writer of Schnackenburg's stature had no need to refer to a view that (even in 1963!) could be perceived as an idiosyncrasy of the English commentary tradition.

[18] For the question about the reference of the words *in this* (Greek: *en toutō*) in John's Gospel and First Epistle, see note 8 in chapter 3.

[19] Brown, *Epistles*, p. 379.

CHAPTER 6

Learning to See Christian Love

(1 John 3:10b-23)

The apostle has now made perfectly clear the one and only basis on which a child of God may be manifested. This can only come about by doing righteousness. Since "whoever is born of God does not sin," and "cannot sin," sin can be no part of such a manifestation.

The idea that the children of God are manifested by a *diminution* of sin, or by its *increasingly sporadic occurrence* in a Christian's life, is totally foreign to John's thought. Sin is always, and only, a work of the devil and all sin finds its source in this adversary of God. Sin is contrary to both the Person and work of Christ, who came to abolish it completely.

But granted that God's children can only be manifested by the doing of righteousness, in what does that righteousness consist? How can we recognize it when it is on display?

Many people today might answer such a question in terms of morality. But there are unregenerate people who are highly moral, and there is nothing distinctively Christian about this morality, however admirable it may be. What is unique to *Christian* morality is its demand for a *brotherly love* based on our mutual faith in Christ. Where one or both of these things are missing, there can be no actual *manifestation* of a truly Christian righteousness (cf. 1 John 3:23).

Accordingly, the section of the epistle that begins with 3:10b turns to the subject of Christian, or brotherly, love. Up to this point in the epistle, the Greek noun for "love" (*agapē*) has occurred only three times (2:5, 15; 3:1) and the verb "to love" has occurred only four times, two in the warning against loving the world (2:10, 15 [twice]; 3:1). From 3:10b–4:21, the noun occurs fourteen times and the verb twenty-one times. The new theme is clearly *love*.

C. By Learning to See Christian Love (3:10b-23)

1. What Love Is Not (3:10b-15)

John begins his new discussion of love by considering what the absence of Christian love is really like. He thereby prepares the way to discuss what characterizes such love (3:16-18).

> **[10b]Whoever does not practice righteousness is not of God, nor *is* he who does not love his brother.**

The discussion of righteousness (cf. 2:29; 3:7) is now left behind as the writer makes a transition to the more specific subject of **love**. In fact, the reference to **righteousness** in this verse is the last in the entire epistle. But this is understandable if we keep in mind that, for John, there is no such thing as a Christian **righteousness** which does not include **love** for one's **brother** (3:23). To speak of loving one's brothers is thus to speak also of **righteousness** in a truly Christian sense.

In this transitional statement, John affirms that what is true of **whoever does not do righteousness** is true also of whoever **does not love his brother**. In both cases, the person is **not of God**. (Once again, the NKJV translation "practices" is infelicitous and we should render the Greek verb as "do": cf. KJV, "doeth." See the discussion under 3:7).

As was the case with the phrase *of the devil* in verse 8 (see discussion there), it is completely unfounded to take the phrase **not of God** (Greek: *ek tou Theou*) as though it meant "not born of God." The NIV rendering here, "Anyone who does not do what is right is not a child of God," is a classic example of theologically motivated translation run amuck. It not only paraphrases the text but misinterprets it at the same time! There is nothing in this text about not being a child of God. How could there be? One *must be* a child of God before one could hate *his* **brother**. An unsaved man has no Christian **brother** to hate (cf. discussion under 2:9).

A close analogy in the Greek New Testament to the phrase **of God** is found in Gamaliel's statement to the Sanhedrin about the Christian movement: "'...for if this plan or this work is of men [Greek: *ex anthrōpōn*], it will come to nothing; but if it is of God [Greek: *ek Theou*], you cannot overthrow it'" (Acts 5:38-39). Gamaliel's obvious meaning is that if the

Christian movement originates with God—if God is behind it—it cannot be defeated. Similarly, in Acts 11:2, "those of the circumcision" (Greek: *hoi ek peritomēs*) means something like "those who favored circumcision" or "those belonging to the circumcision party." Or again, in Galatians 3:12, the words "the law is not of faith" (Greek: *ouk estin ek pisteōs*) mean something like "the law is not based on faith."

The Greek behind the phrase **of God** must not be compelled to do heavy theological duty. It employs a flexible Greek expression that must always be adapted to its context. Since we have already been told that all sin is "of the devil" (3:8), one who is unrighteous cannot be said to have his actions sourced in God. He is **not of God** in the sense that God is not behind what he is doing. He is not on God's side. He is doing the devil's work and not God's work. Brown is correct to state, "The main theological usage of *einai ek* is in the Johannine dualistic worldview to indicate origin from and/or adherence to one side or the other. The *good side* is described 15 times explicitly or implicitly in terms of being 'from God (the Father)'..." (italics in the original).[1]

It must be noted that in this transition verse, John moves from a broader to a narrower theme. The words **whoever does not practice [do] righteousness** can refer to *anyone* who lacks righteous conduct, whether saved or unsaved. But the words **he who does not love his brother** introduce a specific kind of righteousness that only a Christian can manifest or fail to manifest. This becomes even plainer in the following verse.

> **[11]For this is the message that you heard from the beginning, that we should love one another,**

The failure to love one's brother is nothing less than an infraction of the Savior's command to **love one another** (John 13:34). It is striking that the original command was expressed by the Lord Jesus *only after* Judas had left the Upper Room (John 13:30). His audience was therefore composed entirely of regenerate men. Such a command would have had no bearing on Judas, who was not a child of God.

Thus, the new subject matter in this unit of the epistle (3:10a-23) has to do with a command that was given only to believers and can be fulfilled, or not fulfilled, only by a born again person. With respect to the readers, this **message** about love had been given to them **from the beginning** of their Christian experience (cf. 2:7 and discussion there). Since the Revisionists were not far from John's thoughts (cf. 3:7), no doubt the command to **love one another** was one of those things that the readers had **heard from the beginning** and must hold onto over against those who brought new doctrines (cf. 2:24). If the Revisionists rationalized sin (cf. verse 7 and discussion), they may also have dismissed the command for brotherly **love** as trivial and/or irrelevant.

> ¹²**not as Cain *who* was of the wicked one and murdered his brother. And why did he murder him? Because his works were evil and his brother's righteous.**

The classic example of brother-to-brother hatred is, of course, the case of **Cain** and Abel (Genesis 4:1-15). Even this illustration shows that throughout the discussion the author is thinking of a genuine relationship of brotherhood between the one who hates and the object of his hatred.

Cain, of course, **was of the wicked one**, in that what he did was derived from satanic influence rather than from anything related to God (cf. verses 8, 10b and discussions in those places). As our Lord had said, Satan "was a murderer from the beginning." Whether or not **Cain** was ever regenerate is a question that cannot be answered from the biblical information. But even so grievous a crime as **murder** is not regarded in the New Testament as impossible for a Christian to commit. (Cf. the warning in 1 Peter 4:15: "But let none of you suffer as a murderer...") Yet it is clear that if a Christian were to be guilty of this, the influence of **the wicked one** would be obvious.[2]

The apostle's next words are telling. **Why did he murder him? Because his works were evil and his brother's righteous.** It was thus a case of spiritual envy that led to the first murder in human history. And whenever Christians feel guilt because their behavior is contrary to God's will, they will find it easy to experience hatred toward those whom they know God approves. Indeed, as Paul recognized, divisions within churches are all too often a clash between those who have God's approval and those who do not. So he said, "For there must also be factions among you, that those who are *approved* may be recognized among you" (1 Corinthians 11:19; italics added).

Conflict among Christians in which harsh and unloving words and actions occur is unfortunately far too common in Christian churches. Envy and jealousy, from which such situations arise, are likewise common. The New Testament epistles reveal these things in the early church, sometimes in painful detail. The proposition that no true Christian could possibly hate another Christian is so unrealistic on its face that it is astounding that this is often maintained in regard to the text before us. Nothing John says here gives the slightest support to this view. Its proponents are reduced to saying that **his brother** must really mean something like "his purported brother." However, this is nothing but reading *into* the text what one wishes the text to say.

¹³Do not marvel, my brethren, if the world hates you.

While brother-to-brother hatred is wholly inconsistent with our Lord's command "to love one another" and is therefore not to be the expected experience, the same cannot be said of **the world**. The world's hatred, as Jesus taught, *is* to be expected (cf. John 15:18-19). The readers should not be surprised by it.

In the statement under discussion, the Greek words for **the world** (*ho kosmos*) are in an emphatic position at the very end of the sentence. We could capture the emphasis by italics in English or by the proper oral stress on these words: **do not marvel...if *the world* hates you**. While the readership might well **marvel** at hatred from a brother, the world's hatred is to be anticipated. The apostle will pursue the implications of this in the following verses.

¹⁴We know that we have passed from death to life, because we love the brethren. He who does not love *his* brother abides in death.

This statement begins in Greek with an emphatic pronoun, **We**. The pronoun is thus juxtaposed with the emphatic words "the world" which conclude the previous verse. The pronoun "you" in Greek immediately precedes the words "the world." The result of this conjunction of words is that "you—the world—**We**" are brought into close proximity.

In two other places in the epistle, where John has the antichrists in mind, we meet a similar close conjunction which we may call a "we-you-they" combination which refers to the apostles ("we"), the readers ("you") and the antichrists ("they"). The first instance is in 2:19-20 where the "us" of verse 19 refers to the apostles, the "they" of verse 19 to the antichrists, and the "you" of verse 20 (emphatic in Greek) refers to the readers. Equally clear are 4:4-6 where each verse is led off with an emphatic Greek pronoun and the same three groups are referred to (see discussion under 4:4-6).

It seems most likely that we have the same combination here in verses 13-14. Since, according to 4:5, the antichrists are "of the world," the reference to "the world" hating the readers ("you," verse 13), probably has particular reference to the present manifestation of the world's hatred through its agents and representatives, the Revisionists. If this is the case, then the emphatic **we** (Greek: *hēmeis*) no doubt refers to the apostles themselves. In contrast to "the world," the apostles **love** their fellow Christians, and especially in this context, the readers. At the same time, John wishes to say more than this about the apostolic experience of **love**.

Indeed, John declares, **we** apostles **know that we have passed from death to life, because we love the brethren.** This is more than an assertion that they do **love** their fellow Christians. It is also a claim to a certain quality of experience. The apostles are able to recognize their experience of **love** as an experience of **life** rather than **death**.

The phrase translated **passed from death to life** is a famous one, although it occurs only one other time in the New Testament in the well-known statement of John 5:24. There we read the words of Jesus: "Most assuredly, I say to you, he who hears My word and believes in Him who sent Me has everlasting life, and shall not come into judgment, but *has passed from death into life*" (italics added). The wording of the phrase in Greek is identical to that in our verse, except that in John 5:24 the singular verb is used rather than the plural here. That the apostle had his Lord's words in mind here is hard to doubt.

But it would be a mistake to read the statement as if the apostles were sure of their eternal salvation **because** they loved **the brethren.** There is no reason why this should be true for them or any other Christian. Assurance of salvation is based on the testimony of God (see 5:9-13 and discussion there). Instead, in a perfectly normal use of the word **know**, John declares that he and his fellow apostles have a direct and immediate knowledge of their passage **from death to life** through the experience of loving their Christian brothers.[3]

Perhaps the classic biblical use of the word *know* in this sense is to be found in the declaration God made to Abraham after the patriarch showed himself willing to offer his son Isaac as a sacrifice. On that occasion God said to him: "...now I *know* that you fear God, since you have not withheld your son, your only son, from Me" (Genesis 22:12). It goes without saying that God already *knew* this before Abraham did anything at all, but now God *knows* it as a manifested reality.

The Greek verb used here (*oida*) has a well-recognized semantic category under which it may mean to "*understand, recognize, come to know, experience.*"[4] The standard lexicon cites, for example, a use in Diognetus 12:1 which it renders, "'*You will experience* [Greek: *eisesthe*] what God bestows.'"[5] This kind of direct, immediate knowledge can be seen, for example, in Paul's observation in 1 Corinthians 2:11, "For what man *knows* the things of a man except the spirit of the man which is in him?" The idea is the unique, experiential self-knowledge that an individual possesses about himself.[6]

John is saying here that he and his fellow apostles have first-hand knowledge and experience of the fact that they **have passed from death to life**. This knowledge is theirs **because** they **love the brethren**. The underlying implication is that the passage **from death to life**, which occurs at the point of salvation (John 5:24), can be experientially known and appreciated through Christian **love**. Since John wants his readers to "have fellowship" with the apostolic circle (cf. 1:3), it is obvious he wants the readers to share this same experiential knowledge of the "life" they possess as children of God.

By contrast it may be said that **he who does not love *his* brother abides in death**. There is no way a Christian who fails to **love his brother** can have the immediate knowledge of **life** which John has just spoken about. On the contrary, such a person **abides** ("dwells") **in death**. If love is an experience of "life," John is saying, hatred of our brother is an experience of **death**. That, of course, is where the world lives in its hatred of Christians (cf. verse 13), but emphatically *not* where the apostles live.

Many interpreters of First John have a reflex response to the word **death** here and conclude that the persons spoken of must be unsaved people. But this conclusion is theological, not exegetical. It also ignores the fact that in almost any highly developed language the word-group "die-dead-death" has an extremely broad semantic range. This, of course, is true in English. We may say, "My hopes have died," or, "He talked the subject to death," or, "That course of action is a dead end." Examples could be multiplied indefinitely.

A similar semantic range for this word-group is found in the Greek language. So Paul, for example, can speak of Abraham's "body" as "already dead" and of "the deadness of Sarah's womb" (Romans 4:19). He can call on us to "put to death" our sinful practices (Colossians 3:5). The writer of Hebrews speaks of "repentance from dead works" (Hebrews 6:1). And we are told that the widow "who lives in pleasure is dead while she lives" (1 Timothy 5:6)! One might also note Philo's comment, "What is good and virtuous constitutes life; what is bad and evil constitutes death."[7]

Of particular relevance to our text here are some statements by Paul in Romans 7. Speaking of the effect of the law upon his Christian experience, he writes, "I was alive once without the law, but when the commandment came, sin revived [Greek: came back to life] and I *died*. And the commandment, which was to bring life, I found to bring *death*" (Romans 7:9-10; italics added). This certainly cannot describe Paul's unsaved days, since there is no reasonable sense in which he could be said to have been "alive without the law" at that time. But as a Christian experience it is easily intelligible. He was experiencing his new life until confronted by a legal demand, and then "sin, taking occasion by the commandment, deceived me and by it *killed* me" (Romans 7:11; italics added). In other words, the experience of Christian life and joy evaporates as sin takes dominion again.

There is thus no reasonable objection to the concept of a Christian "abiding" **in death** in the sense that he has lost touch with the experience of God's life.

The key word here is **abides**. This is John's favorite word for the experience of discipleship to Jesus Christ (cf. discussion under 2:5-6). It is also the key word in the thematic statement of 2:28, which gives the fundamental appeal of the epistle to its readers to "abide in Him [i.e., Christ]." The man **who does not love *his* brother** lives out in the cold, dark sphere of **death** (cf. 2:11).

158

It should be observed that there is no Greek word standing for *his* in the phrase *his* **brother**. This is in sharp contrast with 2:9-11; 3:10, 12. The Greek phrase does contain the definite article (*ton adelphon*) which could carry a force equivalent to *his*. But this departure from his repeated habit of using the Greek pronoun for "his" with "brother" suggests that the omission is deliberate. Since we are talking in this context about *the world's* hatred, as well as about the hatred of one brother for another, it is possible to see a slight shift in meaning.

Thus our text could be translated by rendering the article (Greek: *ton*) by "a," so that we could read it as **he who hates** *a* **brother**—meaning *any particular* brother, or Christian. (This use of the Greek definite article to designate a particular instance of the class referred to is seen clearly in John 3:10, where we ought to translate, "Are you *a* teacher of Israel?" in the manner of the KJV rendering. But we should definitely not translate this as "*the* teacher of Israel" [so NKJV], since Nicodemus was but one of many.) The statement of our verse can then apply not only to Christians who might hate a particular Christian **brother**, but also to anyone else who might hate such a **brother**.

It makes no difference who is doing the hating. Hatred of a Christian is an experience in the realm of **death**.

> **15Whoever hates his brother is a murderer, and you know that no murderer has eternal life abiding in him.**

Hatred of one's **brother** is not only an experience of death; it is also an experience of murder. The person who **hates his** Christian **brother** is really no different from Cain (cf. verse 12), even though he may not commit the overt act of physically killing **his brother**. The spirit of hatred is that we want "to be rid" of our brother and would not really care if he died. But this is the spirit of **a murderer**.

Someone will perhaps meet the apostle John in the kingdom and ask him, "What did you mean when you said that 'no murderer has eternal life'? What about King David?" If so, John will certainly reply, "I never said, 'No murderer *has* eternal life.' What I said was, 'No murderer has eternal life *abiding* in him.'" Once again, the key to this text is the concept of "abiding" (see discussion above under verse 14). Moreover, John's concept of **abiding** is always that it is a reciprocal relationship, even as Jesus said: "Abide in Me, and I in you" (John 15:4; see discussion under

1 John 2:27). Since Christ Himself *is* eternal life (cf. 1 John 5:20), to say that someone does not have **eternal life abiding in him** is equivalent to saying that he does not have Christ **abiding in him.**

Clearly, in the subsection concluded by this verse, John has been stigmatizing hatred for one's **brother** as an action that separates the Christian from all real experience of the eternal life which he possesses as one who has "passed from death to life." Although **eternal life** is the possession of each and every believer in Christ (cf. 1 John 5:1), hatred of one's brother reflects the spirit of **a murderer** who is "abiding" in a realm of death where all vital experience with God's **life** is lost.

2. What Love Is (3:16-18)

If hatred of one's brother is the very antithesis of the experience of eternal life, what then is true Christian love? How do we know it if we see it? The following three verses answer this question.

> **¹⁶By this we know love, because He laid down His life for us. And we also ought to lay down *our* lives for the brethren.**

Christian love can be recognized by its conformity to the supreme model found in Christ's death **for us.** Although Christ died for the entire world (cf. 2:2), when we consider our own obligation to love we should focus on the fact that it was **for us** that He did this. As the personal beneficiaries of His great sacrifice, we should be prepared to make a similar sacrifice **for the brethren.**

This is obviously the direct opposite of Cain who *took* his brother's life (cf. verse 12). Cain and Christ, therefore, stand as Johannine polarities. We should recognize that hatred of our brother makes us like Cain, while love for our brother makes us like Christ. The words **we know** represent a Greek verb in the perfect tense which (as mentioned under verse 6) suggests a state or situation arising from a past event or action. Here the idea seems to be that once we have understood the love of Christ for us, we have come to a definitive knowledge of what Christian *love* is really about.

> [17]**But whoever has this world's goods, and sees his brother in need, and shuts up his heart from him, how does the love of God abide in him?**

Sometimes, however, it is easier to profess a willingness to die for our brethren than it is to actually aid them in their time of **need**. John therefore wishes to test the reality of a Christian's love for his brother by offering an example more likely to occur than an opportunity to die for a brother.

The English necessarily conceals a link with verse 16. In that verse John speaks of laying down one's life for the brethren. The Greek word for "life" there is psyche. Here he employs another Greek word for "life" (*bios*) which refers to "life" in its earthly and/or material aspects—hence the translation **goods**. We could almost render: **but whoever has this world's** *life!* The connection of thought suggested by this is that sharing with other Christians the material things which *sustain* life is, at heart, a way of laying down "our lives" for them. If what might keep *me* alive is given to a **brother in need**, then I have acted in the spirit of self-sacrifice for which the Lord Jesus offered the model.

If, instead of doing this, however, a Christian **shuts up his heart** from his needy brother, this speaks pointedly about his relationship to God. The Greek expression **shuts up his heart** (*kleisē ta splanchna autou*) could even be translated by "locks up his sympathies." The Greek word here for **heart** referred in a literal sense to the area of the stomach and intestines (which were thought to be the seat of the feelings and emotions). Thus, the translation of the old KJV nicely conveys the idea, "and shutteth up his bowels of compassion from him." The more discreet NKJV rendering loses some of the vividness implicit in the KJV.

But the Christian who acts so uncompassionately is not having a vital experience of God's *love*. John's rhetorical question, **how does the love of God abide in him?** means simply that God's **love** does not **abide in him**. The calloused action of refusing help to **his** needy **brother**, even though he possesses the means, **this world's goods**, is clear evidence that here is one in whom neither Christ, eternal life, nor **the love of God** are "abiding." As Brown puts it, "The person described…is blocking the movement of divine love, which would lead him to treat his brother as Christ treated us, so *divine love does not function in such a person*" (italics added).[8] The uncompassionate Christian is not walking as his Master walked (cf. 2:6) and thus is not living the abiding life.

> **[18]My little children, let us not love in word or in tongue, but in deed and in truth.**

The apostle now concludes his characterization of real love (verses 16-18) by urging his readers to love in a truly Christian way. They must not think that they have expressed love if that expression is merely verbal (**in word**) and requires only the use of the **tongue**. Loud professions of love are no substitute for actions that express it concretely. Christians often give *lip service* to love and carelessly tell people, "I love you," when in fact they are not prepared to act sacrificially for those to whom they say this.

True love requires action (= **in deed**)[9] and conformity to the **truth**. By the words **in truth** John could simply mean something like "genuinely." But because he so often uses the word **truth** in reference to the Christian revelation (cf. 1:6, 8; 2:4, 21; etc.), it is likely he also means that their love for other Christians should conform to the Christian manifestation of love in the person of Christ (cf. verse 16). Clearly, self-serving acts done in the name of love are excluded by this standard, since in no sense did our Savior act selfishly in giving Himself on the cross. Christians are not above deceiving themselves and/or others by performing actions that actually serve their own interests better than they do those of the recipients. Ananias and Sapphira (Acts 5:1-10) made a mockery of their own professed sacrifice of property in order to protect their own concerns. They did not love **in** accordance with the **truth**.

3.   What Love Does for Believers (3:19-23)

John now approaches the climax of the second major unit of the body of his epistle. In the first major unit, he has shown us that the child of God is manifested only by righteousness (2:29–3:10a). Thus far in this unit we have seen that this righteousness is inseparable from genuine Christian love for the brethren and is expressed through concrete acts of love (3:10b-18). The apostle will now conclude the unit by showing how Christian love can embolden us in the presence of God in prayer. By surfacing the concept of "boldness" for the first time since the thematic statement of 2:28, he signals an advance toward the consummation of his theme of "boldness" *at the coming of the Lord.*

> [19]**And by this we know that we are of the truth, and shall assure our hearts before Him.**

As an experienced shepherd of God's people, John would have known that the theme of Christian love, modeled after the Savior's own love, could produce feelings of guilt and self-reproach. The issue involved is not the assurance of salvation, but whether one participates in **the truth** with respect to Christian love. The believer in Christ can easily ask himself, "Can I love as *He* loved? Am I really doing *that?*"

The words **of the truth** obviously are an echo of the exhortation of verse 18 that we are to love "in deed and *in truth.*" The introductory words **And by this** should be referred backward to the exhortation of verse 18.[10] On this understanding, **And by this** is essentially equivalent to "And by doing this" (i.e., by loving "in deed and in truth"). That is to say, when we act in love with deeds that reflect **the truth** about love as revealed in Christ, **we** can **know** that **we are of the truth.**

As we have seen in the discussions under 3:8 and 3:10b, phrases like "of the devil," "of God," etc., are to be handled in a supple fashion, since they involve an extremely common Greek idiom that is very malleable in context. The same thing can be said here about the phrase **of the truth.** Its sense must be grasped in context.

If the Christian doubts that he is able to express Christian love to his brethren, essentially he is doubting whether he can relate to, or participate in, **the truth** revealed in Christ about that kind of love. He may feel guilty for past failures or he may have a strong sense of inadequacy, but by acting in love as verse 18 directs, he can actually know that by such actions he *is participating in* **the truth**—that is, he is **of the truth.** Another way of saying this is, that by so loving one can know that his actions *have their source in* **the truth.**

The words that follow, **and shall assure our hearts before Him,** are best taken with the words of the next verse and will be considered there.

²⁰**For if our heart condemns us, God is greater than our heart, and knows all things.**

The NKJV treats this verse as a separate sentence. But this is almost certainly wrong. The NKJV rendering glides over, and omits, a repetition of the initial word of the Greek sentence. This is the Greek word *hoti* (rendered as **For** by the NKJV); but *hoti* is repeated in the Greek in front of the clause beginning (in the English) with **God is greater** and is left untranslated in NKJV. The most natural way to take the second *hoti* is as resumptive of the first one, but in that case *hoti* in both instances is not a causal conjunction meaning "for" or "because." Even if the second *hoti* is left out in English, the first *hoti* ought to be taken in the sense of "that," which is its common meaning after the verb for "assure" (verse 19; Greek: *peisomai*; followed by *hoti* = "that" in Romans 8:38; 15:14; 2 Corinthians 2:3; Galatians 5:10; etc.).

The translation will then be linked with the last clause of verse 19 and would be as follows, "…and we shall assure [or, persuade] our hearts before Him that, if our heart condemns us, that God is greater than our heart, and knows all things."

John's meaning in verses 19-20 is that by acting with deeds of love ("by this," verse 19), we can know we are "of the truth." But also, by so acting, we can quiet our condemning heart **if our heart** accuses us of failure in the expression of Christian love. Every sincere Christian knows what is involved in this experience. Whatever we try to do in love, a sensitive conscience often **condemns us** for having done too little, or for not making up for past failures, or for any number of things. Our instincts, in our sinful flesh, are so selfish that we may even in the midst of acting in Christian love suspect ourselves of impure or unworthy motives. **Our heart** thus *does not take account of* our actions and continues to accuse us.

But **God is greater than our heart** and what the **heart** refuses to take into account, **God,** who **knows all things** does take into account. When we have loved "in deed and in truth" God is very much aware of that, even when our hearts tend to ignore it. At such times we should *assure* (i.e., *persuade* [verse 19, Greek: *peisomai*]) our hearts that **God is greater than our heart** in that He knows perfectly well the love we have expressed by our actions. Nothing escapes His eye.[11]

It should be pointed out that in verse 19, in the statement "we shall assure our hearts before Him," the words "before Him" are emphatic in the Greek text. As the following verses make clear, John is thinking about our experience before God *in prayer.*[12] It is precisely when we kneel before God in prayer that we are most likely to struggle with the reality of our own failure to love in contrast to His own measureless love to us in Christ. Such self-condemnation can reduce to almost zero our expectation that our prayers will be answered. But the apostle's advice is that when we approach God's throne of grace, we should count on God knowing (even if **our heart** does not!) what we have *actually done* in love.

A slight paraphrase of 3:18-20 may serve as a summary of these verses:

> My little children, let's not love with words only or with our speech, but in action and in reality. That, you see, is how we recognize our participation in the truth and that's how we can convince our heart—if our heart makes us feel guilty—that God is greater than our heart and He takes account of all we have done.

21Beloved, if our heart does not condemn us, we have confidence toward God.

As we come before God, perhaps **our heart does not condemn us** for failure to express Christian love. This could be because our heart readily accepts the fact that God takes cognizance of our love manifested "in deed and in truth" (cf. 18), or because we have "persuaded" it to do so (verse 19). In any case the result is **confidence toward God.**

The word for **confidence** here (Greek: *parrēsia*) is the same one used in 2:28 in the thematic statement about having *"confidence...before Him at His coming."* Though John picks up the thematic word of 2:28, we do not have here an *inclusio* rounding off the entire discussion. That will come at 4:17. Obviously, if we do not have confidence before God when we kneel *in prayer* (cf. verse 22), it is even less likely we will have such confidence *"at His coming."* For at His Second Advent we will have been instantly transformed by the sight of Him (cf. 3:2) and there is no possibility then of hiding from our past failures to love.

Yet even here and now our **confidence** "before Him" can be real if it is based on our obedience to His commands (verse 22). This is such a wonderful spiritual state to be in that, in expressing it, John addresses his audience as **Beloved**. Only the great love of God could give us the status of children who can pray *boldly* to their heavenly Father (cf. 3:1). Clearly there is hope that such *present* boldness can lead to *future* boldness at His return.

> ²²**And whatever we ask we receive from Him, because we keep His commandments and do those things that are pleasing in His sight.**

As indicated by the emphatic words "before Him" in verse 19 (see comment under verse 20), John has been thinking in this immediate context of "confidence" *in prayer.* (He will return to this subject again in 5:14-17.) The result of "confidence" toward God in prayer is, of course, answered prayer. Thus, **whatever we ask we receive from Him.**

The reason for this kind of answered prayer is twofold: **because** (1) **we keep His commandments,** and (2) we **do those things that are pleasing in His sight.** However, these are not likely to be two separate conditions at all (cf. verse 23) since obviously to obey God's **commandments** is to do something that is **pleasing in His sight.** No doubt the addition of the words **do those things that are pleasing in His sight** is intended as a reminder that God is pleased with our obedience. Thus, His pleasure in our obedience becomes a motive for His response to the prayers we offer.

Christians sometimes forget the simple truth that God is *pleased* when we obey. He never takes our obedience for granted, or fails to appreciate it. But just as an earthly father is happy over an obedient son or daughter, so also is our heavenly Father as well (cf. Malachi 3:16). The realization of this will augment our "confidence" in His presence as we pray.

It is also true that the Christian who is actively seeking to please God will not **ask** for things that are *not* **pleasing in His sight!** As John states later in the epistle, we can expect answers to our prayers when we ask "according to His will" (cf. 5:14-15). Since the obedient Christian is seeking to do God's "will" by keeping His commands, he will naturally make all his prayers subject to that will when he is in doubt about what God truly wishes to do. This is not sidestepping, since the best example of a request made subject to God's will is the prayer of our Lord Himself in the Garden of Gethsemane: "Father, if it is Your will, take this cup away from Me; nevertheless not My will, but Yours, be done" (Luke 22:42).

When prayer arises, therefore, from the heart of one in whose life the will of God is first and foremost, then **whatever** he asks of God will be received **from Him** precisely because he is asking "according to His will" (5:14). Like our Lord, the man or woman of prayer will always seek that will first; in our Lord's case, the actual answer was not in the removal of the cup of suffering (Jesus drank that!) but in the accomplishment of His request, "Not My will, but Yours, be done"! Prayer for the will of God to be accomplished is thus one of the primary ways in which obedient Christians can pray (cf. Acts 21:14). At the same time, where Scripture makes God's will clear, the Christian may pray directly for that. One such specific request is discussed in 5:16-17.

> **²³And this is His commandment: that we should believe on the name of His Son Jesus Christ and love one another, as He gave us commandment.**

John concludes the subunit (verses 19-23), as well as the larger subsection (3:10b-23), with a summary of what it means to "keep His commandments and do those things that are pleasing in His sight" (verse 22). That this is indeed a summary is seen by the transparent shift from the plural "commandments" (verse 22) to the singular **commandment** here. Answered prayer (cf. verse 22) finds its basis fundamentally in our adherence to this **commandment**.

The **commandment**, however, has two aspects. The first of these is that **we should believe on the name of His Son Jesus Christ**. There is no word for **on** in the Greek text. Instead, we have a construction in which **the name** functions as the object of the word **believe**. This is slightly different than the construction found twice in 1 John 5:13 where the word *in* (NKJV) translates the Greek word *eis*. The construction with *eis* is the one John consistently uses in his Gospel when he speaks of "believing in/on His name" (John 1:12; 2:23; 3:18; etc.). The construction in our verse might therefore be rendered without the word **on** as **believe the name of His Son**.

It is hazardous in the Johannine literature to draw sharp distinctions between alternative constructions, and if any distinction is to be felt here, it would be no doubt a subtle shading only. Still, this is a context that has dealt with prayer. John may therefore wish to suggest both (1) "believing **the name**" in the sense of believing that **Jesus** is the **Christ** (its standard meaning in the Gospel; cf. John 20:30-31), and also (2) "believing **the name**" of **Jesus** to be effectual before God in prayer (cf. John 14:13-14; 15:16; 16:23-24).

Clearly John here links faith and love together as a single commandment for Christian people. They are properly indivisible in Christian experience. It is precisely our knowledge that faith in **the name of His Son Jesus Christ** imparts life to all believers and constitutes them our brothers or sisters, that gives us the proper object for our love when we are told to **love *one another***. If we did not know this truth, we would not know *whom* to love (cf. 1 John 5:1 and discussion there). Moreover, as John will later tell us, we can pray confidently (in faith) for a brother who does not sin "unto death" (cf. 5:16-17 and discussion). Believing **the name of** God's **Son** is a prerequisite, and an essential component, of love for **one another**. John is surely justified in speaking of but one **commandment**.

Finally, the fact that love (with faith) summarizes all that the Lord Jesus commanded His disciples is consistent with Paul's own observation on the subject. After writing that we should "owe no one anything except to *love one another* (Romans 13:8a; italics added), he adds, "For he who loves another has fulfilled the law...Love does no harm to a neighbor; therefore love is the fulfillment of the law" (Romans 13:8b, 10).

The closing words of the verse, **as He gave [us]**[13] **commandment**, are not at all redundant, but they should not have been set off by a comma as in the NKJV. The reference is to Jesus Himself from whom the commandment to love one another directly came (John 13:34). We should read the text with the proper differentiation of the pronouns as follows: **that we should believe on the name of His** [God's] **Son Jesus Christ and love one another as He** [His Son] **gave [us]**[14] **commandment**. God's will, therefore, can be summarized as faith in *His Son's name* and obedience to *His Son's commandment*.

With these words John concludes the unit on love that comprises 3:10b-23. Though he still has much to say with regard to loving one another, he has certainly made plain in these verses the parameters within which any discussion of Christian love must operate. The Christian who hates his brother acts utterly out of touch with God, exemplifies the murderous spirit of Cain, and is "abiding" in the sphere of death (verses 10b-15). By contrast, the loving Christian takes Christ's own self-sacrificing love as the model by which he himself should love in actual deeds and in accord with the truth (verses 16-18). If he does so, he can quiet a guilt-ridden heart, achieve a superb confidence before God in prayer, and expect answers to his prayers precisely because he is pleasing God (verses 19-23).

This is truly a lofty level of Christian experience to which the apostle is pointing each believer, but obedience to God's commandment is the only route by which it can be reached.

ENDNOTES

[1] See Raymond E. Brown's whole discussion of this construction in *The Epistles of John*, AB (Garden City, NY: Doubleday, 1982), pp. 312-13. While I might quibble here and there with his statements, on the whole his discussion is solid.

[2] For references to extra-biblical materials related to Cain in Jewish tradition, see Brown, *Epistles*, pp. 442-43.

[3] To be rejected are statements like: "The proof that a person possesses eternal life is that he shows love for his brothers" (I. Howard Marshall, *The Epistles of John*, NICNT [Grand Rapids: Wm. B. Eerdmans Publishing Co., 1978], p. 191); and, "Only so, by obedience to the divine love command, can membership of God's people be determined; for love is a summation of the obedience and service which are required of the Christian" (Stephen S. Smalley, *1,2,3 John*, WBC [Waco, TX: Word Books, 1984], p. 189). In Johannine theology, personal assurance of salvation rests on the testimony God has given about His Son (cf. 1 John 5:9-13 as well as the numerous guarantees of eternal life in John's Gospel based only on faith: John 3:15-17; 5:24; 6:47, etc.). When commentators refuse to acknowledge the obvious, it is not surprising that false theology results.

[4] Bauer, Walter. *A Greek-English Lexicon of the New Testament and Other Early Christian Literature* (Chicago: University of Chicago Press, 1979), p. 556.

[5] Ibid.

[6] Commentators sometimes perceive rather sharp distinctions in meaning between the two verbs John uses for knowing, namely between *ginōskō* and *oida* (cf. Brooke Foss Westcott, *The Epistles of St John: The Greek Text with Notes* [Grand

Rapids: Wm. B. Eerdmans Publishing Co., 1966], p. 46; and John R. W. Stott, *The Letters of John: An Introduction and Commentary* TNTC [Grand Rapids: Wm. B. Eerdmans Publishing Co., 1988], pp. 94-95). But such differentiations break down frequently and the effort to maintain them consistently produces labored and untenable explanations. (Brown, *Epistles*, p. 250, rightly points to "the impossibility of a sharp distinction.") It is correct to say with Marianne Meye Thompson (*1–3 John*, IVPNT [Downers Grove, IL: InterVarsity Press, 1992], p. 52) that "no meaningful distinction can be attributed to the author's use of the two verbs for knowing..." However, one could enter the caveat that, of course, native speakers know when one semantic choice seems better than another. Careful English speakers will no doubt often use the verbs "to understand" and "to perceive" interchangeably, but will have a feel for when one is preferable to the other (e.g., in the first line of this note I prefer the word "perceive").

[7] Philo, *On Flight and Finding,* 11.58.

[8] Brown, *Epistles*, p. 450. This view obviously presupposes that the phrase **the love of God** does not mean "love for God" (a grammatical possibility), but rather "God's own love." By shutting up "his heart from" his Christian brother, such a Christian shows that "God's love" is not "making its home" (abiding) within him (cf. again, John 14:23).

[9] I like Marianne Meye Thompson's note here on the NIV rendering: "The NIV translates a singular 'action' (*ergon*) with a plural *actions*, which can be misleading. The phrase *en ergō* implies living out our commitments" (*1–3 John*, p. 106).

[10] So John and Joy Anderson, "Cataphora in 1 John," *NoT* 7 (1993): 41. See the discussion in note 8 in chapter 3. The initial **And** before **by this** does not affect the reference backward (*anaphora*), though this is the only place in the epistle where anaphoric *en toutō* is preceded by *kai* (but cf. *gar* with anaphoric *en toutō* in John 4:37), whereas cataphoric *en toutō* is preceded by *kai* at 2:3 and 3:24. The initial *Kai* of 3:19 does indeed stand in brackets in Nestle-Aland (27th ed.) and UBS (4th ed.) to signal the editors' uncertainty (see also Bruce M. Metzger, *A Textual Commentary on the Greek New Testament,* 2nd ed. [Stuttgart, Germany: Deutsche Bibelgesellschaft and United Bible Societies, 1994], p. 643). But the manuscript attestation for omission is very slender (less than a dozen mss cited in UBS) and Hodges/Farstad, *MajT*, print it without hesitation as the Majority reading.

[11] Needless to say, the commentators on this passage (1 John 3:19-21) go all over the waterfront in their explanations. It would hardly be profitable to go through all the permutations in their views, especially since those who are interested can find a full treatment (as usual) in Brown, *Epistles*, pp. 453-60. Brown is not at his most gracious when he writes: "We have already seen that

the epistolary author is singularly inept in constructing clear sentences, but in these verses he is at his worst. Most commentators kindly call the passage a *crux interpretum;* less charitably Loisy, *Évangile-Épitres* 559, dubs it 'gibberish' (*un galimatias*)" (p. 453). But might it not be that the problems perceived by commentators are due, not so much to grammatical difficulties in the text, but to a widespread lack of empathy toward the experience the apostle is describing? Sensitivity of conscience to the scriptural demand for Christlike love is a natural reaction in the believer. I doubt very much that the first readers (or, hearers) were perplexed by the text when it was read aloud in their congregations.

[12] The reference of **before Him** (verse 19) is not yet to the day of judgment (cf. 4:17), or to God as Judge, as some have thought (e.g., Rudolf Bultmann, *The Johannine Epistles: A Commentary on the Johannine Epistles,* Herm [Philadelphia: Fortress Press, 1973], p. 56; Smalley, *1,2,3 John,* pp. 201-202). J. L. Houlden (*A Commentary on the Johannine Epistles,* HNTC [New York: Harper & Row, 1973], p. 102) is correct: "The reference in these verses is not, as in ii. 28, to the Last Day, but to regular Christian life; and the purpose of Christian confidence is not to appear before God at the End, but in the present, in the act of intercession."

[13] The **us** is bracketed here since it does not appear to be the original reading and is found, for example, in only 25 of the manuscripts examined by Richards (*The Classification of the Greek Manuscripts of the Johannine Epistles.* No. 35: Society of Biblical Literature Dissertation Series [Missoula, MT: Scholars Press, 1977], p. 239) over against 55 that lack it—a better than 2-1 ratio for omission.

[14] Ibid.

CHAPTER 7

Learning to See the God of Love

(1 John 3:24–4:19)

We now reach the climactic section of the body of the epistle, to which we have given the title: *The Life That Leads to Boldness Before Christ's Judgment Seat.* The apostle is now ready to tell us precisely how this goal is achieved.

To reach this point, it has been necessary for John to make plain that the one and only way in which the child of God can, or does, manifest himself, is by doing righteousness. Indeed, righteousness is the *only* possible way for the child of God to express himself, since he cannot sin (2:29–3:10a). John has also taken care to define love sufficiently so that when we see it in action it can be recognized as such. In its essence it is the direct opposite of the murderous hatred of Cain. It finds its true Model in God's Son, Jesus Christ, who "laid down His life for us," and it leads to boldness before God in prayer (3:10b-23).

We should take note of a special feature of Johannine style. His units of thought are marked off at their commencement by the introduction of new subject matter. They may be concluded by what is called an *inclusio* (the repetition at the end of a unit of a word, phrase or idea found at the beginning). An *inclusio* marks the unit as complete. It is an element of Greek style that is frequently found outside of John and of which this author makes good use.

Thus in 2:28, the thematic statement introduces the idea of "manifestation" which runs through 2:28–3:10a, where the word "manifest" is the *inclusio* marking the unit as complete. The theme of love for one's brother emerges in 3:10b (only previously referred to in 2:10) and concludes with the restatement of the Savior's command to "love one another," again an *inclusio* (3:23). The new theme that now emerges is the theme of God "abiding" *in* believers: "...abides in Him, *and He in him*" (3:24). The *inclusio* that terminates this unit is found in the words of 4:16, "...abides in God, *and God in him.*"

It may come as a surprise to some readers of the First Epistle of John that John has not yet directly spoken of God, or Christ, "abiding" *in* believers. To be sure, prior to 3:24 the Greek word for "abide" (*menō*) has occurred in the Greek text of First John no less than fifteen times. Yet the closest John comes to speaking about God "abiding" *in us* occurs when he tells his readers that "the anointing...*abides in you*" (2:27) and when he affirms of the one who hates his Christian brother that "no murderer has eternal life *abiding in him*" (3:15). As suggested under the discussion of each of these statements, no doubt John knew his readers could identify "the anointing" as the Holy Spirit and "eternal life" as Christ (cf. 5:20). But his artfulness in not saying so directly is a demonstration of the care and skill with which he has crafted his epistle.

With this discussion of the subject of God abiding *within* the obedient believer we reach the pinnacle of the mountain up which John has been leading us.

D. By Learning to See the God of Love (3:24–4:16)

1. God's Indwelling Affirmed (3:24)

> **24Now he who keeps His commandments abides in Him, and He in him. And by this we know that He abides in us, by the Spirit whom He has given us.**

The key to boldness before God in prayer, John has just told us (verse 22), is obedience to **His commandments**. But something else is true of the person who keeps these **commandments**: such a person **abides in Him** [i.e., in God or Christ] and, in addition, **He** [God or Christ] abides **in him** [the obedient believer]. Here we meet again the reciprocal relationship which is an integral part of our Lord's doctrine of abiding (cf. John 15:4-5; see discussion under 1 John 2:24). If a Christian is abiding in Christ (or God) then Christ (or God) is also abiding in that Christian. Although John has not said so directly until this point, now this truth becomes a central fact in the progression of his thought, namely, that the obedient believer has God making "His home" within him. Such an experience fulfills the words of Jesus that, "If anyone loves Me, he will keep My word; and My Father will love him, and We will come to him and make *Our home* with him" (John 14:23; italics added). In this statement, the word *home* is the Greek word *monē*, belonging to the same word group as *menō* (to abide, live, dwell).

Obviously such an experience with God is the ultimate form of *fellowship* with God, which the apostle John declared from the beginning was the goal of his epistle (cf. 1:3). Thus, here in this climactic section of the body of the epistle, the theme enunciated in the prologue (*fellowship*) and the one enunciated in 2:28 (*abiding in Him*) merge as John develops the concept of the indwelling God.

But along with the first direct mention of God abiding in us, there is also the first direct mention of the Holy **Spirit**. Although the **Spirit** has been referred to under the designation of "the anointing," He is now mentioned specifically. If God indeed **abides in us**, we can know this **by the Spirit He has given us**. Since all Christians possess the Holy **Spirit** (Romans 8:9), they have the means by which they can discern the reality of God abiding within them. Just exactly how this discernment is achieved is developed later in this unit of the letter.

1 JOHN 4

2. God's Spirit Recognized (4:1-6)

> **¹Beloved, do not believe every spirit, but test the spirits, whether they are of God; because many false prophets have gone out into the world.**

The mention of the Holy Spirit (3:24) causes John to pause for a warning that has been needed in every age of the Christian church. The Christian who possesses the Holy Spirit must not be so naive as to think that God's Spirit is the only spirit at work in **the world**. Satan has many **spirits** who serve him here, as is shown by the fact that **many false prophets have gone out into the world**.

In this verse and the following one, John seems to be trading on the fairly fluid meaning of the term **spirit**. The word itself can refer not only to a human **spirit**, or to supernatural **spirits** like satanic angels or demons, but also to an attitude or disposition (e.g., "a spirit of fear" or "of power and of love and of a sound mind" 2 Timothy 1:7). John does not necessarily imply here a separate supernatural **spirit** for each **false prophet**, for he will shortly speak of "*the* spirit of the antichrist" (verse 3). In all likelihood John is not trying to be specific on this point and is warning at the same time against **every** malevolent **spirit** of Satan, **every** human

spirit who becomes his agent, as well as **every** manifestation of "the spirit of error" (cf. verse 6) which characterizes satanic doctrine.

It may well be that in speaking here of **false prophets** John is thinking of individuals who speak under the immediate influence of some inspiring **spirit**. At the time of writing (before A.D. 70; see Introduction), Christian prophecy seems to have been very much alive in the Christian church (cf. Acts 19:6; 21:9-10), and satanic counterfeits were to be expected in accordance with our Lord's prediction concerning them (Matthew 7:15-20). Of course, such counterfeits have not ceased, even to the present day.

According to the Lord Jesus, **false prophets** were to be tested "by their fruits" (cf. Matthew 7:16-20). Contrary to popular interpretation, this does *not* mean that they were to be tested by their *works*. On the contrary, as Matthew 12:33-37 proves, their fruits are their *words!* Indeed, as the Lord Himself said, they "come to you in sheep's clothing" so that they *look like* sheep when in reality they are "ravenous wolves" (Matthew 7:15). Their *behavior* does not set them apart from the sheep, but their *message* does! Here, in our epistle, this is precisely the kind of test that John goes on to specify.

> ²**By this you know the Spirit of God: Every spirit that confesses that Jesus Christ has come in the flesh is of God,**

The test that can be applied to **Every spirit** is its willingness, or unwillingness (cf. verse 3), to confess **Jesus Christ** incarnate.

The words **By this you know** are often taken to refer forward to the rest of verse 2 and to verse 3. But we have earlier found reason to believe that the phrase **By this** refers only forward when followed by some kind of explanatory subordinate clause (see note 8, chapter 3), which is not the case here. In accordance with this structural clue, a reference *backward* is more probable and this makes perfect sense. The statement will mean, "This is how [i.e., by testing the spirits] you know the Spirit of God" [or, as in the *MajT*, "This is how the Spirit of God is recognized"].[1] A period, rather than a colon, should follow the statement, with the words **Every spirit** beginning a fresh sentence.

On this understanding, verses 2b-3 give the substance of the test that is to be used to recognize God's Spirit. Verses 1-2a insist that under the circumstances (with many claims to prophecy) only those willing to *test* the spirits will be able to recognize *God's* Spirit. If they "believe every spirit" they will really not know which of them is truly God's. The warning is urgently needed today.

The conjoining of **the Spirit of God** with the words **Every spirit that confesses** no doubt is intended to link the Holy **Spirit** with **every** *human* **spirit** that make this confession. The phrase **of God** (at the end of the verse), as we have seen before (cf. 3:7, 10b, 18 and discussions in those places), is malleable in context. Here it points to the fact that **Every spirit that confesses** Christ is "acted upon" to do this by **the Spirit of God**. The person who makes this confession is of God because he has been enlightened and motivated by God's **Spirit**.

The confessional statement **that Jesus Christ has come in the flesh** can indeed be translated as in the NKJV. But a more likely translation is this, [**Every spirit that confesses**] **Jesus** as **Christ having come in the flesh**. There is no word for **that** and no finite verb in the Greek text. The form rendered **has come** by the NKJV (Greek: *elēlythota*) is more naturally taken as a modifier of the word **Christ**. Moreover, John's principal theological concern is that **Jesus** should be recognized as the **Christ** (cf. 2:22) and this truth is, for John, a saving one (1 John 5:1; cf. John 20:30-31). It is thus very likely that the confession is an affirmation of John's fundamental doctrine, and that **come in the flesh** is designed to assert a truth about the **Christ** that the Revisionists may have denied.[2]

As will be considered further under 5:6, some or all of the Revisionists may have held to the doctrine that **Jesus** was a mere man and that the divine **Christ** was an incorporeal, spiritual being who descended on Him at His baptism, but departed from Him before He died. But to assert this was to sever the human **Jesus** from the divine **Christ** in the interests of a spiritualized, but false, Christology. **Jesus** and the **Christ**, in this view, were not the same being.

> [3]**and every spirit that does not confess that Jesus Christ has come in the flesh is not of God. And this is the *spirit* of the Antichrist, which you have heard was coming, and is now already in the world.**

In contrast with "Every spirit that confesses" Christ is **every spirit that does not confess Jesus** as **Christ come in flesh** (for an explanation of the altered translation, see previous verse).[3] As the former "spirit" is "of God" in making its confession, so **every spirit** that does *not* make this confession **is not of God**. That is to say, the source and inspiration of such a **spirit** is found elsewhere than in God. That source, in fact, is satanic, since such a spirit exemplifies **the *spirit* of the Antichrist**.

It is noteworthy that John does *not* say **every spirit that** *denies*, but rather **every spirit that** *does not* **confess**. Heretical teaching can mask the full extent of its deviation from the truth by simply failing to affirm some pivotal biblical truth. This is often done to make its false doctrine more palatable to the Christian audience it seeks to reach. But, says John, even the failure to *confess* **Jesus** as **Christ come in flesh** is a clear indication that the religious outlook in question **is not of God**. If a religious leader or movement cannot speak loud and clear about the fundamental Christological and soteriological truth that **Jesus** is the **Christ**, then that leader or movement does not have its source, or dynamic, in **God**.

Indeed, the denial of this truth is **the *spirit* of the Antichrist**. Since for the apostle John **the Antichrist** is the ultimate manifestation of false prophecy, the "many false prophets" (4:1) are his precursors. (For this end-time figure, also called the False Prophet, see discussion under 2:18.) The spirit in which the false prophets speak, as well as the spirit (ultimately, Satan) who works through them, are identical with **the spirit** (though absent from the Greek, **spirit** is correctly supplied by NKJV) of the False Prophet who is yet to come.

The readers already have been taught about the end times and know that "the Antichrist is coming" (2:18), so that here they are also said to be aware (**you have heard**) that his *spirit*...**was coming**. The Greek grammar makes clear that the word **which** refers to *spirit* rather than to **the Antichrist**, but the meaning of the statement here is essentially the same as in 2:18. Yet because the context (3:24–4:3) is dealing with the theme of "spirit," it is appropriate to draw this sharp contrast between God's Spirit and the Antichrist's *spirit*. What the Revisionists have to say has nothing to do with the truth, but is the polar opposite of the influence of the Holy Spirit.

⁴You are of God, little children, and have overcome them, because He who is in you is greater than he who is in the world.

As John has consistently maintained, his readers have spiritual strength and are capable of successfully resisting the antichrists (cf. 2:12-14, 20-21). Though addressed here with the tender, paternal term **little children**, they also have the status of knowledgeable "fathers" and vigorous "young men" (see discussion under 2:12-14). In particular, as "young men" they have previously been said to **have overcome** the wicked one (2:13-14). The readers, therefore, are **of God** because they stand firmly in the truth (for other discussions of this type of expression, see under 3:8, 10b, and 19).

The statement here that the readers **have overcome** the false prophets, or Revisionists, may possibly indicate that they have already encountered some of them and rejected their claims. On the other hand, the past tense here may be proleptic and simply anticipate that they will be victorious when the encounter occurs. In the absence of more specific information about the situation of the recipients of First John, we cannot decide between these alternatives. But if encounters *have* occurred, the general tenor of the book shows that the danger is far from over.

The reason they have been, or will be, victorious lies in their possession of the Holy Spirit, who was in them as He is in all Christians (cf. 3:24; Romans 8:9).⁴ It is precisely **because He** (God's Spirit)...**is greater than he** (Satan) **who is in the world**, that victory over the world's deceptions is possible. Since, as John will later say, "the whole world lies under the sway of the wicked one" (5:19), to have victory over the world's deceptions is to have victory over Satan's deceptions. John is very confident that the Holy Spirit will enable his readers to repulse the attempted incursions of the antichrists.

But it should always be remembered, whatever the level of our spiritual growth, that we are not, in and of ourselves, immune to false doctrine and satanic deception. If we have victory at all it is because the Holy Spirit within us is mightier than the Archdeceiver, and we must rely on Him to keep us cleaving to God's truth.

⁵**They are of the world. Therefore they speak *as* of the world, and the world hears them.**

The **They** which begins this verse represents an emphatic Greek pronoun (*Autoi*) just as did the "You" (*Hymeis*) which began verse 4. The antichrists, or Revisionists, are here viewed in sharp contrast with the readership. Whereas the readers are "of God," the Revisionists are **of the world**. The origin of their conceptions lies in the satanic perspective of the world (cf. 5:19) and represents some or all of the world's constituent elements, which stand in opposition to God (2:15-16; see discussion there).

Accordingly the Revisionists bring a "worldly" message: **they speak...of the world**. There is no Greek word that corresponds to **as,** which has been supplied to make the meaning clearer. The precise Greek phrase for **of the world** (*ek tou kosmou*) occurs twice here and this illustrates the flexibility of this sort of phrase, of which John is very fond (cf. discussions under 3:8, 10b, and 19). The Revisionists are **of the world** in that they are fundamentally in league with the godless world system. They **speak of the world** in the sense that their message is worldly in content and perspective. Not surprisingly, **the world hears them.**

This last statement suggests that the antichrists received a good hearing from many who were part **of the world**. It has been true down through the centuries that heterodoxy has a far greater appeal to worldly people than does orthodoxy. Very many religious movements are composed mainly of unsaved people who find the false theology of the movement attractive. In particular this has proved true in connection with the truth that "whoever believes that Jesus is the Christ is born of God" (1 John 5:1). The worldly perspective is that this is far too easy and cannot possibly be true. Works-oriented churches thus have great attracting power for many who are outside of Christ, not to mention Christians who may also fall into this trap (cf. Galatians 5:4).

If we wonder why false theology seems to run rampant in the professing Christian church, the statement of this verse is the biblical answer.

⁶We are of God. He who knows God hears us; he who is not of God does not hear us. By this we know the spirit of truth and the spirit of error.

As in the case of verses 4-5, this verse begins with an emphatic pronoun, **We** (*Hēmeis*). Thus we have in verses 4 through 6 three contrasting pronouns, "You—They—**We**." It can hardly be doubted that three distinct groups are intended, the "You" referring to the readers, the "They" referring to the Revisionists, and the **We** referring to the same group designated as "we" in the Prologue (1:1-4). In other words, the **We** refers to the apostles.

Only the apostles of the Lord Jesus Christ could ever correctly make the statements that are made here. As the authoritative representatives of the Risen Lord of the Church, they were the only teachers whose doctrine was the touchstone of Christian orthodoxy. In the fullest sense, they were **of God** because their doctrine came directly from Him and was not only true but fully sufficient, since what they had not personally learned from Jesus Himself the Holy Spirit had taught them (cf. John 14:25-26; 16:12-15).

They could thus confidently affirm that **He who knows God hears** ("listens to") **us**. As noted under the discussion of 2:3 (see also 2:13-14), in this epistle the concept of "knowing" God suggests progress beyond mere spiritual infancy (cf. discussion under verse 7 below). While it is true that immature Christians are often swayed by false doctrine (cf. Ephesians 4:14; Hebrews 5:12-14), it is a mark of the mature Christian that he is responsive to apostolic teaching as over against "worldly" teachings (cf. previous verse and Ephesians 4:14). The knowledge of God is thus inseparable from apostolic truth, a fact that needs reemphasis in our own day and time.

It follows, of course, that **he who is not of God does not hear** ("listen to") **us**. As has been frequently pointed out in this Commentary (e.g., under 3:8, 10b, and 19), expressions such as **of God** (or, "of the devil," "of the truth," etc.) signal concepts whose meaning is determined by context. Here it may be suggested that John is thinking of anyone out of touch with **God** (not under His influence or that of His Spirit) as the kind of person who rejects apostolic authority and teaching. Such a person could be a believer or an unbeliever.

The words, **By this we know**, can be naturally taken of the apostles, who are the subject of the earlier statements of this verse. Had John had the readers particularly in mind here, a switch to "By this *you* know" would be expected (in light of the "You" in verse 4). Here again the phrase **By this** refers backward to the statements he has just made.[5]

The apostles themselves, who were, after all, only men, were able to make appropriate discriminations between **the spirit of truth and the spirit of error** on the basis of each spirit's submission, or lack of it, to apostolic truth. That this was needful even for the apostles should be plain upon reflection. In the early church, with its open meetings, there was ample room for verbal expression (cf. 1 Corinthians 14:12-32), and Paul himself enjoined the principle that "the spirits of the prophets are subject to the prophets" (1 Corinthians 14:33). Paul also felt constrained to say, "No one speaking by the Spirit of God calls Jesus accursed" (1 Corinthians 12:3), as though this had happened under some pretense to inspiration. In the context of the early church, where the gift of prophecy existed, the apostles themselves had at times to determine whether what was said in the churches came from God. But if there was a refusal to "confess Jesus as Christ come in flesh," **the spirit** that spoke (whether supernatural or human) was "that of the Antichrist" (verse 3) and therefore not a **spirit of truth** but **of error**.

This statement about apostolic knowledge of **the spirit of error** underlines their role in protecting the church from the ravages of false teaching. A great number of the New Testament epistles were written with precisely this goal in view. That is most emphatically true of the present epistle. So when John condemns the Revisionists as "false prophets" who are "of the world" (verses 1-3, 5), the judgment he makes about them is authoritative and final.

3. God's Indwelling Recognized (4:7-16)

> **[7]Beloved, let us love one another, for love is of God; and everyone who loves is born of God and knows God.**

The apostle now leaves behind his discussion about the many false spirits which "have gone out into the world" to allure Christians into worldly ideas. These ought to be rejected, of course. But if this was done, the readers could then focus on **love** for **one another**.

What might at first appear to be an abrupt change of thought is not that at all. As will shortly appear, the writer is returning to the theme of God abiding in us, which he introduced in 3:24. The Holy Spirit, he has told us, is the means by which we can know the reality of the indwelling God (3:24b). The section in 4:1-6 is somewhat parenthetical in nature, designed to warn readers about spiritual counterfeits, which are marked as such by their failure to speak the truth about Jesus Christ in the way God's Spirit does. In turning away from the subject of counterfeits, the writer now stresses a genuine mark of the Holy Spirit's activity: the expression of Christian love.

John has said (verse 6) that those who listened to the false teachers, and not to the apostles, were "not of God." But if the readers (who were **Beloved** both to God and to John), obeyed the command to **love one another**, they would be carrying on an activity that was distinctively sourced in their heavenly Father. The reason for this is that **love** itself **is of God**. In other words, true Christian love, whenever expressed, finds its source in, and takes its character from, **God** Himself.

It follows, then, that of **everyone who loves** two things may be safely said: (1) such a person **is born of God and** (2) he also **knows God**. It should be carefully noted that John here treats these concepts as two different things. This is especially observable when he goes on to say (in verse 8) that "he who does not love does not know God." It would have been both natural and easy to say, "He who does not love, *is not born of God and* does not know God" in direct antithesis to the statement of this verse.

But this is precisely what *cannot be said*. Already John has talked about a person who "hates *his* brother," which is a feat quite impossible for a non-Christian since a Christian is not *his* brother (cf. 2:11; 3:10b; 3:15; 4:20). The proposition is often stated that if a person is genuinely saved, he *will* love his Christian brother. In fact, this very epistle is often cited to prove this point. But there is not a scintilla of evidence in First John for this point of view, and to extract it from the epistle one must engage in eisegesis (reading into the text what one wants to find there). Indeed, in the effort to discover this teaching in First John, expositors are compelled to conclude that the apostle was incautious in talking about a person hating *his* brother, since this is technically not possible for an unregenerate man. And in verse 8 they must say that John really *meant* that the unloving person was not regenerate, even though he does not say it directly!

This kind of special pleading carries its own refutation on its face. It is a fact, both of Scripture and of Christian experience, that one Christian *can* hate another. There is no biblical doctrine to the contrary. Those who teach that a Christian *cannot* hate another Christian are teaching a myth.

⁸He who does not love does not know God, for God is love.

But since a born again Christian *can* fail to **love**, if **he does not love** it would show that he has not really come to **know** the **God** who is his heavenly Father (cf. discussion under 2:3). The **God** who has begotten him *is* **love**.

Here we meet the second of First John's two great affirmations about God. The first, found in 1:5, affirms that "God is light." The second one, here, declares that **God is love**. The former, as we noted under 1:5, points to His perfect holiness, His freedom from all sin or deception. This statement affirms that His basic nature is characterized by **love**. Naturally the statement does not mean that God has no other attributes, such as wisdom and justice. But it does indicate that **love** is fundamental to what **God** is and to what He does.

The question is often asked how a God who is love could ever send anyone to eternal hell. Although a commentary like this is not the place to address this question in detail, the probable answer is not as mysterious as it is sometimes made to seem. In creating the world, God took all eventualities into account and made the choices regarding the ultimate outcomes of human experience that were most consistent with all His attributes, including love. Since it is in the very nature of love that it must be *spontaneous* to be genuine, a world of human "robots" who could do nothing other than to love would be an artificial world which did not allow human beings to truly experience what their Creator experiences in the giving or receiving of love.

The Scriptures clearly declare God's love for the whole world (John 3:16, cf. 1 John 2:2). If man in his sin rejects that love and goes to hell, this is not what God *wishes* (1 Timothy 2:3-6) but what He in His wisdom *allows*. God does not coerce either the giving or receiving of love. For this reason, too, the love of Christians for their fellow Christians is not automatic or coerced. God by His Spirit *enables* us but does not *compel* us to "love one another."

> **⁹In this the love of God was manifested toward us, that God has sent His only begotten Son into the world, that we might live through Him.**

The apostle now reminds his readers of the supreme expression of **the love of God**—an expression which fully justifies the claim he has just made that "God *is* love." What could possibly make this fundamental truth about God's nature more evident than the fact that **God has sent His only begotten Son into the world** for our salvation?

This concept is a striking indication that the God of the Bible is also the God of creation. The highest manifestation of His **love...toward us** involves His parental love for His Son. In this way God's love becomes comprehensible to humanity because of our common earthly experience of parental love. It is instinctive, even with sinful people, to love their offspring, although the depraving effects of wickedness can blot out even this. Yet it remains true today, in Western culture, no matter how distorted, that there is a wide consensus that the welfare of children must be vigilantly guarded. Sensitive and loving parents can empathize with the profound sorrow that losing a child can bring, and many have actually had this tragic experience. It would be hard to devise a better way to demonstrate exceptional *love* than by the surrender of, not simply a son, but an **only begotten Son**.

Linguistic discussions of the Greek term for **only begotten** (*monogenēs*) often observe that its root idea is simply "one of a kind" or "unique." Hence the translation preferred today is simply the word "only," so that we often get the rendering "only Son" (so, e.g., the Jerusalem Bible, and the NIV ["one and only"]). The Greek term is found in the Greek Bible mainly, but not exclusively, in reference to children. It probably carried the nuance of a filial relationship in everyday usage. The translation of "only Son" is acceptable. If the familiar "only begotten Son" is retained (as it is by the NKJV here and in John 1:14, 18; 3:16, 18), we need to keep in mind that there is no suggestion in the word itself that the Son of God was actually "begotten" at some point in eternity past. But "only begotten" remains an acceptable rendering so long as it is taken to refer to the filial relationship itself without suggesting a point of origin for God's eternal Son. The discussion of this word by Westcott is still helpful.[6]

God's purpose in sending **His only begotten Son** was **that we might live through Him**. Unstated here, though plainly indicated in verse 10, is the fact that God's **Son** had to *die* **that we might** *live*. Thus, when **the love of God was manifested toward us**, this manifestation involved two quite opposite experiences: *death* for God's **Son**, *life* for **us**. That God would allow this for His beloved **Son** so **that we might** have eternal life speaks volumes about the greatness of that **love**. This greatness is further magnified when we consider that the **Son** was perfectly sinless and we were wretchedly sinful (cf. Romans 5:8; 2 Corinthians 5:21).

The words **toward us** translate the Greek: *en hymin*, more literally meaning "among us." This latter sense is preferable here since the words obviously anticipate the concept of God's love "among us" in verses 12-15 (see discussion there).[7]

> [10]**In this is love, not that we loved God, but that He loved us and sent His Son** *to be* **the propitiation for our sins.**

The previous verse began with "In this the love of God was manifested" while this one begins **In this is love**. The former verse stressed the way God's love was *revealed*. Here we have that in which this **love** *consisted*. This is to say, the manner in which God's love was displayed is specified in verse 9, while here its basic character is discussed.

It should be noted that the words "of God" do not occur here in the phrase **in this is love**. John is saying, in effect, here is what **love** (by whomever expressed, God or the Christian) really is all about. Since "God is love" (verse 8) it is necessary and proper that we draw our understanding of the character of **love** from His perfect display of it in the sending of **His Son** for us.

To begin with, we note that God's **love** was not a response to ours: **not that we loved God, but that He loved us**. Love which is displayed only toward those who already love us does not measure up to this standard. Thus Jesus Himself said, "For if you love those who love you, what reward have you? Do not even the tax collectors do the same?" (Matthew

5:46). True Godlike **love** for our Christian brother does not require that our brother love *us!*

Second, we can note that God's **love** sought to meet our *spiritual* need: **and [God] sent His Son *to be* the propitiation for our sins.** God's **love** for us was not deterred by our sinful condition or by the need to sacrifice **His Son** to make **propitiation for our sins.** Instead, the **Son** became precisely the **propitiation** that was required. (For the word **propitiation**, see the discussion under 2:2.) Although John wishes us to be concerned for our brother's *physical* need (3:17), we should also be concerned for his *spiritual* need (cf. 5:15-17 and discussion there). In the light of the powerful example presented in this verse, we can never excuse our failure to love our brother by the claim that he is too sinful and therefore unworthy of our love. The fact is that the worst sinner in the Christian church—indeed in all the world—is covered by the propitiatory work of Christ (cf. 2:2). Since no one in all humanity is beyond the reach of our Savior's sacrificial death, no brother or sister should be beyond our sacrificial love.

> [11]**Beloved, if God so loved us, we also ought to love one another.**

In the simplest terms John applies the truth of the two great statements he has just made about how **God...loved us.** The lesson is: **we also ought to love one another.**

The use of the word **so** (Greek: *houtōs*) makes the total phrase, **God so loved us,** redolent of the famous words of John 3:16, "For God so (*houtō[s]*) loved the world..." It is almost as if the apostle presciently anticipated that John 3:16 would become one of the most widely known and appreciated statements in the Bible. Since the Lord spoke these words in John's hearing so many years before, they no doubt had become richly valued by John and by those he taught. (In fact, there are echoes of John 3:16 in the two verses that precede this one, verses 9-10.) He thus chooses an echo of John 3:16 on which to ground his insistence that **we also ought to love one another.**

In the well-loved hymn, "When I Survey the Wondrous Cross," the hymn writer has caught the essence of what the apostle John is doing here. The apostle is asking us to look to the cross and see God's "love so

187

amazing, so divine" and then to look back at our brother as the appropriate object for *our* love as well. As those who are so deeply **Beloved** of God, our profound obligation and privilege is to love our brother who is equally **Beloved** by Him. At the foot of the cross a failure to love one for whom Christ died is a failure whose proportions can be measured only against the divine love which sacrificed His Son for that same brother.

> [12]**No one has seen God at any time. If we love one another, God abides in us, and His love has been perfected in us.**

In verses 9-11, John has clearly delineated the true nature of Christian love. It is modeled after the supreme expression of God's love which was displayed at the cross. Although this truth had already been introduced (in 3:16), 4:9-11 elaborates it in a powerfully compelling way. But what John now says might seem surprising. The invisible **God**, whom **No one has seen...at any time**, actually abides in those who **love one another**.

With this verse, therefore, the author has brought us straight back to the theme of the unit enunciated in 3:24, namely, the indwelling God. We were told in 3:24 that "he who keeps His commandments" is the one in whom "He [i.e., God or Christ] abides." But in the preceding verse those commands were summarized as *one* command ("His commandment") involving two indivisible aspects: "that we should believe on the name of His Son Jesus Christ and love one another" (3:23).

In the light of this fusion of faith with love, we can see more clearly why the "many false prophets" of 4:1ff must be rejected. Faith in God's incarnate Son is indispensable to expressing Christian love. The whole model of Christian love is predicated on the fact that it was God's Son, the Christ, who actually died on the cross as a manifestation of God's love to us (4:9-10). The denial of this truth makes it impossible to express true Christian love.

By denying "Jesus as Christ come in flesh" (cf. 4:2-3 and discussions there), the Revisionists were also denying that the physical death of Jesus was the death of God's Son, the Christ. Thus the death of Jesus could not be the supreme model of love that John had called it, since in the view of the antichrists God was not really surrendering "His only begotten Son" (verse 9) on the cross for us. But as John insists, there can be no real Christian love that is not modeled after the love God expressed at the cross in the death of Christ. We must, therefore, as 3:23 made clear, "believe on the name of His Son Jesus Christ" if we are also to "love one another"!

When real Christian love, modeled on God's love, is truly exercised by the Christian community, God is "at home" in those who exercise it: **If we love one another, God abides in us**. That is to say, the invisible **God** whom **no one has seen** is *actively living* in such a body of believers. (For John's basic concept of abiding, see discussion under 2:5-6.) The full importance of this will be stated shortly (verse 14). But here we must note that the words **in us** may also be rendered "among us" (as suggested for the same words in verse 9). In the present verse, John may intend to convey both senses ("in" and "among"), since both are true in a loving community of worshipping Christians.

Yet not only does **God** abide in believers who **love one another**, but also **His love has been perfected in** (or "among") them. The idea of the perfecting of God's love in obedient Christians was first mentioned in 2:5 (see discussion there). The Greek words for **has been perfected** (*teteleiōmenē estin*) are in a form (the perfect tense) that somewhat stresses the effect of **His love** being **perfected,** namely, the resulting exercise of Christian love. The Greek verb for **perfected** (*teleioō*) indicates "*to complete,*" "*to finish,*" "*to bring to its goal,*" "*to bring to full measure,*" and similar ideas.[8] The implication in this text is that God's **love** achieves its goal and reaches its full measure **in us** when that **love** is reproduced in us and reflected through us by loving **one another**.

What John describes here is nothing less than the pinnacle of Christian experience in which we who are "beloved" of God become the vessels and conduits for that **love** as we **love one another**. No form of fellowship with God could attain a higher level than this, namely, the fulfilling of our Lord's superlative "new commandment" (John 13:34).

¹³By this we know that we abide in Him, and He in us, because He has given us of His Spirit.

When this verse is considered along with the previous one, we have come full circle from the opening verse of this subsection, that is, from 3:24. There we were told for the first time in this epistle that the person "who keeps His commandments, abides in Him, *and He in him*." That is, we hear for the first time in 3:24a about the fully mutual nature of the "abiding" relationship. In the same verse we are also told that "by this we know that He abides in us, by the Spirit which He has given us" (3:24b).

In other words, 4:12-13 comes close to being a repetition of 3:24. However, in place of "keeping His commandments" as in 3:24, here we find "loving one another" as the key to this mutual "abiding" relationship. But as we saw from 3:22-23 (cf. discussion there), these are but two sides of the same coin for the apostle: the obedient Christian *is loving* and the loving Christian *is obeying*. We should also note again that the phrase **in us** can mean "among us" (see discussion under verse 12). The community's experience is primarily in view, as verse 14 shows.

One other alteration from 3:24 is very significant here. Whereas in 3:24 John wrote that we know the inward abiding of God "by the Spirit whom He has given us," here we are told that this is known **because He has given us of His Spirit**. The Greek constructions are different in that in 3:24 "His Spirit" is what God is said to have given us, while here we are told that **He has given us** *out* **of His Spirit**. That is to say, we *participate in the same* **Spirit** that God has. In the context, this can only mean that we participate in a "spirit of love" which is nothing less than **His Spirit**, since "God is love"! (The elasticity of the Greek word for "spirit" allows the word to suggest both a Person and an attitude; cf. 4:1 and discussion there. In 4:13 we might almost be tempted to write **S/spirit** to suggest both meanings.)

Taking 3:24 and 4:13 together, it is clear that John regards the Holy Spirit as the Person within us who can make evident the inward abiding of God; He does this when we find ourselves loving one another. Since love in the likeness of God's love, revealed at the cross, could be produced in us only by the Holy Spirit, when such love *is* produced in us, the Holy Spirit is manifesting the reality of the indwelling God. That is to say, the God of love is loving our brethren through us by the power of His Spirit. And when we thus partake **of His S/spirit** of love, we can know that **He** abides **in us**.

> **[14]And we have seen and testify that the Father has sent the Son *as* Savior of the world.**

No verse in the First Epistle of John is more critical to understanding the entire epistle than this one. Clearly the initial statement, **And we have**

seen...that the Father has sent the Son, suggests an apostolic experience such as was declared in the prologue. There John tells us that he and his fellow witnesses "have seen, and bear witness, and declare to you that eternal life which was with the Father and was manifested to us" (1:2).

That such was indeed the apostolic experience is beyond question. But it must be recalled that in the prologue John also affirmed, "That which we have seen and heard we declare to you, that you also may have *fellowship with us*" (1:3; italics added). Most readers do not pause to consider these words from the prologue. They assume that John simply means that he *will tell his readers about* what the apostles saw and heard so that they can know what the apostles know. But John means more than this.

The crucial question for interpretation in this verse is exactly how wide is the range of the **we** (*hēmeis*), which is emphatic in the Greek. It might be thought at first that once again we have the "apostolic we" which we met, not only in the prologue but also at 2:19, 3:14, and 4:6. But in all these places there is a contrasting "you" nearby (cf. 1:2-4; 2:20; 3:13; 4:4). This does not occur here.

The subject "**we**," which runs through this passage, begins in 4:7 with the words, "Beloved, let *us* love one another." That the readers are included in this is undoubted. But they are also transparently included in "us" and "we" in verse 9, in the "we," "us," and "our" of verse 10, in "us" and "we" of verse 11, in "we" and "us" (twice) in verse 12, and in "we" (twice) and "us" (twice) in verse 13. There is no reason at all to suddenly change the reference of the "**we**" in this verse. In fact, the passage makes excellent sense with a continuing inclusion of the readership in all the first person plurals of the unit from verse 7 through verse 14.[9]

This is evident when we take account of John's flow of thought. "No one has seen God at any time," he tells us (verse 12). Yet, "if we love one another" this unseen God *abides* within us, as is demonstrated by our active participation in His S/spirit of love (verses 12-13). But that S/spirit of love is nothing less than an expression of the kind of love which was demonstrated at the cross (verses 9-10), and when we "so" love one another (verse 11) there is, so to speak, a *re-display of that love* within the loving Christian community. And that very *re-display* is also a living *testimony* (cf. **testify**) to the reality of God's love to **the world** in Christ. Did not Jesus, in giving His "new commandment" (John 13:34), say also, "By this all will know that you are My disciples, if you have love one for another" (John 13:35)? The Church has no more effective way to **testify** to *the world* about the Saviorhood of Jesus than by the *re-display* of the Savior's love in the fellowship of His disciples.

We should remember that the Greek word translated **And** (*Kai*) at the beginning of our verse can be taken in its well-recognized sense of "And so." With this in mind we can paraphrase the words of the verse, **And** *so,* when we love like this, **we** [both the readers and the apostles] **have seen** the reality, *and* we **testify** to the reality **that the Father has sent the Son** *as* **Savior of the world**. Thus, by loving one another, the readership can *have fellowship* with the apostles in what the apostles had *seen*, precisely as the prologue had promised (1:3a). And, of course, this was nothing less than *fellowship with the Father and with His Son Jesus Christ* (1:3b).

It should be noted in passing that the Greek verb for **we have seen** (*tetheametha*) is in the perfect tense, implying that the act of seeing has some present result. The verb for **testify** (Greek: *martyroumen*) is in the present tense and is probably intended to express the result of the seeing. The idea is likely to be: **we have seen and** by this experience we bear testimony **that the Father sent the Son**... That acts or deeds may indeed "bear testimony" is established in Johannine usage (cf. John 5:36; 10:25; cf. also 1 John 5:7-8; 3 John 3). However, verbal testimony is not excluded; see under verse 15.

We must now recall that the prologue does not explicitly name the Lord Jesus as the object of the apostolic experience. When John spoke of "that...which we have heard, which we have seen with our eyes, which we have looked upon, and our hands have handled," we are told only that this concerned "the Word of life" (1:1). In the same way, John does not say that Christ was manifested, but that "the *life* was manifested" (1:2a) and that what the apostles "declare to" them is "that eternal life which was with the Father and was manifested to us" (1:2b). We can now see that this careful articulation of the apostolic experience was deliberate.

If the readers were to "have fellowship" with the apostles in what the apostles had "seen" (1:3), that fellowship could not be the visible Person of Jesus Christ Himself. But it definitely *could be* an experience of seeing "that eternal life which was with the Father and was manifested" to the apostles. All that John has been saying from 2:29 to the present verse has laid the groundwork for this. Thus in 2:29–3:10a, John has affirmed that the born again child of God is manifested by, and only by, the doing of righteousness. In 3:10b-23, he asserts that this manifestation takes the form, not of brotherly hatred like Cain's, but of self-sacrificing love like Christ's. And in 3:24–4:13, he teaches us that such love demonstrates the presence of the indwelling God whose S/spirit of love we share. Thus, "that eternal life which was with the Father and was manifested to" the apostles (1:3) is *re-manifested* within the loving Christian community. When it is re-manifested among the readers, they *along with the apostles* can be said to **have seen...that the Father sent the Son** *as* **Savior of the world**. Since this manifested Christian love is nothing less than the manifestation of *eternal life* within the loving Christian fellowship, those who so manifest this *life* are *living witnesses* to the reality that **the Son** who saved them really is the **Savior of the world** (cf. John 13:35).[10]

(It should be noted that here we meet John's only use of the term *Savior* [Greek: $\overline{so}\overline{te}r$] in the epistle. John's only other use of the word is in 4:42 of his Gospel where the Samaritans give this same title to Jesus: "the Savior of the world." In both places the universal scope of His saviorhood is in view. In John 4:42 it is used by the believing Samaritans, a race despised by the Jews, and here it is used in a context of Gentile faith where *testimony* is rendered to that same universal saviorhood. See also John 1:29 and 1 John 2:2!)

In other words, the visible manifestation of *eternal life* through Christian love, so that this *life* can be **seen** in that love, is an enormously effective way to **testify** about the Saviorhood of Christ. It goes without saying that such a "seeing" is a "seeing" of faith expressed in the confession of **Jesus** as the world's **Savior**. Though there are *concrete acts* of love to be literally **seen**, the significance of these acts is perceived through the community's faith in God's **Son**.[11]

> **15Whoever confesses that Jesus is the Son of God, God abides in him, and he in God.**

What John has spoken of in verse 14 was "fellowship" with the apostles in what they had "seen" (cf. 1:3), but the readers were also to have "fellowship" in what the apostles had "heard" (cf. 1:3 and the discussion there of the two verbs). What the readers can *hear* in the midst of the loving Christian community is nothing less than a confession **that Jesus is the Son of God.**

In the case of John himself, it is virtually certain that he was originally a disciple of John the Baptist. There is little reason to doubt that John was the unnamed disciple mentioned along with Andrew in John 1:35-40. For this reason he and Andrew are both likely to have actually *heard* the words of the Baptist (which John alone records), that gave testimony to Jesus, "I saw the Spirit descending from heaven like a dove, and He remained upon Him. I did not know Him, but He who sent me to baptize with water said to me, 'Upon whom you see the Spirit descending, and remaining on Him, this is He who baptizes with the Holy Spirit.' And I have *seen and testified that this is the Son of God*" (John 1:32-34; italics added).

The words of the Baptist that he had *seen and testified* reflect the wording of our previous verse (verse 14), which states that "we have seen and testify," while the Baptist's words *that this is the Son of God* reflect our present verse: **that Jesus is the Son of God.** Thus the "testimony" mentioned in verse 14 is not to be limited to the visible manifestation of eternal life in the form of Christian love, although this is a part of it. But John is thinking of a congregational context where there would also regularly be the confession of **Jesus** as God's **Son.** This confession would take place in prayer, in the singing of hymns about Christ, and in teaching and preaching.

In the kind of church context John had in mind, the visible manifestation of Christian love, accompanied by this confession of **Jesus**, reproduced what the apostles themselves had *seen* in Jesus and what they had *heard* about Him from His forerunner and prophet, John the Baptist. *John's goal of leading his readership into this kind of fellowship with the apostolic circle (1:1-3) has now been reached.*

We should also note that what John could say of those who loved one another, he could also say of **Whoever confesses that Jesus is the Son of God.** He has just stated (verse 12) that "if we love one another, *God abides in* (or "among") us." Of anyone who **confesses that Jesus is the Son of God,** John now also says that **God abides in him, and he in God.** That is to say, the mutual "abiding" relationship (God in us and we in God) exists also for the one who makes this confession in the context of Christian love, so that the confession is fundamentally the testimony of God Himself. That is, it is a confession of the Spirit of God by whom the indwelling of God is known and recognized (cf. verse 13). Indeed, the Holy Spirit Himself is recognized by this confession (cf. 4:2).

We must not reduce this confession to the low common denominator that it often has in modern-day religion. For John, the fact that **Jesus** was **the Son of God** was inseparable from the reality that He was God's Christ. Thus in the thematic statement for the Fourth Gospel, found in John 20:30-31, we are told, "But these [miraculous signs] are written that you may believe that Jesus is *the Christ, the Son of God*, and that believing you may have life in His name" (verse 31; italics added). Just exactly what the role of *the Christ, the Son of God* was, for John, is clearly delineated in Jesus' famous exchange with Martha.

In that critical passage, standing in connection with the last and greatest of the signs in John's Gospel (the raising of Lazarus), we read, "Jesus said to her, 'I am the resurrection and the life. He who believes in Me, though he may die, he shall live. And whoever lives and believes in Me shall never die. Do you believe this?'" (John 11:25-26). Martha's reply is a full-fledged *confession*, "Yes, Lord, I believe that You are *the Christ, the Son of God*, who is to come into the world" (John 11:27; italics added). When Jesus is confessed as **the Son of God**, He is being confessed as *"Christ come in flesh"* (cf. 1 John 4:2) and as the Guarantor of eternal life and future resurrection to every believer. Therefore, "Whoever believes that Jesus is the Christ is born of God" (1 John 5:1) and this eternal life is a *promise* that the Revisionists evidently deny (cf. 1 John 2:25-26). Against this background of Johannine thought, it is clear that only those who grasp John's concept of the title **Son of God** can truly make the confession that John speaks of here.

When Peter made his great confession, "You are the Christ, the Son of the living God" (Matthew 16:16), Jesus immediately responded by saying, "Blessed are you, Simon Bar-Jonah, for flesh and blood has not revealed this to you, but My Father who is in heaven" (Matthew 16:17). The genuine (as over against a "pretended") confession of **Jesus** as **the Son of God**, i.e., as the Christ who guarantees eternal life to every believer, *can be made only on the basis of divine illumination* (cf. also 1 Corinthians 12:3). Thus, when it is made in the context of Christian love, it can be said that **God abides in** the confessing one, **and He in God**. The Spirit of God within is the source of the confession.

We can now see that it is possible for a Christian community to recognize the reality that God "abides" within its membership if (1) they
love one another, and if (2) they confess **that Jesus is the Son of God.**
Thereby that community is keeping "His commandment" which enjoins
us that "we should believe on the name of His Son Jesus Christ" and that
we should "love one another" (3:23). In recognizing and experiencing
such a reality, a Christian community enters into real fellowship with the
apostles and, at the same time, "with the Father and with *His Son Jesus
Christ*" (1:3, italics added). What the apostles "have seen and heard" (1:3)
is significantly shared (though not, of course, in its totality) by any Christian church that is obeying "His commandment."

> [16]**And we have known and believed the love that God has
> for us. God is love, and he who abides in love abides in
> God, and God in him.**

Once more, as in verse 14, we can take the opening word **And** in the
sense of **And** *so.* In fact, it seems quite clear in the Greek text that this
verse is deliberately made parallel in structure to verse 14. Both verses
utilize the emphatic pronoun **we** (Greek: $\bar{h}emeis$) as the subject of a com-
pound verbal statement: "And *we* have seen and testify..." (verse 14); **And
we have known and believed**...(here). Three of the four verbs are also
in the Greek perfect tense ("testify" in verse 14 is in the present). The
author apparently intends that both verses show the results of the community experience of love that he has been discussing. (On the reference
to **we,** see discussion under verse 14.)

But between the two verses John has pointed out the role of confessing Jesus (verse 15) as an additional sign that God indwells the members
of a loving Christian community. Therefore, when believers in a church
enjoy such an experience as this, they are brought face to face with the
reality of **the love God has** toward them. At the level of personal experience they *have come to know* it. Here the perfect tense of the verb *know*
(Greek: $egn\bar{o}kamen$) has the same force as it did in 2:3-4 (see discussion
there) and signals knowledge *attained* and *possessed.* They now know **the
love that God has** toward them, not by apostolic testimony alone (valid
though that was), but by first-hand experience, like the apostles. They
have come to know it in the living experience of loving one another,
because God Himself is loving each of them through their brethren.

In addition they have also **believed** this **love**. John does not mean to say, of course, that they had not believed it before, but rather that the expression of Christian love in the believing community produces a fresh surge of confidence in the reality of **the love** of **God**. It is in the very nature of faith that fresh evidences of the truth can produce fresh responses of belief in that truth. For example, it seems quite clear that the disciples of Jesus mentioned in John 1:35-50 had already believed in Him at that time. But later, in response to the miracle of turning water into wine we are told, "This beginning of signs Jesus did in Cana of Galilee, and manifested His glory; *and His disciples believed in Him"* (John 2:11; italics added). So impressive was that miracle that one might say that the disciples believed *all over again!* Indeed, every Christian who has any significant experience of answered prayer knows how such an experience can call up a new conviction about the truth of God's word.

It should be pointed out that the words rendered by the NKJV as **the love that God has for us** could also be translated **the love that God has among** (Greek: *en*) **us**. (The Greek could also mean "in" us, but this is less suitable in context.) While the NKJV rendering is possible, it is less natural for the Greek than the translation "among," so that the stress here is once again upon the corporate experience of God's **love**. Therefore, God's **love**, as originally exemplified in the giving of His Son, is in a sense "reincarnated" in the midst of the believing community.

Thus the bottom line of the experience of the loving Christian community is that this experience produces *knowledge of* and *faith in* God's **love**. How often have hostile, quarreling Christians produced in the immature believer serious doubts about the validity of the Christian faith? No body of believers will really be any stronger than the extent to which they manifest God's *love* by loving one another. If **the love** of **God** is evident in the midst of a Christian church, such a church will flourish in its discernment of, and confidence in, the redeeming love revealed in Jesus Christ God's Son.

In addition, anyone who so lives **abides in love** and, because **God is love**, he also **abides in God and God** [abides][12] **in him**. We have now come full circle from the thematic statement of 3:24 where the idea of *our* abiding in God or Christ is explicitly joined, for the first time, with the idea of God or Christ abiding in us. All who are part of the corporate experience that John has been describing (for Christian love cannot be exercised apart from other Christians) are actually "dwelling" **in love**. (For John's concept of "abiding" as a term for living as a disciple, see 2:5-6 and discussions there.) And they are also "dwelling" **in God**. At the same time **God** is "dwelling" in them. In other words, in the exercise of mutual love, the Christian individual who participates in this experiences the fully interactive character of "abiding" in that he **abides in God and God** [abides] **in him**.

The statement **abides in God and God** [abides] **in him** forms an *inclusio* with the statement "abides in Him, and He in him" in 3:24. That is, it picks up this earlier statement and marks the unit as complete. It should be noted that the very similar words in 4:15, "God abides in him, and he in God" are not the same sequence as 3:24 and 4:16. Though they prepare for the *inclusio* found in verse 16, they do not really end the section as verse 16 does. John has thus completed his discussion of what it means to "abide in Him," which was the exhortation he gave in the thematic statement of 2:28 (see discussion there). He is now ready to speak of the astounding results of this experience.

E. Conclusion: Having Boldness at the Judgment Seat (4:17-19)

In the theme verse of the main section (body) of First John, the apostle has urged the readership to "abide in Him, that when He appears, we may have confidence [boldness] and not be ashamed before Him at His coming" (2:28). In elaborating on the subject of "abiding" in Christ, or God, John has shown this experience to be one of "dwelling" in love and therefore an experience in which a person "dwells" in God and God "dwells" in him (4:16). This is an experience of such closeness to God, who *is* love (4:16), that it ought to be productive of a confident relationship to Him.

> **[17]Love has been perfected among us in this: that we may have boldness in the day of judgment; because as He is, so are we in this world.**

John has already spoken twice of the perfecting of God's love in Christians as they love one another (cf. 2:5; 4:12). Both of these contexts suggest that God's love reaches its fullness and maturity in us only as we learn to pass it on to our brothers and sisters in Christ. God's love is not

perfected in a Christian whose heart is simply a reservoir in which to receive it, but only in one whose heart furnishes an aqueduct to convey it to others. But John will now describe another aspect of this perfecting: namely, the acquisition of **boldness in the day of judgment**.

The words **in this** at the end of the introductory clause actually stand at the beginning of the Greek statement and mark a new point of departure for the discussion. By placing them at the end of the clause the NKJV makes clear that they refer to what follows.[13] That is, they introduce the result of the fact that **Love has been perfected among us**.

It is worth noting that John does not speak here explicitly of *God's love*, but simply of **Love**. Of course, it *is* God's love that John is thinking of, but the stress obviously falls on **Love** as a specific kind of experience that has a specific result. That result is realized when **Love has been perfected among us**. The words **among us** translate the Greek phrase *en hymin*, which elsewhere in First John occurs only at 4:12 (twice); 4:13; and 4:16. In all of these places the NKJV translates "in us," except 4:16 where it is handled as "for us." But in this last place, "among us" would have been preferable (see discussion under verse 16). Here either translation is possible, and it may be that the author himself did not intend a sharp distinction at this point. The **Love** he has been talking about could be said to have **been perfected** both **among** the Christians who were loving, and also in them individually.

The result of this perfecting of **Love** is **that we may have boldness in the day of judgment**. This carries us back to 2:28 and to the concept of "*confidence*...before Him at His coming." Both the word rendered "confidence" there and **boldness** here represent the same Greek word (*parrēsia*). As has been pointed out before, there is no such thing as a judgment for the saved to determine their destiny in heaven or hell, since that is already settled (cf. John 5:24; Romans 8:31-34). But Christians will give an accounting of their Christian lives at the Judgment Seat of Christ (Romans 14:10-12; 2 Corinthians 5:10-11).

It is clear, however, that the Judgment Seat of Christ should not be thought of as simply some kind of great awards celebration. After speaking of the fact that "we must all appear before the Judgment Seat of Christ" (2 Corinthians 5:10), Paul goes on to say, "Knowing, therefore, *the terror* [Greek: *phobos*, fear] of the Lord, we persuade men" (2 Corinthians

5:11; italics added). In another place, Paul states that our works "will be revealed by fire," and that "the fire will test each one's work, of what sort it is." The possibility is held out that "if anyone's work is burned [Greek = burned *up*], he will suffer loss; but he himself will be saved, yet so as through fire" (1 Corinthians 3:13, 15). And John himself, standing in the presence of the Lord Jesus and seeing Him as God's appointed Judge, "fell at His feet as dead" (Revelation 1:17).

In light of these Scriptures, the Judgment Seat of Christ must be viewed as utterly solemn and potentially productive of fear. Even a transformed believer, who knows he is in no danger of hell, will be capable of feeling the fear which the presence of God always produces in those with holy sensibilities. We forget the awesomeness and majesty of Jesus Christ our Lord if we think otherwise.

For this reason the idea of having **boldness in the day of judgment** is truly a stunning concept. Reasonable Christians, even though fully assured of their salvation, will share with Paul a realization of "the terror of the Lord." The possibility of triumphing over that "terror" is challenging indeed. Yet this is possible, John teaches us, if we "abide in love" (verse 16).

The specific reason why one who "abides in love" can expect **boldness** at the Judgment Seat is **because as He is, so are we in this world**. As John has already told us twice, "God is love" (4:8, 16), so that the one who loves is like **He is**, even though the loving Christian is still **in this world**.[14] This of course does not mean that this Christian is sinless, but that he or she is keeping God's basic command that "we should believe on the name of His Son Jesus Christ and love one another" (3:23). Whatever other faults may cling to us in our sinful humanity (and we are never without them: see 1:8), the manifestation of eternal life through us, by means of faith and love, is indeed a manifestation of the God who abides in us (cf. verse 16) and therefore represents a true likeness to Himself.

As often is the case in John's Epistle, the pronoun referring to God may also be a reference to Jesus Christ as well, who is "the true God and eternal life" (1 John 5:20). As John himself recorded, "The Father judges no one, but has committed all judgment to the Son" (John 5:22). Thus, it is before the Son that we stand at the Judgment Seat; yet we also stand before God the Father as Paul says, "So then each of us shall give an account of Himself to God" (Romans 14:12). Thus John's frequent

ambiguity in his references to God the Father or Christ with words like
"He" or "Him" is no doubt deliberate and also a tacit acknowledgment
of the full deity of Jesus Christ.

> [18]There is no fear in love; but perfect love casts out fear,
> because fear involves torment. But he who fears has not
> been made perfect in love.

The experience of **fear** and **perfect love** are incompatible. If a Christian has **been made perfect in love**, he does not have **fear** of, or at, the
Judgment Seat.

Once again, by **perfect love**, the writer does not mean sinlessness
(cf. again 1:8). The word translated "perfect" (Greek: *teleios*) is of the
same root with the verb rendered **has…been made perfect** (Greek:
teteleiōtai), a verb also used previously at 2:5; 4:12 and 17. Here, as in
those places, the concept is of a matured **love** that has reached its goal or
objective (see discussion under 2:5). John's point is that when God's **love**
to us has reached its goal in us, by making us channels for that **love** to
one another, this experience **casts out fear**.

A little reflection will show that once a Christian knows on the authority of God's word that he is keeping God's command to love others,
he can realize that any anxiety about his future accounting at the Judgment Seat is unnecessary. For if God is pleased with our lives, we can
expect His approbation before His tribunal. It is an important step to
reaching this point, however, to remember what the apostle taught in
3:18-23. Indeed that passage is a kind of midpoint between the thematic
statement of 2:28 and the realization of that theme here in 4:17-19.

In 3:18-23 John invites the readers to assure themselves that they are
participating in true Christian love by doing actual deeds of love. This is
the means by which they can silence a condemning heart when they come
before God in prayer; and the "confidence" (Greek: *parrēsia, boldness*) which
this quieting of the heart produces leads to answered prayer. It is no
accident that, up to this point in the epistle, this word has occurred only
three times: in the theme verse (2:28); in the midpoint passage (3:21); and
here in the conclusion to the main unit covering 2:28–4:19. (The word
occurs one final time, in 5:14; see discussion there). Thus the author of
this epistle once again is seen as a skilled craftsman leading his discussion
through its necessary stages to the impressive climax in 4:17-19.

If a believer has not yet quieted his condemning heart before God, this signals a need to experience what 3:19-23 describes. But if the experience of confidence before God in prayer, on the basis of obedience to His commandments, is realized, then the Christian can also look forward to having "boldness in the day of judgment" as John describes that privilege here.

However, in the absence of this, the disobedient Christian will experience God's discipline, since the presence of **fear involves torment**. The word rendered **torment** (Greek: *kolasis*) would probably be better translated *punishment*.[15] Though obviously **fear** *is* a form of **torment**, it is more likely that John has in mind the truth that "whom the Lord loves He chastens, and scourges every son whom He receives" (Hebrews 12:6). In fact, this New Testament truth is found on the lips of the Lord Jesus in John's last book, "As many as I love, I rebuke and chasten" (Revelation 3:19).

If a Christian experiences **fear** as he anticipates being evaluated by his Lord at the Judgment Seat, and if the conscience cannot be quieted as specified in 3:19-23, then this experience of **fear** can be properly regarded as a *punishment* intended to awaken the Christian to his need to correct his behavior. Unpleasant as it is, like all divine discipline (Hebrews 12:11), it is nevertheless a signal of God's love for us and of His desire to see us **made perfect in love**. If the Christian responds to this kind of discipline, the discipline is effective and "yields the peaceable fruits of righteousness" (Hebrews 12:11) which for John are inseparable from **love**.

¹⁹We love Him because He first loved us.

John's climactic statement closing the main unit, or body, of this epistle, is an impressive one. In regard to the Christian's exercise of love, he has up to now spoken of that love as directed toward other Christians, i.e., toward "one another." Here, however, he speaks for the first time in the epistle of loving *God*. (It should be noted that the standard critical editions of the Greek NT omit **Him** and so do the translations based on them [e.g., NIV, NASB, JB, etc.]. The omission is most unfortunate, since the reference to loving God is pivotal here: see verse 20.)[16]

In the background of John's entire doctrine of the "abiding" life (as previously noted) are the crucial words of Jesus spoken in the Upper

Room and recorded in John 14:19-24. In that passage Jesus predicates obedience to His commands on the disciples' love for *Him*. He states: "He who has My commandments and keeps them, it is he who loves Me" (John 14:21), and, "If anyone loves Me, he will keep My word…" (14:23). "He who does not love Me does not keep My words" (14:24). Clearly, the one whose obedience to God results in his being "made perfect in love" is one of whom it can truly be said that he loves God.

Yet if this is true, another fact remains equally true. Our **love** for God is sourced in His love for us. As John has already reminded us, His love "was manifested toward us" in the sending of "His only begotten Son into the world, that we might live through Him" (4:9) and we find our very definition of love in His own superlative act of love (cf. 4:10). Consequently, if we love one another, and also **love** God, there can be only one reason. It is **because He first loved us**!

ENDNOTES

[1] In Hodges/Farstad *MajT*, verse 2 begins thus: "By this [i.e., by testing] the Spirit of God is recognized." The same verb (Greek: *ginōskō*) is used both in *MajT* and in the critical editions, but in *MajT* it is passive in form (Greek: *ginōsketai*). This rather exceptional use of the passive of *ginōskō* (the active predominates in First John) was evidently an irresistible temptation to some ancient scribe or editor, who harmonized it with John's familiar active (e.g., 2:3, 5, 18, 29; 3:19, 24; etc.).

[2] The NKJV rendering is also the rendering of KJV, NIV, NASB, JB, NACE, NRSV, and is accepted (though not discussed) by F. F. Bruce, *The Epistles of John: Introduction, Exposition and Notes* (Old Tappan, NJ: Fleming H. Revell, 1970), p. 105. Close to this is the view that the whole phrase is the object of the verb *confesses*, i.e., "confesses Jesus Christ come in flesh" (so Raymond E. Brown, *The Epistles of John,* AB [Garden City, NY: Doubleday, 1982], pp. 492-93; A. E. Brooke, *A Critical and Exegetical Commentary on the Johannine Epistles,* ICC [Edinburgh: T. & T. Clark, 1912], p. 109; Brooke Foss Westcott, *The Epistles of St John: The Greek Text with Notes* [Grand Rapids: Wm. B. Eerdmans Publishing Co., 1966], p. 141; I. Howard Marshall, *The Epistles of John,* NICNT [Grand Rapids: Wm. B. Eerdmans Publishing Co., 1978], p. 205; Stephen S. Smalley, *1,2,3 John,* WBC [Waco, TX: Word Books, 1984], p. 222). The translation, "confesses Jesus Christ *as* come in flesh," is favored by Alfred Plummer (apparently), *The Epistles of St. John* (Cambridge: University Press, 1886 [reprint ed., Grand Rapids: Baker Book

The First Epistle of John

House, 1980]), p. 95; Rudolf Bultmann, *The Johannine Epistles: A Commentary on the Johannine Epistles,* Herm (Philadelphia: Fortress Press, 1973), p. 62; and by others cited in Brown, *Epistles,* pp. 492-93. The view which we have presented in the text of this Commentary ("confesses Jesus as [or, to be] Christ come in flesh") is shared by J. L. Houlden, *A Commentary on the Johannine Epistles,* HNTC (New York: Harper & Row, 1973), p. 107; and John R. W. Stott, *The Letters of John: An Introduction and Commentary,* rev. ed., TNTC (Grand Rapids: Wm. B. Eerdmans Publishing Co., 1988), pp. 157-59. In our judgment, the fact that the antichrists denied that Jesus was the Christ, according to 2:22, should be decisive in favor of this option.

³ The words of verse 3, **that does not confess that Jesus Christ has come in flesh** (but see previous note) are reduced to "that does not confess Jesus" in the critical editions (Nestle-Aland, UBS) and the shorter text is followed by NIV, NASB, JB, NACE (which also replaces "confesses" [Greek: *homologei*] with "severs" [Greek: *luei*], a famous reading that can claim no extant copy of First John in its favor!) It is argued that the original, short reading (*that does not confess Jesus*) "was expanded by copyists with additions derived from the previous verse" (Bruce M. Metzger, *A Textual Commentary on the Greek New Testament,* 2ⁿᵈ ed. [Stuttgart, Germany: Deutsche Bibelgesellschaft and United Bible Societies, 1994], p. 645). But the manuscript evidence, though including Codex Alexandrinus (A) and Codex Vaticanus (B), is extremely sparse (less than a dozen can be cited out of a total of some 600 mss). It is far more likely that the omission arises out of an ancient papyrus exemplar whose dimensions were similar to those of Papyrus Bodmer II (𝔓⁶⁶), of around A.D. 200, in which the number of letters per line averages between 18 and 28. The omitted words in Greek contain 23 letters and perhaps constituted a complete line in this exemplar so that the entire line was accidentally skipped by the scribe. Anyone who has examined the layout of ancient papyri (like 𝔓⁶⁶) will know how easily this could happen.

⁴ As so often in the epistle, the pronoun reference to deity is not always clear in terms of which Person of the Godhead is referred to. Since Christ is often said to be "in" us, and even the Father is so spoken of (Ephesians 4:6), the reference could be to either. But the contextual emphasis on the Spirit of God makes a reference to the Spirit's indwelling presence much more likely. Contrary to Marianne Meye Thompson's comment (*1–3 John,* IVPNT [Downers Grove, IL: InterVarsity Press, 1992], pp. 116-17), the use of a masculine pronoun in this verse is *not* an argument against a reference to the Spirit (a neuter noun in Greek). See John 16:13-14 where *to Pneuma* (neuter, verse 13) is picked up by *Ekeinos* (masculine, verse 14).

⁵ See note 8 in chapter 3.

[6] Westcott, *Epistles,* pp. 169-72. For a more modern discussion, see D. Moody, "God's Only Son: The Translation of John 3:16 in the Revised Standard Version," *JBL* 72 (1953): 213-19.

[7] The words may also be translated "in us" or "within us," but since the reference is to the Incarnation (before we loved God), a reference to an interior realization of His love is not at all likely.

[8] See Bauer, Walter. *A Greek-English Lexicon of the New Testament and Other Early Christian Literature* (Chicago: University of Chicago Press, 1979), pp. 809-10.

[9] This point has been widely overlooked, or misconstrued, in the commentary tradition. Thus the **we** of this verse is restricted by some to the actual eyewitnesses to the historical Incarnation (so Brooke, *Epistles,* p. 121; Stott, *Letters,* p. 169). By others it is applied to the church as a whole (or, to the so-called Johannine community) viewed in solidarity with the original eyewitnesses (Westcott, *Epistles,* p. 153; Marshall, *Epistles,* p. 220; Brown, *Epistles,* pp. 522-23; Bruce, *Epistles,* pp. 110-11; Smalley, *1,2,3 John,* p. 251; C. H. Dodd, *The Johannine Epistles,* MNTC [New York: Harper & Row, 1946], pp. 115-16 [who takes exactly the same view in 1:1-4 (!), cf. pp. 9-16]; Thompson, *1–3 John,* pp. 124-25). But this is very tenuous, to say the least, and rests on an unfounded assumption that Christians who had not really seen anything could say **we have seen** as though they had. Thompson adduces John 4:42, "where the Samaritans say, 'We have *heard* for ourselves, and we know that this man really is the Savior of the world.'" She adds: "There is no substantive distinction between 'seeing' and 'hearing' this truth" (*1–3 John,* pp. 124-25). But surely there is. The corporate-witness interpretation is clearly forced and in no way self-evident. By contrast (ironically) Bultmann handles the text with the most dexterity, writing: "*Tetheametha* points back to v 12 and emphasizes that there is a *theasthai* ('seeing') of God, in spite of the fact that 'no man has ever seen God.' However, the seeing is precisely not direct...but indirect. If this seeing in v 12 was the relationship to God fulfilled in love for one another, then according to v 14 the relationship to God has its basis in God's act of salvation in sending his Son. The seeing of faith evinces its certainty in the fact that it carries its testimony with it: *kai martyroumen* ('and testify'). What faith sees and testifies to is stated in almost the same words as in v 9: *hoti ho patēr apestalken ton huion sōtēra tou kosmou* ('that the Father has sent the Son as savior of the world')" (Bultmann, *Johannine Epistles,* pp. 70-71). Correctly, Bultmann perceives the seeing here as a seeing of faith related to the fulfillment of our relationship to God through love for one another.

[10] It is to be noted that in John 13:35, the words translated by the NKJV as "love for one another" might be more literally rendered "love *among* (Greek: *en*) one another." This obviously is the basis for John's phrase *en hēmin* ("among us") in 1 John 4:9, 12, 13.

The First Epistle of John

[11] Cf. the quotation from Bultmann at the end of note 9.

[12] The word **abides** (Greek: *menei*) is placed in the text by Hodges/Farstad *MajT*, though it was absent from the text translated by the KJV (most likely Beza's 5th edition [1598] of the Textus Receptus), and thus also from NKJV. In the manuscripts surveyed by W. L. Richards (*The Classification of the Greek Manuscripts of the Johannine Epistles.* No. 35: Society of Biblical Literature Dissertation Series [Missoula, MT: Scholars Press, 1977], p. 246), he finds the inclusion of *menei* supported by 49 (59.8 percent) of them; its omission by 25 (30.5 percent); while 8 (9.8 percent) render no testimony at this point. This is not an unambiguous margin for *menei*, but lacking a genealogical reconstruction of the transmissional history of First John, it is the most probable reading. The loss of *menei* in some early exemplar is highly probable since the scribes dropped single words with great frequency.

[13] See note 8 in chapter 3.

[14] Brown (*Epistles*, p. 529) approaches this idea, without quite reaching it, when he writes: "The author is offering a reason why we should have confidence on Judgment Day, a judgment to be rendered by Christ, as the author previously indicated when he said, '...that we may have confidence and not draw back in shame from him at his coming' (2:28). The reason for the confidence is that already in this world we have a resemblance to Christ, for we are in mutual union and indwelling with God, just as Christ *is*...Already we are children of God, just as Christ is... In other words the author is repeating the reason he gave for confidence when he first spoke about the parousia: 'We are God's children right now' (3:2)." This illustrates quite well the impact of theology on interpretation, whether consciously or unconsciously. Brown thinks in terms of a "Judgment Day" in which the fact of our being God's children is decisive for our eternal destiny, whereas for John there is no such judgment (John 5:24). Brown misses the New Testament teaching of a judgment for Christians only, in which not their eternal destiny but their future rewards are determined (see 1 Corinthians 3:11-15, where even the man whose works are burned up is "saved" [verse 15]). Thus the statement of 3:2 does not connect directly with John's statement about **boldness in the day of judgment**. As a result, Brown overlooks the fact that the lifestyle of love described in the *immediately preceding context* is the grounds for this boldness. Brown does not seem to detect the progression of Johannine thought from 2:28 through 4:16.

[15] Cf. BGD, p. 441.

[16] Unfortunately, the standard Greek critical editions of First John omit the Greek word *Him*. The evidence for this omission is quite slender in terms of the Greek manuscripts. Only the famous codices, Alexandrinus (A) and Vaticanus (B), plus nine later manuscripts are cited in UBS, 4th ed. (along with some minimal

versionary evidence, plus Augustine [various times])–out of the approximately six hundred known manuscripts containing the Johannine Epistles in whole or in part. The accidental omission of the Greek word for *Him* (*auton*) was no doubt made in an early copy from which most of the few Greek manuscripts omitting it are probably derived. However, a simple scribal error like this might occur more than once, since short words were quite frequently dropped by the scribes. Nevertheless, the omission is followed in many modern translations (e.g., RSV, NASB, NIV, JB, etc.).

CHAPTER 8

Conclusion: How to Live Obediently

(1 John 4:20–5:17)

John no doubt intended his letter to be read publicly to all the members of each congregation—even if the addressed readers of First John were the elders, or leaders, of the church or churches to which this letter went. This public reading would have a twofold effect. First, it would buttress the authority of the local leadership so that they could stand more effectively against the Revisionists. Since the author was an apostle, his endorsement both of their doctrine and personal qualifications (cf. 2:12-14) was vital. But second, it would make the letter a teaching vehicle to all the Christians who heard it, and later to untold millions who would read, study, and hear it preached.

Since the apostle John was unquestionably one of the greatest teachers the church has ever had, he must have known perfectly well that the level of experience he described might seem hard to some of the less mature in his audience. In the final segment of his epistle, which serves as a conclusion to all that has gone before, the writer addresses the practical concerns that his teaching on Christian experience might raise.

V. CONCLUSION: LEARNING HOW TO LIVE OBEDIENTLY (4:20–5:17)

A. What Loving Our Brothers Means (4:20–5:3a)

John's first step in addressing the issue of *how* we can actually love one another as God has commanded us to do, is to clarify what it really means to love our Christian brothers and sisters. In the process, potential excuses for not doing so are dealt with.

> **20If someone says, "I love God," and hates his brother, he is a liar; for he who does not love his brother whom he has seen, how can he love God whom he has not seen?**

One of the easiest ways to avoid responsibility is to sidestep it. As a traveling teacher, John must have encountered many examples of this.

When convicted of lovelessness toward his Christian brothers, the guilty Christian might evade the issue by saying, "Well, at least **I love God!**"

As we have insisted in this Commentary (see especially under 4:7-8), those who claim that a Christian *cannot* hate fellow Christians, are living in a dream world. Their theology has support neither from Scripture nor from experience and is an exercise in futility. To deny the capacity of a regenerate person to hate is to prepare the way for massive self-deception, not to mention the deception of others. Those who think like this must lie to themselves about the lovelessness of which their own hearts are all too aware. This is why their theological assertions should not be taken seriously by any attentive reader of John's Epistle. A verse such as the present one suggests the possibility of hate by one brother for another. Every discerning pastor understands this!

To a Christian it might seem easier to **love God whom he has not seen** than to **love his brother whom he has seen**. This is due to the simple fact that while **God** seems perfectly deserving of our **love**, our **brother** often does not. We can easily *see* all the faults that *he* has! But we must not forget that, for John, **love** is *not* basically an emotional word. This particular Greek verb (*agapaō*) is often rather colorless; it does not have the passionate overtones of the verb for romantic love (Greek: *eraō*) or the implied warmth of the word for affectionate, or friendly, love (Greek: *phileō*). The related New Testament Greek noun (*agapē*) has been found so far only once in secular literature.[1]

For John, "to love" is to behave in a way that meets the need of one's fellow Christian (see 3:16-18 and the discussions there). To hate, therefore, is to refuse to meet our brother's need (3:16-17). There can be no doubt that our emotional reactions to our fellow Christians can profoundly affect how we act (whether in love or hate). Still, it is by our *actions*, rather than our *feelings*, that John assesses the reality of our love for one another: we are to love "in deed" and therefore "in truth" (3:18). Our emotions normally follow our actions, so that when we repeatedly override our negative emotions toward others by acting in love toward them, we usually find those emotions subsiding and even changing. Of course, we need God's help in all this! John will speak of that shortly (cf. 5:14-17).

But since *action*, not *emotion*, is the critical issue in Christian love, it is obvious that there is actually no basic difference between expressing our love for **God** and our love for our Christian **brother,** since the test of our love for *Him* is our obedience to His commandments (see discussion under 4:19). If we do not obey God's commandments, we do not **love** Him, no matter what we say or feel. Thus the person who says, "**I love God,**" but does **not** obey God's command to **love his brother, is a liar.** No profession of deep feelings can substitute for actual obedience.

> **²¹And this commandment we have from Him: that he who loves God *must* love his brother also.**

John now states clearly the connection between love for **God** and love for one's **brother.** The two things are in fact part of the same **commandment.** The **commandment** is so stated that the presence of one kind of love necessitates the presence of the other.

It is possible, of course, that when John refers to **this commandment** which **we have from Him,** he is thinking of a specific command given by Jesus which is not recorded in the New Testament. After all, John himself in his Gospel reports only a small fraction of the things actually spoken by our Lord (cf. John 20:30; 21:25). An otherwise unrecorded **commandment** may well be what John has in mind.

But it is just as likely that the form in which John expresses **this commandment** is determined by such statements as those recorded in John 14:19-21 and 23 (see discussion above under 4:19). Since these statements by Jesus insist that obedience to His commandments is the test of His disciples' love for Him, then the presence of true love for Him dictates love for our brethren. Very close to our present verse is the command spoken by Jesus in John 14:15, "If you love Me, keep My commandments."

There is no word corresponding to the NKJV's ***must*** in John's text. More literally the command may be translated: **that he who loves God *love* his brother also.** But the English word *love* by itself would be a rare use of the English subjunctive in an indirect command. (Compare, for example, "My instructions are that he *finish* his homework.") Perhaps instead of the **must** of the NKJV we could translate: **that he who loves God *should* love his brother also.**

1 JOHN 5

¹Whoever believes that Jesus is the Christ is born of God, and everyone who loves Him who begot also loves him who is begotten of Him.

The chapter break in our Bibles is unfortunate since John is continuing the discussion begun in chapter 4. A Christian cannot truly say he loves God unless he also loves his Christian brother (4:20-21). Nor can the Christian evade this command by claiming that he does not know who his brother is. In the simplest possible terms his brother is **Whoever believes that Jesus is the Christ**.

We can recall here the evasion used by the Jewish lawyer when trying to address the law's demand, "You shall love...your neighbor as yourself." When Jesus said, "You have answered rightly; do this and you will live," the lawyer replied, "And who is my neighbor?" (Luke 10:27-29). It is a natural response, when people feel their guilt, to attempt to soften the extent of their failure by defining the responsibility away. The apostle will not allow his readers to do this.

John's definition of a Christian brother is simple and direct. **Whoever** (there are no exceptions!) **believes that Jesus is the Christ is born of God**. In this verse John recalls the thematic statement of his Gospel. There, speaking of the reason for recording the miracles ("signs") contained in his book, he writes, "...but these are written that you may believe that Jesus is the Christ, the Son of God, and that believing you may have life in His name" (20:31). There is no other way that John ever defines a Christian.

Of course, many modern theologians do it differently. So do more than a few expositors of this epistle. But a Christian is *not defined* by lifestyle, good works, or obedience to God. A Christian is defined only by faith in Christ.

This strips a well-known excuse from the hands of those who might wish to use it: "I don't need to love *him*. The way *he* lives he could not possibly be a Christian!" The church has more than a few "fruit inspectors" like this, who are more than ready to tell us who is saved and who is not. But many such "inspectors" have never been born again *themselves,* because they have never understood the grace of a God who "imputes righteousness apart from works" (Romans 4:6).

When it comes to loving a Christian brother, whether or not he is living worthily of his Christian faith is totally irrelevant. My reason for loving him has nothing to do with his performance. The real reason is now stated by the apostle: **everyone who loves Him who begot also loves him who is begotten of Him**. Why do I love the child of God? Because I love the Father of that child! And if I do *not love* the child, I am simply lying if I say that I *love* his Father (4:20).

> ²**By this we know that we love the children of God, when we love God and keep His commandments.**

The apostle now makes explicit what was implicit already in the discussion thus far (4:20–5:1). If I want to **know** whether I really **love the children of God**, this can be truly verified if I **love God and keep His commandments**. Here the words **By this** refer forward and are explained by the clause beginning with **when**.²

At first glance this seems almost to reverse what John has been saying.³ Earlier he had declared that a claim like "I love God" (4:20) is falsified if I hate my brother. Now he says that my love for **the children of God** is verified by my love for **God**. Of course, there is no contradiction. The key to both perspectives is wrapped up in keeping God's **commandments** (see next verse). Since **God** has commanded us to love one another, I cannot say that I love God if I do not keep that commandment. But by the same token, obedience to God by keeping **His commandments** is the way I demonstrate that I *do* love my brother, since love for my brother is one of those **commandments**.

But this new perspective subtly introduces a new thought. John does not speak here of a single commandment (as he did in 3:23 and 4:21), but rather of keeping God's **commandments**, plural. It is not merely our obedience to the specific command to love our brother that shows we do love him, though it is true that specific acts of love must be a part of the whole process (cf. 3:18-19). Rather it is our obedience to all that God commands of us that verifies **that we love the children of God**. This is an important concept.

What better thing can I do for my Christian brothers than to live a life of obedience to God before them? It is true this will move me to reach out to any whose need I might be able to meet. But it is also true that the model of a life devoted to the Lord does even more for my brother than any single act of love can do. As my brother observes this model of obedience, I am actually showing him the kind of life which he most needs to experience. By my example, I am aiming him toward, or confirming him in, the pathway which will best meet any personal needs he has. Thus, while God is pleased with what I do (cf. 3:22), my brother also is truly served. The plural word **commandments** is therefore a point of real significance in John's discussion.

> **3aFor this is the love of God, that we keep His commandments.**

Not surprisingly, John now insists that **the love of God** is fundamentally a matter of keeping **His commandments**.

The NKJV translation (**the love of God**) might easily be misread as God's **love** for us (subjective genitive). Though the Greek permits this idea, it is certainly not the correct one in this context. Instead, we should understand the phrase as referring to *our* **love** for God (objective genitive, cf. verse 2). John is here following a series of steps, for which this statement is the climax. First we are told that the person who "loves Him who begot [i.e., God] also loves him who is begotten of Him [i.e., the child of God]" (5:1). Next we are told that the person who loves "the children of God" is the one who loves God and keeps His commandments (5:2). Finally we are told here that **love** for **God** consists in keeping **His commandments**. The result of this sequence is to point up the fact that when we **keep** God's **commandments** we can know (1) that we love God and (2) that we love the children of God.

John does not leave us adrift on a sea of emotional introspection. Our internal feelings are often unreliable indicators of our spiritual state. We should test our lives always by God's **commandments** and not by whether we have what we imagine to be the required emotional response. Of course, some of our feelings are definitely wrong and we should lay them aside, as Peter advises us (cf. 1 Peter 2:1). But we should be careful not to measure our love for God or our brothers by some perceived failure to rise to a high level of emotional response to Him or to them. The only relevant question then is, "Am I doing what God has commanded me to do?"

The final words of this verse introduce a new subsection. They should actually be read with the next verse and will be considered there.

B. What Actually Empowers Our Love (5:3b-15)

If love for our fellow Christians actually boils down to keeping God's commandments, how can we do that? Is that a difficult, or even impossible, task? The apostle will now address this natural concern which every Christian feels at one time or another.

> ³ᵇAnd His commandments are not burdensome. ⁴For whatever is born of God overcomes the world. And this is the victory that has overcome the world—our faith.

In the NKJV translation, the closing words of verse 3 are made into a complete sentence. But this is not at all likely to represent the Greek correctly since this verse starts with the Greek subordinating conjunction *hoti* (*because*; translated here as *For*). It would be much better to read the text this way: **And His commandments are not burdensome,** *because* **whatever is born of God overcomes the world.**⁴

If both love for God and love for our brethren can be summarized by obedience to God's commands, the next obvious question is, "But aren't those commands really hard?" In fact, just such a claim might have been made by the Revisionists about the commands Christians were taught to keep. As we have already suggested, the Revisionists may have taught that both light and darkness could be found in God, and so Christians could participate in both without moral concern. If they did teach something like this, they may have argued that Christianity was too rigid and **burdensome.** If so, John would be conscious of contradicting them here. Indeed the following verses (5:6 ff.) suggest that the Revisionists are in his mind.

In any case, John asserts clearly that **His commandments are not burdensome** (verse 3b). Of course, the Lord Jesus Himself had said this in His well-known words, "'For My yoke is easy and My burden is light'" (Matthew 11:30). So John is echoing the words of his Savior when he affirms that the Christian life is not at all an overwhelming yoke or burden. The reason for this is now given.

The reason God's commands **are not burdensome** is because **whatever is born of God overcomes the world**. It is striking that John does not say "whoever" but **whatever** (Greek: *to gegennēmenon*, neuter gender).[5] This suggests that there is something inherently world-conquering in the very experience of being **born of God**. We are now immediately told what this is: **and this is the victory that has overcome the world— our faith**. (The *MajT* edition prints the reading *humōn*, "your" instead of the "our" [= *hēmōn*] of the NKJV. But the evidence of the *MajT* is divided here and the original reading is uncertain. We comment on the NKJV text in this place since "your" would scarcely affect the meaning.)

In full accord with his own theology elsewhere, John is here telling us that **our faith** in Christ (cf. next verse) **has** already **overcome the world**, since **whatever is born of God** is the product of that **faith** (cf. 5:1).[6] **The world** is a system that is hostile to God (2:15-17). Since the world's representatives, the antichrists, deny "that Jesus is the Christ" (2:22), it is a great victory to believe this truth and so to be born again. With every instance of new birth, the satanically inspired world system suffers a significant and permanent defeat.

In fact the Bible presents Satan as actively engaged in trying to prevent people from coming to faith in Christ (cf. 2 Corinthians 4:3-4; Luke 8:5, 12). Whenever a person is born again he can be said to have been "delivered...from the power of darkness and conveyed...into the kingdom of the Son of His love" (Colossians 1:13). He has been turned "from darkness to light, and from the power of Satan to God" (Acts 26:18). Since **the world** "lies under the sway of the wicked one" (5:19), every defeat the wicked one suffers is a defeat for **the world**.

Thus, the very fact of new birth is a spectacular **victory** accomplished by **our faith**. **Victory** over **the world** is, so to speak, a constituent element in **whatever is born of God**. It hardly needs to be said that this initial victory does not *guarantee* subsequent victory in Christian living. John's point is that the victory achieved by the very fact of new birth makes obedience to God's commands an achievable goal. His readers should not regard these commands as impossibly **burdensome**, but doable with God's help (see 5:14-15 and discussion there). Neither here nor

216

in Revelation 2 and 3 are believers regarded as automatic "overcomers" in Christian experience. The *seeds* of victory are found in our new birth; but, as the whole New Testament testifies, these must be nurtured until they ripen into mature, victorious Christian living.

> ⁵**Who is he who overcomes the world, but he who believes that Jesus is the Son of God?**

Very specifically John now identifies the "world-conqueror" (**he who overcomes the world**) as one and the same as **he who believes that Jesus is the Son of God**. This belief has saved that person, brought to pass his regeneration to eternal life (cf. John 20:30-31), and constituted him a "world-conqueror" (see discussion under previous verse).

The Greek constructions here translated as **he who overcomes** (Greek: *ho nikōn*) and **he who believes** (Greek: *ho pisteuōn*) consist of present participles preceded by the Greek article. This construction in Greek is essentially timeless and characterizes an individual (or, individuals) by some act or acts he has (or, they have) performed, without specifying how often these were done or even whether they still continue. In this respect such statements have their closest analogy to many English nouns (often ending in –er) that express completed and/or ongoing action. For example, "he is a murderer," "she is a cheater," "he is a supporter," "she is a winner."⁷ In such cases, the person may be described this way based on *one instance* of murder, cheating, support, or winning, or on the basis of many such acts.

John is thus saying that "the overcomer of the world" is one and the same as "the believer in Jesus Christ, God's Son." As is made clear by the past tense of verse 4 (*"has* overcome") this is *already true!* But since John is discussing the fact that keeping God's commandments is not "burdensome" (verse 3b), the implication is that such victory can continue and that the key to it is *faith!* This implication will be developed a little further on by John (cf. verses 12-13), but for now he must pause to clarify an essential point related to this faith, which was evidently challenged by the Revisionists.

In suggesting, as he does here, that the key to the Christian life is *faith*, John stands (as he so often does) on Pauline ground. Was it not Paul who said, "...and the life which I now live in the flesh, I live *by faith* in the

Son of God, who loved me and gave Himself for me" (Galatians 2:20; italics added)? The writer of Hebrews also taught this in his famous chapter on faith (Hebrews 11). It is an impressive fact that just as the Christian life *begins* at the moment of saving faith in Christ, so also that life is *lived* by faith in Him: "For we walk by faith, not by sight" (2 Corinthians 5:7).

John is now leading his readers toward a fresh understanding of this vital truth.

> **⁶This is He who came by water and blood—Jesus Christ; not only by water, but by water and blood. And it is the Spirit who bears witness, because the Spirit is truth.**

The meaning of this text has been much discussed. It is reported in some ancient Christian literature that there was a certain Cerinthus who lived in Asia Minor. He is said to have taught that Jesus was a mere man and that the divine Christ descended on Him at His baptism and left Him at the cross. Thus only the human Jesus, not the divine Christ, died and rose. This ancient Christian literature also portrays Cerinthus as an arch-foe of the apostle John.[8]

This information is likely to be essentially true. It certainly satisfactorily explains the statements of this verse. (Of course, Cerinthus himself need not be in view in First John, but rather people who were his theological forerunners.) Under this understanding of the verse, the reference to **water** is a reference to the *baptism* of Jesus, while the reference to **blood** is a reference to His *death*. These two occasions are of course the two horizons of His earthly ministry as the Messiah, or **Christ**. Thus it can be said that **He came by water and blood**. That is, these two events were focal points to His coming to earth to carry out His Messianic work.

With this understanding, the Greek phrase **by water and blood** (*di hydatos kai haimatos*) should be understood as using the Greek preposition *dia* in its well-recognized usage called "attendant circumstance."[9] So we might translate it *with respect to, in relationship to*, or something similar. John is saying that **Jesus Christ** (one person) **came** (His whole first advent) *in relationship to* **water and blood**. That is, He came to be baptized and to die. Not just to be baptized, however (**not only by water**), as the Revisionists probably taught. But also *to die* (**but by water *and* blood**).

The baptism of Jesus should be given its full significance here. In the New Testament it is evidently the formal inauguration of Jesus as the messianic Savior, i.e., as the **Christ**. Since the Hebrew and Greek words for Messiah indicated "the Anointed One," Peter describes "Jesus of Nazareth" as the One whom "God anointed...with the Holy Spirit and with power" (Acts 10:38). No doubt this occurred at the baptism. In fact, we are told in the Fourth Gospel that the Holy Spirit attested to the Messianic identity of Jesus by descending and remaining on Him at His baptism (John 1:33). Therefore, John the Baptist said, "'I have seen and testified that this is the Son of God'" (John 1:34). We have already seen the Holy Spirit referred to by John as an "anointing" (cf. 2:20, 27). His abiding presence on and with **Jesus Christ** was the sign of our Lord's messianic office.

The words **it is the Spirit who bears witness** accurately describe the role of the Holy Spirit at the baptism of Jesus. (The Father also bore witness, of course, by speaking from heaven, "This is My beloved Son, in whom I am well pleased" [Matthew 3:17].) It is quite possible that the Revisionists distorted the event of the baptism by making **the Spirit** represent the "divine Christ" who descended on the human Jesus at that time, only to leave Him when He died on the cross.[10] If this is what they taught, then John's words correct a misrepresentation of the Holy Spirit's role in relationship to the messiahship of Jesus. **The Spirit** is a witness, but He remains a distinct Person not to be identified as the **Christ**.

Moreover, the Spirit's testimony is reliable **because the Spirit is truth**. **The Spirit** can be said to be **truth** in much the same sense as "God is love" (cf. 4:8). The very nature and character of **the Spirit** is to be truthful and therefore His testimony can be relied on.

In the light of this verse it is possible to surmise what the more specific theology of some, or all, of the Revisionists may have been. As we have seen throughout this epistle, they claimed that Jesus was *not* the Christ (2:22). Quite possibly then, the Revisionists regarded the "Christ" as a spiritual being (the Spirit?) who descended on the man Jesus at His baptism but left Him to die alone. Thus, the work of the cross was not a sacrifice offered up by God's Son, but the death of a mere man. Therefore, what saving value could it have?

This may have been as well the basis on which the Revisionists challenged the assurance of the readers that they had eternal life (cf. 2:25 with 26 and see discussions there). Those who believed that Jesus was the Christ would then be believing a falsehood. Hence they were not born of God as apostolic doctrine taught that they were (cf. 5:1).

That this was a grave and fundamental challenge to basic Christianity is obvious indeed. If the readers' belief that Jesus is the Son of God was false (cf. verse 5) there had been no victory over the world through that faith (cf. verses 4-5). Moreover, there was no hope of ongoing victory over the world if the fundamental faith of the Christian readers had been misplaced.

John obviously had to deal with this issue directly before proceeding with his discussion of victorious Christian living.

> **[7]For there are three that bear witness [in heaven: the Father, the Word, and the Holy Spirit; and these three are one. [8]And there are three that bear witness on earth:] the Spirit, the water, and the blood; and these three agree as one.**

These verses are famous because they involve the addition of material that is inadequately attested by the Greek manuscripts. The words enclosed above in brackets are well known because they were first introduced into an early printed edition of the Greek New Testament by Erasmus, the editor.[11] They are often called 'The Johannine Comma' and they became part of the KJV when they were adopted by the translators of the first edition of 1611. But they are not found in the overwhelming majority of the surviving Greek manuscripts of First John. Although a few writers have tried to defend them, their absence from virtually all Greek manuscripts (with the exception of a few late ones) cannot readily be explained. Without a credible explanation for their disappearance from most Greek manuscripts, their absence from these is a fatal argument against their originality.

This is the only place in this Commentary where it becomes necessary to set forth the text in a way substantially different from the NKJV. To do this properly requires also that the revised material be connected with the last sentence of verse 6. We will now give this text in revised form so that we may comment on it:

> [6b]And it is the Spirit who bears witness, because the Spirit is truth—[7]because there are three that bear witness: [8]the Spirit, the water, and the blood; and these three agree as one.

John has affirmed that **the Spirit** *is* reliable—He is **truth**—and this is not just **because** of His nature as **truth**, but also **because** His testimony follows the biblical law of verification which required two or three witnesses. This Old Testament principle appears in various places in the New Testament, for example in Matthew 18:16, "'By the mouth of two or three witnesses every word will be established'" (cf. Deuteronomy 17:6; 19:15; John 8:17-18). Of particular interest for the present text is John 5:31-40 where the three witnesses are: (1) John the Baptist (verses 33-35), (2) Jesus' works (verse 36), and (3) the Father through the Scriptures (verses 37-39).

In the text before us, the Spirit's truthful testimony is supported by testimony from the baptism (**the water**) and from the crucifixion (**the blood**). John is likely to be thinking here of the fact that these historical events stand fully authenticated in their own right and thus add two further witnesses to that of **the Spirit**. It must be remembered that the epistle began with the claim that the truth "concerning the word of Life" had been verified by the direct apostolic experience of seeing, hearing, gazing on, and touching the realities involved (1:1-2). Perhaps he refrains here from a direct appeal to this apostolic testimony precisely because he and his fellow apostles were far from being the only witnesses to these events. We must remember that this was the first age of the church and many witnesses to the events of our Lord's life and death were still alive. Paul, in fact, once claimed as evidence for the resurrection of Jesus Christ the experience of "over five hundred brethren at once," of whom he could say "the greater part remain to the present" (1 Corinthians 15:6).

There was thus no reason to disbelieve the events surrounding the baptism and the death of Jesus, since they were so firmly attested that they themselves could be said to **bear witness** along with **the Spirit** and to be fully in accord with Him: **these three agree as one**. Behind John's words stands the fact that at *the baptism* God spoke from heaven to declare, "'This is My beloved Son, in whom I am well pleased'" (Matthew 3:17). John the Baptist personally "bore witness" to this event and to its meaning (cf. John 1:32-34) as well. In addition, *the crucifixion* was foreseen by the Scriptures (cf. John 13:18; 19:24, 28, 36, 37) and was attested by apostolic witnesses (John 19:35; 21:24, where one should note the "*we know*"). Thus **the water** and **the blood** are fully attested in their own right, both by divine testimony and by witnesses divinely called to do so.

What John is doing here is similar to what we do when we say that the resurrection of Jesus Christ is a witness to His deity and to the completeness of His sacrificial work. We mean, of course, that the resurrection is so well authenticated that it counts as "evidence." Thus **the Spirit, the water, and the blood** all **agree** that the Person who was baptized and crucified, Jesus Christ, is indeed "the Son of God" (cf. verse 5). They bear concordant testimony to the single, indivisible identity of Jesus Christ.

> **⁹If we receive the witness of men, the witness of God is greater; for this is the witness of God which He has testified of His Son.**

God has borne witness to the identity of Jesus Christ, His Son, through "the Spirit, the water, and the blood" (verses 7-8). But there is something further that **He has testified of His Son**, which John is about to state.

The opening words of the verse probably look both backward and forward. Their backward reference would be to the testimony specified in verses 7-8. Their forward reference will be to the witness of God that is stated in verses 11-12. They make the point that inasmuch as we do receive human testimony and treat it as valid, how much more should we be able to do this with **the witness of God** which, considering the Source, is obviously **greater** and thus much more deserving of reception.

The conditional statement, **If we receive the witness of men**, is presented in Greek in a form that takes the matter for granted. John does not mean to say that we *always* accept human testimony, but that in fact we *do* do so. He is probably thinking again of the Jewish rule of witness that required two or three witnesses to be considered valid (see discussion under verses 7-8). His point is that if we can regard **the witness of men** as valid when adequately supported, surely **the witness of God** should be treated as valid too.

But God has given additional testimony about **His Son**. That this too had all the requirements for valid testimony is not explicitly stated. But John claims that **God has testified of His Son** and the words that follow in verses 11-12 show that this testimony is derived directly from words spoken by Jesus Himself in the hearing of the apostles. Since Jesus is "the Son of God" (cf. verse 5), properly attested as such (verses 6-8), His own words are equivalent to the very words of **God**. John hardly needs to state here that these words (which he now draws on) were attested to by the other apostolic hearers of them as well. In a sense, however, he has *already said* this when, in the prologue, he states, "That which *we* have seen and *heard we* declare to you" (1:3; italics added).

John will now state this further testimony from **God** (verses 11-12), after a brief but significant observation in the next verse.

> **¹⁰He who believes in the Son of God has the witness in himself; he who does not believe God has made Him a liar, because he has not believed the testimony that God has given of His Son.**

These words should probably have been placed in parentheses by the NKJV. They constitute a brief side comment before the "witness of God" is actually stated (cf. verse 11). In this comment John draws the contrast between believing and not believing **the testimony** about God's **Son**.

The phrase **believes in** (Greek: *pisteuō eis*) reflects an expression which is extremely common in the Fourth Gospel (cf. John 1:12; 2:11, 23; 3:15-16, 18, 36; and *passim*) and is a standard way for John to convey the idea of faith in Jesus for eternal life. (Efforts have been made to claim that "spurious" faith is indicated in John 2:23; 8:30; and 12:42, but all these attempts are without valid support in John's text and represent an effort to read into his text a preconceived theology.)[12] The idea of "believing *in*" Jesus is identical in force with the idea of "believing *that* [Greek: *hoti*] Jesus is the Christ" (John 11:27; 20:31; cf. 8:24; 13:19). This is shown by the fact that either Greek construction can be said to express the means of receiving eternal life (cf. 20:30-31 with John 3:15-16, 18, etc.). One should compare 1 John 5:1 above, "Whoever believes *that* [Greek: *hoti*] Jesus is the Christ is born of God" (see discussion there).

The person who exercises this faith, John says, **has the witness in himself**. That is to say, God's testimony about **His Son**, which John will state in the next verse, is *internalized* when a person **believes in the Son of God**. This statement reflects the New Testament recognition that when the word of God in the gospel is believed, that word is a life-giving seed planted within the believer. (Cf. 1 Peter 1:23 and Luke 8:11-15 where "the seed is the word of God" and the ground on which it falls is the human heart.)

By contrast, the person **who does not believe God** (that is, disbelieves **the testimony that God has given of His Son**) for all intents and purposes **makes** God out to be **a liar**. This is true because he is saying, in effect, that God's **testimony** is false. It is clear that the issue for John is very simply the truth or falsity of what God says about **His Son**. Neither here nor anywhere else does John introduce the complications often proposed by theologians. There is nothing here about "head or heart belief," or about a "faith that yields to God as over against mere intellectual assent," etc. The Bible does not complicate faith like that. Once we have understood the message, the issue is: Is it true or false? Do we believe it, or do we not?

> [11]**And this is the testimony: that God has given us eternal life, and this life is in His Son.** [12]**He who has the Son has life; he who does not have the Son of God does not have life.**

These two verses are best considered as a unit. The words **and this is the testimony** should be taken as covering both verses which, taken together, state God's testimony about **His Son**.

The connection between this opening statement and the final statement of verse 9 is partly obscured by the use of the word "witness" in verse 9 and the word **testimony** here. The Greek word in both places is *marturia*, which can be rendered both ways. It may help the reader of this Commentary if we set out the text a bit differently than in NKJV, as follows:

> [9b]for this is the *testimony* of God which He has testified of His Son—[10]he who believes in the Son of God has the witness in himself; he who does not believe God has made Him a liar, because he has not believed the testimony that God has given of His Son—[11]and this is the testimony:...

From this layout it is easier to see that verse 10 serves as a parenthesis and that the statement in verse 9b is picked up again in verse 11.

What then is God's **testimony?** It consists of two closely related affirmations. The first is an affirmation about what God has bestowed (verse 11), and the second is an affirmation about the exclusive character of this bestowal (verse 12).

It must be remembered here that First John is not an evangelistic tract. It is written to people who "know the truth," not to people who "do not know" it (cf. 2:22 and 2:12-14, and discussions in both places). The **testimony** of God is thus phrased in terms of what was *actually true* of John and his readers, not in terms of what *could be true*. In other words, it was not an *offer* of eternal life as John 20:30-31 is, but rather a *confirmation* of what God had actually done for them. That this is the case is verified by verse 13.

According to the divine **testimony**, it can be said **that God has given us eternal life** and that this gift is bestowed **in His Son.** And since this gift is bestowed **in His Son**, its only possessor is the person who possesses **the Son**, since **He who has the Son has life**; but, **he who does not have the Son does not have life**.

As we have seen, the Revisionists appear to have called into question the readership's belief that they possessed **eternal life** (cf. 2:25 and discussion there). And since the Revisionists also denied that Jesus was the Christ, the Son of God (cf. 2:22), they would quite naturally have affirmed that there was no *eternal life* available in Jesus. Thus, in the eyes of the Revisionists, John's readers did not really possess such life. In all probability they taught that *eternal life* (or, what passed for such in their theology) was to be sought somewhere else.

John counters all this by asserting that he and his readers *do* have **eternal life** because **God** has **given** it to them **in His Son** and that this **life** is to be found *in Him and nowhere else*. If someone doesn't **have the Son**, that person doesn't **have** this **life**.

It should be noted that the concept of "having" the *Son* is not found in John's Gospel. Of course, it is implicit in Jesus' words to Thomas in the Upper Room, "I am…the life" (John 14:6; see also John 11:25-26). If *He* is the life, then one who has life will also have *Him*. But in the Fourth Gospel this never becomes an explicit way of describing the experience of new birth. (Of course, the idea of "having" is common there [cf. John 3:15-16, 36; 5:24; 6:40, 47; 10:10; etc.].) John's particular way of phrasing the issue here seems clearly dictated by his desire to cut off any suggestion that **this life** can be found anywhere other than **in God's Son**.

When one considers **the testimony** of God, based on all that John and his fellow apostles had heard (cf. 1:1, 3), one could correctly conclude that Jesus Christ, and He alone, is the repository for the gift of **eternal life**, and that apart from Him no one possesses that **life**. One recalls here the words, apparently of John the Baptist, "He who does not believe the Son shall not see life" (John 3:36).

> [13]These things I have written to you who believe in the name of the Son of God, that you may know that you have eternal life, and that you may *continue to* believe in the name of the Son of God.

The reason John has been speaking about the "testimony that God has given of His Son" (verses 6-12) is to assure the readership that they do indeed **have eternal life** and to encourage continuing faith **in His name**.

Strangely enough, the idea has taken hold in some circles that the words **These things** refer to the contents of the whole epistle. This view is a centerpiece for the school of thought that treats the entire epistle as a test of its readers' salvation. We have already noted how completely far afield this perspective really is (cf. 2:12-14 and the discussions there). So far from wanting the readership to engage in self-examination to see if they are born again, the writer proclaims the high level of their spiritual attainments (again, cf. 2:12-14, 21).

The view, therefore, that the epistle is intended to test the validity of the readers' eternal salvation, is an idea that grotesquely distorts the actual intention of the author, whose focus is on fellowship (1:3).

The phrase **These things** (Greek: *Tauta*) by no means refers to the entire content of the epistle, but rather to verses 6 through 12. Indeed, this near reference is consistent with John's style elsewhere in the letter.[13] Thus in 1:4, the words "these things [Greek: *tauta*] we write to you" refer to what has just been mentioned in the prologue (1:1-3). In 2:1, the statement "these things [Greek: *tauta*] I write to you, so that you may not sin," refer to the previous discussion on sin found in 1:5-10. In the same way, the words of 2:26, "these things [Greek: *Tauta*] I have written to you concerning those who try to deceive you," obviously refer to the preceding discussion about the antichrists in 2:18-25.

In considering this, it is important to note the progress of John's thought in 5:6-12. A brief summary will help us do this.

According to verse 5, the "world-conqueror" is the one who "believes that Jesus is the Son of God." But when one believes this, he is believing in the one, indivisible Person of Jesus Christ whose messianic coming was marked by His baptism and His crucifixion (verse 6a). To this reality, witness has been borne by the Holy Spirit and the historical events of His baptism and death themselves (verse 6b-8). Furthermore, God has given additional testimony to His Son, and this testimony assures us that He has imparted eternal life to us in His Son, in whom alone this gift can be found (verses 9-12). It follows from this that those who have believed in the Son's name can know, on God's testimony, that they do indeed have **eternal life** (verse 13).

The words **to you who believe in the name of the Son of God** do *not* mean **to** those of **you who believe**. There are, of course, ways of conveying that idea in Greek (e.g., *tois ex hymōn*), but none of them is used here. Instead the Greek (*hymin tois pisteuousin*) simply means "to you believers." Never once, throughout his epistle, does John even hint that he thinks some of those he addresses might be unregenerate. Needless to say, he is not writing *to* the Revisionists, but *about* them (2:26).

John addresses his audience as "believers." Although the Revisionists are telling them that they do not have eternal life, John is reminding them that they do. It is their world-conquering faith in Jesus as the Son of God that has given them this, and God's testimony about His Son verifies this fact beyond all controversy or contradiction.

There are any number of statements in the Fourth Gospel that affirm this truth, but as an illustration it would be hard to do better than John 5:24, "'Most assuredly, I say to you, he who hears My word and believes [in] Him who sent Me has everlasting life, and shall not come into judgment, but has passed from death to life.'" (The word *in* [NKJV] does not appear in the Greek and should be left out.)

What is striking here is that the Lord Jesus speaks of those who hear *His* word and who *believe the One who sent* Him! That is to say, if they accept

His word as true they will be believing *God!* Thus He says, "'My doctrine is not mine, but His who sent Me'" (John 7:16). Similarly, "'I have many things to say and to judge concerning you, but He who sent Me is true; and I speak to the world those things which I heard from Him'" (John 8:26). And, "'I have not spoken on My own authority; but the Father who sent Me gave Me a command, what I should say and what I should speak'" (John 12:49). So the words of Jesus are the words of God.

But what kind of testimony does God give in John 5:24? Precisely the kind of testimony that John appeals to in 1 John 5:9-12. Namely, that the believer "has eternal life" and is in no danger of coming "into judgment," but has already "passed from death into life." This testimony from God, spoken through the lips of His Son, is the kind of testimony John wishes his readers to rely on so that they will **know that** they **have eternal life**.

Of course, when they initially believed, they *knew* they had **eternal life**. In the same way, every believer *knows* at the point of saving faith that he has this **life**, because the promises he believes guarantee it (cf. John 11:25-26). But the believer is not immune to doubts and uncertainties after he is saved (cf. John the Baptist: Luke 7:18-19). The antidote to such doubts is always God's promises to the believer. These promises can always be referred to again and again as a fresh source of assurance. And no book of the Bible contains more of these straight forward guarantees than John's Gospel itself (John 3:16, 18, 36; 5:24; 6:35-40, 47; etc.). In our text, John is recalling his audience to the testimony of God that they have already believed, and to which he himself testified.

The logic of John's argument is evident. Since the believers he writes to have believed **in the name of the Son of God** (whose identity is attested by "the Spirit, the water, and the blood," verse 8), then they should rest securely on the testimony that God has given *about* and *through* His **Son**. This "testimony" (found in John 5:24 and in so many other places in John's Gospel) assures the believer that he does *have* **eternal life**. If Jesus said so, God said so—and there the matter should rest!

It should be said here that all true assurance of salvation and *eternal life* must rest on the "testimony of God," for only that testimony has full reliability and solidity. The many professing Christians who think that a more stable basis for assurance can be found in the lives they lead are only deceiving themselves. There is never a time at all in our Christian experience where we are free from sin (cf. 1 John 1:8). To suggest that Christian experience can stand on some relatively equal level with the "testimony of God" as a grounds for assurance is nearly a blasphemy, since it compares human experience in its multitude of flaws with the flawless word of God.

Those who are willing to look at themselves with complete honesty will find more grounds to doubt their salvation than to be assured of it. Some even teach that this uncertainty is healthy! But this does not reckon with the fact that the apostle John expected his readers to **know that** they had **eternal life**. The irony is that once Christian experience is made the grounds for assurance, as some hold First John does, John's statement in this verse about *knowing* becomes a complete impossibility!

The apostle here seeks to *reaffirm* the assurance of his readership. It was the *antichrists* who called that assurance into question!

There is no word in the Greek text for the words **continue to** in verse 13 (which the NKJV places in italics), but there is no reason to object to their introduction for clarity's sake. However, the statement of the Greek text is a shade more subtle than this, and we could translate as follows:

> These things I have written to you believers in the name of
> the Son of God...that you might believe in the name of the
> Son of God.

But if, as the verse also states, they can **know that** they **have eternal life**, why does he admonish them to believe? If the hearers/readers thought that this encouragement to faith was slightly redundant, since they already knew by faith that they were regenerated, they would be wrong. Nor is the reason simply so that they might not lose their assurance. That by itself *should* motivate ongoing faith, even though the loss of assurance does not result in the loss of eternal life. (For the security of the believer in God's Son, see especially John 6:35-40.) Still, the hearer or reader of this epistle might well wonder whether there was more to it than that.

As a matter of fact there was! This continuing faith was to have another object than the "testimony of God" about His gift of **life**. And that object of confidence is now stated.

**¹⁴Now this is the confidence that we have in Him, that
if we ask anything according to His will, He hears us.**

One simple fact now becomes clear. The "name of the Son of God"
(verse 13) can be believed in, not only for *eternal life*, but also for *answered
prayer*. This, too, Jesus had clearly taught His disciples.

While they were in the Upper Room, the Lord Jesus taught His disciples the effectiveness of His **name** in receiving answers to prayer. He
told them, "Most assuredly, I say to you, whatever you ask the Father *in
My name* He will give you. Until now you have asked nothing *in My name*.
Ask, and you will receive, that your joy may be full" (John 16:23b-24, italics
added; cf. also 14:13-14). Obviously, John's shift to the subject of prayer
after his reference to ongoing faith "in the name of the Son of God"
(verse 13), is a natural one, inasmuch as the Son's *name* was also the key to
answered prayer.

To do something in someone's name means to act on his authority
(cf. John 5:43; 10:25). It has nothing to do with simply tacking onto our
prayers a phrase like "in Jesus' name"! John's understanding of His Lord's
authorization to use His name in prayer is made clear in this verse—i.e.,
it means to **ask…according to His** (God's or Christ's) **will**. If this is
done, we can have **confidence that…He hears us**. The word for **confidence** here (Greek: *parrēsia*) is the same as the one in 3:21, which also
deals with prayer. Elsewhere in the epistle it is only used twice, 2:28 and
4:17, both in relation to the Judgment Seat of Christ. (For the essential
correlation between **confidence** in prayer and at the Judgment Seat, see
the discussion of this under 4:18.)

Christians are often puzzled because, in so many matters about which
they pray, they would have to confess that they are not sure that their
request is **according to His will**. How may a Christian know what God's
will is? There is one unmistakable way: His **will** is expressed in His "commandments" (cf. verse 3).

Earlier in this section of the epistle, the apostle has informed us that
love for God and love for our brothers in Christ all boil down to keeping
God's "commandments" (5:2-3a). Further, he has assured us that these
"commandments are not burdensome," because the one who is born of
God is a *world conqueror* by means of his faith that "Jesus is the Son of
God" (5:3b-5). The implication is clear that keeping God's commands is

possible, and therefore not "burdensome," by means of this kind of faith. But how is this so? The answer is now evident.

If our faith in the name of the Son of God enables us to "know that" we "have eternal life" (verse 13a), such belief can also produce further faith in His name, so that we can pray confidently in that name for matters that we know are **according to His will**. And since His *commandments* are the very expression of **His will** for us, we may be sure that we can pray for whatever help or enablement we need to carry them out. The next verse, therefore, follows naturally.

> [15]**And if we know that He hears us, whatever we ask, we know that we have the petitions that we have asked of Him.**

Suppose, then, that I come to God to ask for His help to love my Christian brothers and sisters. Can I expect God to hear and grant such a request? John's answer is emphatically in the affirmative.

Since God's command "to love one another" is beyond all doubt an expression of "His will" for us, if we ask for help to do this, we can **know** that we are being heard (cf. verse 14). And if, in any such matter which is "according to His will" (i.e., **whatever we ask** in His will), we are *heard*, **we** can also **know that we have the petitions** (requests) **that we have asked of Him**. If, therefore, the request is for assistance to *do* God's will by loving our fellow Christians, we can **know** that this assistance will be granted.

John's words, however, should not be misconstrued as though they promised an instantaneous response from God. To say that **we know that we have the petitions** is obviously not quite the same as saying we have the petitions already. John's point is that we can be perfectly confident, in the case of such prayers, that the **petitions** are ours. But of course, God sovereignly determines the means and the timing of His answers. It may well be that a prayer for assistance in keeping God's commands will result in a process of spiritual education that will lead us to the realization of the thing we have asked for. But the point remains: we should "believe in the name of the Son of God" as we pray for matters we know to be according to God's will. Thus, our obedience to God is empowered by a faith in Jesus as the Son of God whose *name* may be appealed to effectively in prayer. When we cast the burden of obedience on Him, His commandments are not "burdensome"!

This truth is also taught by Paul for whom victorious living involves "salvation" from God's temporal wrath against human sin (cf. Romans 1:18-31 with Romans 5:9-10). This can be realized through prayer as we call "on the *name* of the Lord" (Romans 10:13). All victorious Christian experience is totally dependent on the Christian's willingness to rely upon the power of the Risen Christ, whose exalted *name* is our only sufficient source of spiritual strength.

Although the larger context of verses 14-15, the unit covering 5:3b-15, shows that John particularly has in mind the issue he raised in 5:3b-5, the words of these two verses about prayer embody a principle even larger than our concern for living "according to His will." They include also the enormous possibilities for prayer wherever the will of God can be confidently known.

John will now illustrate how such prayer can be turned to the benefit of my Christian sister or brother.

C. What Faith and Love Can Do for Our Brother (5:16-17)

> ¹⁶If anyone sees his brother sinning a sin *which does* not *lead* to death, he will ask, and He will give him life for those who commit sin not *leading* to death. There is sin *leading* to death. I do not say that he should pray about that. ¹⁷All unrighteousness is sin, and there is sin not *leading* to death.

Although a believer in Christ has every right to be concerned about his own obedience to God's commandments, he cannot truly love **his** Christian **brother** if he is unconcerned about that brother's obedience. Indeed, if a Christian has learned to obey the command to love one another by finding the resources for this through prayer in Christ's name, what John advocates here will be an extremely natural extension of his prayer life.

As everywhere in John's Epistle, the words **his brother** refer to a real Christian.[14] The apostle knows only one brotherhood, a brotherhood consisting of everyone "who believes that Jesus is the Christ" (cf. 5:1 and discussion there). If, then, such a **brother** is seen **sinning a sin which does not lead to death**, Christian love should move one to pray for him.

In the phrase **a sin *which does* not *lead* to death**, the words *which does* and *lead* are supplied by the translators and are placed in italics by the NKJV. (This is also true of the word *leading* in verses 16 and 17.) There is nothing particularly wrong with this clarification, except that according to the Bible all **sin** can be said to *lead* to death (Proverbs 11:19; Romans 6:23; James 5:19-20; etc.). It might have been better to use a phrase like: ***which does* not *lead* directly (or immediately) to death**.

In the early Christian church it was known that God could, and sometimes did, inflict **death** more or less immediately in response to certain sins of Christians. The two obvious examples of this are (1) Ananias and Sapphira (Acts 5:1-11), and (2) the Christians at Corinth who ate the Lord's Supper with unconfessed sin in their lives (1 Corinthians 11:27-32). In both cases these deaths are treated as God's judgment and, in First Corinthians, the deaths ("many sleep") are directly attributed to God's chastening of His own people in contrast to the world (1 Corinthians 11:32). Insofar as we may be guided by these two instances, we may be correct in suggesting that **sin *leading* directly to death** is especially possible in cases of a severe breach of the sanctity of the Christian assembly.

The sin of Ananias and Sapphira in Acts 5 occurred in a church where the dynamic of Christian love and sharing were marked evidences of the work of the Spirit of God. This couple's crude effort to deceive their fellow Christians was ultimately lying "to the Holy Spirit" (Acts 5:3). In a similar way, though we do not know all that was involved at Corinth, we do know that there was a notable manifestation of selfishness there which included even drunkenness (1 Corinthians 11:21-22). Such misbehavior at the Lord's Table meant that the Supper was partaken of "in an unworthy manner." To do this was to be "guilty of the body and blood of the Lord" (1 Corinthians 11:27), a serious infraction indeed.

We might expect, therefore, to meet **sin *leading* directly to death** wherever there are serious breaches of what is Spirit-wrought or divinely ordained in the life of the church. But it is hardly possible to be more specific than that. However, John's statements here do not require us to positively identify **sin *leading* directly to death**. It is sufficient if we can identify some **sin *which does* not *lead*** directly **to death,** since it is only when a Christian **sees his brother sinning** in this way that he has an obligation to pray.

John states quite frankly that **there is sin *leading*** directly **to death** and that he is not saying (**I do not say**) that a Christian **should pray about that.** There is no command to **pray** for such **sin,** although equally it must be said that there is no command *not* to, either. In other words, if a Christian suspects that **sin *leading*** directly **to death** is being committed, he is free to pray for the sinning believer, but without any certainty about the outcome of his prayer. Still, as Jonah peevishly observed, God is "a gracious and merciful God, slow to anger and abundant in lovingkindness, One who relents from doing harm" (Jonah 4:2). Although there is no guarantee, it always remains possible that God might grant the sinning Christian repentance and "relent" from His judgment as He did with Nineveh.

John's words do indeed leave this option open, but this is not his major concern. He takes it for granted that it is often possible to recognize when a **brother** is **sinning a sin *which does* not *lead*** directly **to death.** Since most common sins among Christians (like envy, malice, evil speaking, etc.—cf. 1 Peter 2:1) are obviously *not* visited by swift **death,** there is plenty of scope for the kind of prayer John commands.

In fact, this is precisely what John says in verse 17: **all unrighteousness is sin, and there is sin not *leading*** [directly] **to death.** Thus, **unrighteousness** of every kind (it goes without saying that there are many kinds) belongs under the category of **sin,** and the category of **sin** not ***leading*** immediately **to death** actually exists. The assumption underlying this statement seems to be that his readership is fully aware of the need for such prayer. The many forms of **unrighteousness** which give no sign of being **sin *leading*** swiftly **to death** are comprehended in the apostle's command to **pray.**

What then may the Christian expect when he prays for cases where the **sin** is one ***which does* not *lead*** directly **to death?** John affirms that this prayer should take place (**he will ask** is essentially a command) and that as a result **He (God) will give...life for those who commit sin not *leading*** immediately **to death.** Since the **death** in question for the sinning **brother** is not eternal ("And whoever lives and believes in Me shall never die," John 11:26), there is no reason to take **life** here as eternal

234

either. Since, however, all sin leads *ultimately* to physical death, to turn from sin leads to *a lengthening of* one's physical **life**. This truth is taught clearly in Proverbs with statements such as:

Righteousness delivers from death (Proverbs 10:2; 11:4).

In the way of righteousness is life, and in its pathway there is no death (Proverbs 12:28).

As righteousness leads to life, so he who pursues evil pursues it to his own death (Proverbs 11:19).

It follows, therefore, that if a Christian's prayer turns **his brother** away from some sinful pursuit, the effective result can be described as **life**. James also taught this in James 5:19-20.

A very nice touch is given by John's statement that **He will give him life for those who commit sin not** *leading* to sudden **death**. The word **him** is most naturally read as a reference to the Christian who prays (the nearest antecedent is **he will ask**). It is as if the **life** which the sinning **brother** needs is given to the one who prays and then passed on to those who commit **sin**. The Christian who prays with faith in the name of God's Son passes on **life** (albeit physical) to **his brother**, just as Jesus Christ gave him "life" (eternal) when he first believed in His name. The "name of Jesus Christ, God's Son" thus becomes a fountain of **life** from which a believer may draw for himself and for his fellow Christians.

Of course, none of this excludes the possibility that in particular cases the Christian may not be sure about the seriousness of the sin. In such ambiguous instances, he has no command to **pray**, though he is perfectly free to do so. But the command given here *does apply* whenever the Christian **sees** that **his brother is sinning a sin** *which does* not *lead* directly **to death**. If he refuses to **pray**, his own love for his brother is certainly called into question.

It is striking that in these two concluding verses of the unit, which we have called the Conclusion (4:20–5:17), the author neatly enfolds the twin themes of faith and love. As we have seen before, the commandments of God can be summarized as one commandment, "And this is

His commandment: that we should believe on the name of His Son Jesus Christ *and love* one another, as He gave us commandment" (3:23; italics added). Obviously when we pray to God through Christ for our sinning Christian **brother**, relying on the assurance that **He will give him life for those who commit sin not *leading* to** immediate **death**, we are *believing* "in the name of His Son" and *loving* "one another" all at the same time!

With this quite skillful dovetailing of his two great motifs—faith and love—the apostle John concludes his discussion of "How to Live Obediently" (4:20–5:17). No doubt this great servant of Christ would have fully concurred with Paul's words, "For in Christ Jesus neither circumcision nor uncircumcision avails anything, but *faith working through love*" (Galatians 5:6; italics added).

ENDNOTES

[1] For fuller information see W. Günther and H.-G. Link, "*agapaō*," NIDNTT, Colin Brown, gen. ed., 3 vols. (Grand Rapids: Zondervan Publishing House, 1975-78), 2:538 ff.

[2] See note 8 in chapter 3.

[3] I. Howard Marshall finds the statement perplexing ("This, however, is not what we would expect John to say.") and wishes to understand the text as saying: "'This is how we know that we *ought* to love the children of God when we love God and keep His commands'" (*The Epistles of John*, NICNT [Grand Rapids: Wm. B. Eerdmans Publishing Co., 1978], p. 227). But the Greek cannot carry such a meaning here.

[4] So read by Raymond E. Brown, *The Epistles of John*, AB (Garden City, NY: Doubleday, 1982), pp. 513 and 540; and by the Jerusalem Bible (also in the French).

[5] Blass, F., and Debrunner, A. *A Greek Grammar of the New Testament and Other Early Christian Literature* (Chicago: University of Chicago Press, 1961), 138 (1), p. 76, points out, "The neuter is sometimes used with reference to persons if it is not the individuals but a general quality that is to be emphasized," and 1 John 5:4 is cited as the first example. This is likely to be the correct grammatical explanation, despite hesitation by Brown, *Epistles*, pp. 541-42.

[6] The Greek underlying the words **the victory that has overcome the world** is a participial construction (*hē nikē hē nikēsasa ton kosmon*) using an aorist tense for the verb rendered **has overcome**. The time reference in participles is

not a given, even for the aorist participle. If John is thinking of an "event" in which our faith has conquered the world, a reference to the new birth is natural, since the aorist participle tends to refer a time antecedent to the main idea (in this case: **this is the victory**).

[7] See the discussion of the present tense under 3:9. With regard to the present participle, Maximillian Zerwick (*Biblical Greek: Illustrated by Examples* [Rome: Scripta Pontificii Instituti Biblici, 1963], p. 129) reminds us that "**the present participle** does not express time but only the aspect." His examples are worth studying, since the so-called *present* participle can refer to action that is in the past and may have occurred only one time. Thus the man from whom the legion of demons has been exorcised is described as *ton daimonizomenon* (present participle) in Mark 5:15 and we must translate: *the one who had been demon-possessed*. Similarly, in 1 Thessalonians 2:12, it is quite permissible to translate the phrase *axios tou Theou tou kalountos* [present participle] *hymas eis tēn heautou basileian kai doxan* as: "worthily of God who *called* you to His own kingdom and glory." One may understand here that God is "the Caller" without any notion of continuity or repetition in the action of "calling." Sophisticated grammarians know that the present participle is fundamentally descriptive and does not, by itself, signal iterative, or repetitive, action.

[8] For a fuller discussion of Cerinthus and his possible relationship to this epistle, see our Introduction. Eusebius of Caesarea (ca. 265–ca. 339) reports, as a story derived from Polycarp (ca. 70–155/160), a famous encounter by John with Cerinthus: "...John the apostle once entered a bath to wash; but ascertaining that Cerinthus was within, he leaped out of the place, and fled from the door, not enduring to enter under the same roof with him, and exhorted those with him to do the same, saying, 'let us flee, lest the bath fall in, as long as Cerinthus, that enemy of the truth is within'" (*H.E.* 3. 28; trans. C. F. Cruse). Although amusing, the story is not particularly convincing, but it is evidence of the ancient view that John was strongly opposed to Cerinthus and his doctrines.

[9] Bauer, Walter. *A Greek-English Lexicon of the New Testament and Other Early Christian Literature* (Chicago: University of Chicago Press, 1979), p. 180.

[10] This is precisely what Cerinthus *did* do (identify the Spirit with Christ) according to Epiphanius of Salamis (ca. 315-403) in his work on heresies, *Panadarion* (*Medicine Box*), chapter 28. But despite the fact that the views of Cerinthus make an apparently good fit with 1 John 5:6, other interpretations of the verse are often presented. Among the most important of these are the two following: (1) **water and blood** refer to the sacraments of baptism and the eucharist (so C. H. Dodd, *The Johannine Epistles,* MNTC [New York: Harper & Row, 1946], pp. 128-31); (2) **water and blood** refer to Christ's death, at which time, according to John 19:34, "blood and water came out" of His pierced side

The First Epistle of John

(so Brown, *Epistles*, pp. 577-78; see his whole discussion of this text, pp. 573-80; and Marianne Meye Thompson, *1–3 John*, IVPNT [Downers Grove, IL: InterVarsity Press, 1992], pp. 133-35). The view maintained in our Commentary has the support of many modern commentators such as Stephen S. Smalley, *1,2,3 John*, WBC (Waco, TX: Word Books, 1984), pp. 278-80; Marshall, *Epistles*, pp. 231-35; J. L. Houlden, *A Commentary on the Johannine Epistles*, HNTC (New York: Harper & Row, 1973), pp. 125-27; F. F. Bruce, *The Epistles of John: Introduction, Exposition and Notes* (Old Tappan, NJ: Fleming H. Revell, 1970), pp. 118-19; and Rudolf Bultmann, *The Johannine Epistles: A Commentary on the Johannine Epistles*, Herm (Philadelphia: Fortress Press, 1973), pp. 79-80.

[11] Brown, *Epistles*, pp. 779-80, repeats the well-known story about how Erasmus was criticized for leaving the disputed words (the Johannine Comma) out of his first two editions of the Greek New Testament (1516, 1519). One of his critics, an Englishman named E. Lee, confronted Erasmus about the absence of the Comma from his editions and Erasmus replied that if he had found the words in a Greek manuscript he would have included them in his editions. Very conveniently, between May 1520 and June 1521, Erasmus was shown that the Comma was found in Greek in the Codex Montfortianus. This is an early 16th century manuscript copied from an earlier Codex (326 in the standard list) which did not contain the Comma in Greek. Along with some other insertions from the Latin Vulgate, the Comma was undoubtedly translated into Greek and introduced into Montfortianus. Erasmus proceeded to introduce the Comma into his third edition (1522), where it remained also in his fourth and fifth editions (1527, 1535). Since it already appeared in the Greek of the Complutension Polyglot Bible of Cardinal Ximenes (printed in 1514, but only published in 1522), after Erasmus adopted it subsequent editors of this general period tended to include it as well. Thus, it was found in Theodore Beza's 5th edition of the Greek New Testament (1598), which most probably was the Greek Testament used most by the translators of the KJV who put it into their translation. (Cf. F. H. A. Scrivener, ed, *The New Testament in the Original Greek according to the Text Followed by The Authorised Version together with the Variations Adopted in The Revised Version*, New Ed., [Cambridge: at the University Press, 1894].)

The fact remains, however, that the Greek manuscript evidence supporting the Johannine Comma is numerically small and late in date. As presented in Nestle-Aland (27th ed.), the Greek support consists of the following:

a. Have it in the text: manuscripts 61 (Montfortianus; 16th century); 629 (14th or 15th century); 918 (16th century); 2318 (18th century).

b. Have it as a variant reading: 88 (12th century [18th century variant]); 221 (10th century); 429 (16th century); 636 (15th century).

It should be obvious that no reasonable theory of textual criticism can possibly account for such rare, and late, Greek attestation if the Comma was part of the autograph of the First Epistle. Nor does a claim to divine preservation of the original text carry any weight in a case like this, since such a claim carries its own refutation on its face. Clearly the sovereign hand of God on the transmissional process is far better seen when it is admitted that the original text *has been preserved* for 1 John 5:7-8 and that the original did *not* contain the Comma.

[12] For a discussion of John 2:23 and 12:42, see Zane C. Hodges, "Problem Passages in John's Gospel, Part 2: Untrustworthy Believers—John 2:23-25," *Bibliotheca Sacra* 135 (1978): 139-52. For John 8:30, see Zane C. Hodges, *The Gospel Under Siege*, 2nd ed. (Dallas: Redención Viva, 1992), pp. 41-44.

[13] Scholars are divided about the reference of "these things" in 1 John 5:13 (cf. Brown, *Epistles*, pp. 607-608). But as Brown's own summary of the problem shows, the consistency of Johannine style in the use of *tauta + graphein* (cf. 1:4; 2:1, 26 and 5:13) has played an insufficient role in the discussion. This expression is consistently used in the epistle in reference to immediately preceding material. (The phrase found in John 21:24 is a different kind of structure.) Thompson, *1–3 John*, p. 138, holds that, "*These things* refer to the content of the entire letter…Nevertheless, 5:6-12 are especially in view as well, for they spell out the author's understanding of the phrase *Son of God*…As Marshall (*Epistles*, p. 243 n. 1) notes, 5:13 sums up the content of the whole epistle, but its function is to link 5:5-11 and 14-21." But this mediating position is unnecessary once we have admitted that there is really a connection with verses 5-12. One needs simply to let go of the *idée fixe* that there has to be a parallelism with John 20:30-31. The arguments I have offered in the text of this Commentary for the view that the reference is to verses 6-12 were already articulated by A. E. Brooke in *A Critical and Exegetical Commentary on the Johannine Epistles*, ICC (Edinburgh: T. & T. Clark, 1912), p. 142, though he links it with verses 1-12, which is not a material difference since verses 1-5 lead into verses 6-12. Though modern writers adduce "the striking parallel with the language of John 20:31, which gives the purpose of the Gospel as a whole" (Marshall, *Epistles*, p. 243), Brooke is correct to say: "The present verse [verse 13] does not really present an exact parallel to the conclusion of the Gospel (Jn xx. 31)…Even if the reference is to the whole Gospel and not to the *sēmeia* recorded in chapter xx., that reference is determined by the preceding words (*ha ouk estin gegrammena en tō bibliō toutō*)" (*Epistles*, p. 142). A true parallel with John 20:31 would have contained words like "in this epistle"! It is obviously not licit to allow a loose parallel from another book by John (where the reference is made unambiguous by the words Brooke cites) to overrule the author's own usage *within the epistle itself*. It is really the prologue that states the purpose of the epistle ("fellowship") and the flow of thought through

the body of the letter (2:28–4:19) precisely fulfills the purpose of the prologue, as we have tried to show in our exposition. It is time to get beyond the simplistic paralleling of John 20:30-31 with 1 John 5:13, so that we may come to grips with the author's actual intent.

[14] This point is granted by Tim Ward, "Sin 'Not Unto Death' and Sin 'Unto Death' in 1 John 5:16," *Churchman* 109 (1995): 229. His whole article (pp. 226-37) is a useful recent survey of this problem, though he concludes that the sin "unto death" is a sin committed by Christ-rejecting non-Christians, such as the antichrists.

CHAPTER 9

Epilogue: Christian Certainties

(1 John 5:18-21)

John now brings his epistle to a close with a series of statements introduced by the words "We know." Together these statements of certainty plus the closing exhortation constitute a kind of epilogue to John's Epistle. In size it is equivalent to the prologue (1:1-4). This stylistic balancing of prologue and epilogue is a mark of the care the author has taken in the composition of his letter. The fact that verbs whose subjects are "we" predominate in both prologue and epilogue is a further sign of stylistic balance. John is far from being the rambling writer some have imagined him to be, but is a literary artist of high caliber.

The writer's fundamental thought here is that if the readers perceive the truths he mentions, they will be fortified against the allurements of the idolatrous pagan practices around them.

VI. EPILOGUE: CHRISTIAN CERTAINTIES (5:18-21)

> [18]We know that whoever is born of God does not sin; but he who has been born of God keeps himself, and the wicked one does not touch him.

The opening words **We know** (repeated in verses 19-20) evoke a recollection of the "we" statements of the prologue: "that which *we* have heard...which *we* have seen...etc." (1:1-4). But a reference to the apostles only is not likely at this point. Elsewhere in the epistle, outside the prologue, the apostolic "we" appears with the use of an emphatic Greek pronoun for "we" as is the case at 3:14 and 4:6. In both cases, an emphatic "you" is also found close by. This does not occur here in verse 18 and so it is likely that the **"we"** is inclusive of both the apostles *and* the readers.

The truth asserted in this statement is one the apostle has already discussed earlier in his letter at 3:9-10 (see discussion there). He now wishes to remind his readers that **whoever is born of God does not sin**; that is, the regenerate person *as such* is incapable of any *sin*. This leads to the further observation that **he who has been born of God keeps himself** with the result that **the wicked one does not touch him.** The inner man that is born of God has the inborn capacity to resist the pollution of evil and thus lies outside of Satan's reach.

It is not likely that Jesus is referred to in the phrase **he who has been born of God keeps himself.** This view has been supported by the observation that **he who has been born** translates a Greek aorist participle (*ho gennēthes*). This is said to stand in contrast with the Greek perfect participle that is translated in the earlier words **whoever is born of God.** This opinion, however, is a good example of overrefinement in the interpretation of the Greek tenses. The Greek aorist simply picks up the reference of the perfect without the special nuance that the perfect tends to have in terms of state or result. (One might observe that in John 6 the very same action, Jesus coming down from heaven, is described with a present participle [verse 33], a perfect indicative [verse 38], an aorist participle [verse 41], a perfect indicative [verse 42], a present participle [verse 50], and aorist participles [verses 51, 58]! Those who *build* their interpretations on Greek tenses do not understand how these tenses function in the Greek language.)

In saying that the regenerate inward person (cf. Romans 7:22) **keeps himself,** John is not saying of course that our inner self can somehow prevent all sin in the Christian life. John's discussion in 1:5-10 shows he could not mean something like that. What John means is that God's "seed remains in" the regenerate inward self (cf. 3:9) as the controlling element of his born again nature and is impervious to even the slightest contamination from **the wicked one.** Thus not only can Satan not defeat the regenerate inward man, but he cannot even **touch him.**

It is reassuring to remember that, whatever our failures may be, they do not really touch what we are at the core of our being as God's children. In the last analysis our failures are due to the sinful "programming" of our earthly bodies, as Paul himself taught in Romans 7:7-25. Christians need to know this. At the very moment that we are most humbled by our sinful failures, and when we confess them, it is helpful to be confident that those failures have not really changed what we are as children of God.

The enemy, try as he might, cannot really **touch** us. He can only attempt to persuade us that he can, or has. But if we know the truth stated in this verse, he will not be able to deceive us. For if we let him, Satan will use our failures to lead us to further failures. So, after every sin, deeply though we may and should regret it, we ought to rise from our confession to God *knowing* that we are the same inwardly holy persons we were before we failed!

> ¹⁹**We know that we are of God, and the whole world lies** *under the sway of* **the wicked one.**

But there is something else **We** should **know**. If we know the truth stated in verse 18, **We** can also **know** whose side we are on.

For the last time in the epistle, we meet the frequent Johannine phrase *to be of someone or something*. As we have already noted (see 3:10b and discussion), the expression is fluid and must always be understood in context. Used of Christians, it normally suggests a dynamic experiential relationship with God (cf. 3:19; 4:4). Here the words **we are of God** are juxtaposed with the state of **the whole world** which **lies** *under the sway of* **the wicked one**. One might suggest that here the words **we are of God** suggest that we are *on God's side* as over against the world which is *on Satan's side,* being *under* his *sway*. Thus, we do **God's** will and experience fellowship with **Him** (cf. 1:3) with all that this entails as the epistle has expounded on it.

The words *under the sway of* **the wicked one** are a good interpretation of a simpler Greek phrase: *en tō ponerō keitai* = "lies in the wicked one." The phrase is pungent with the suggestion that **the world** passively rests within the operative sphere of God's enemy. By contrast, the Greek phrase *ek Theou* (**of God**) carries a nuance of being "from" *God*. We are, so to speak, His active agents in the midst of a **world** that has chosen simply to "lie down" in the power of the devil!

The Christian should not only be aware of his own sinless inward man (verse 18), but he should likewise be aware of his utter separateness from **the whole world** that lives *under* Satan's *sway*. We whom the enemy cannot "touch" (verse 18) are not a part of **the world** which **lies** passively in **the wicked one**. Thus, as John has earlier said, we must not "love the world or the things in the world" (2:15-17) and we must resist the ideas that **the world** promotes (cf. 2:18 ff.).

It should be remembered, of course, that this letter is written to Christians who are advanced in their spiritual state (cf. 2:12-14; 4:6), probably the leadership. The statements of these closing verses can apply in varying degrees to other believers, depending on the extent to which their own spiritual experience matches that of the readers addressed. But since the letter was no doubt intended to be read in the public meeting, it must have been John's hope that the hearers of it, as well, might be able, at least in time, to identify with his closing declarations.

He is now ready for his final and climactic declaration.

20And we know that the Son of God has come and has given us an understanding, that we may know Him who is true; and we are in Him who is true, in His Son Jesus Christ. This is the true God and eternal life.

The third thing which **we know** is that by virtue of the coming of God's **Son** we have been granted spiritual comprehension (**an understanding**) that makes it possible for us to **know** the **true God**.

The word here translated **understanding** (Greek: *dianoian*) is one that John has not used in his epistle until now. It is close in meaning to the Greek word for *mind* (*nous*) and can refer to the "ability to think, faculty of knowledge, understanding, the organ of *noein* [thinking]."[1] It is hard to choose an exactly suitable word for *dianoia* here, but perhaps the English word *intelligence* is as close as we can get. The idea is that **the Son of God** has granted us the spiritual *intelligence*, or intellect, necessary to **know** God.

Here the apostle is no doubt referring to his earlier teaching regarding the knowledge of God (in regard to **know Him**, cf. 2:3-4 and 2:12-14 and discussions under those verses). As we have seen, this knowledge is attained through fellowship and is verified by obedience to God's commands (2:3-4). John here affirms that the ability to acquire such knowledge, i.e., the necessary *intelligence* for it, is made possible by the fact that **the Son of God has come**.

As John has also made plain, Christian love (obedience) is never absent where God is truly known (cf. 4:7-8 and discussions), but we come to know what love really is only by its expression in the cross of Christ (cf. 4:9-10). There could be no true **understanding** of love or of God had not **the Son of God...come** and died to reveal God's love. Through His death, seen as a manifestation of what God truly is, **the**

Son...has given us an understanding (an *intelligence*) by means of which **we may know** God. That is to say, the obedient Christian possesses the necessary spiritual capacity to know God and this capacity results from the coming of Christ to die.

This assertion by the apostle comes very close indeed to the statement that Paul makes about "spiritual" Christians (as over against "carnal" ones): "But he who is spiritual judges all things, yet he himself is rightly judged by no one. For 'who has known the mind of the Lord that he may instruct Him?' But we have *the mind* [Greek: *nous*] of Christ" (1 Corinthians 2:15-16).

This spiritual comprehension of God is one of the benefits that flows to the child of God as he comes to recognize and imitate the love God has revealed in Christ (cf. again, 4:8-11). It is a priceless spiritual asset that can and should "keep" us "from idols" (see next verse). Thus to **know** God is here said to be to **know Him who is true** (or, "the True One"). The God whom we are to get to **know** stands in infinite contrast to all *false gods* who simply represent a lie. He alone is truly God.

But along with *knowing* God there is the parallel reality that **we are in Him who is true**. The statement that **we are *in* Him** recalls the same expression in 2:5 ("by this we know that we are in Him") which John immediately links to *abiding* in Him (2:6). As we have seen, "abiding" is John's description of the experience of "living as a disciple" (cf. John 15:8). So the words **in Him** have a totally different meaning from Paul's concept of being "in Christ," but refer instead to the "abiding life" of obedience to God's commands.

But to be **in Him**, to abide **in Him**, is not only to abide in **Him who is true** (as John has just described God), but it is also to be **in His Son Jesus Christ**. It should be noted that there is no "and" between the phrase **in Him** and the phrase **in His Son**. To abide in God and to abide in Christ are the same thing, and no Christian can distinguish the experience of abiding in One as over against abiding in the Other. It is the same experience, for God is known to us only through **His Son Jesus Christ**.

The declaration that **This is the true God and eternal life** is one of the most straightforward announcements of the deity of **Jesus Christ** found in the New Testament. The words **This is** at the very least refer back to the words **His Son Jesus Christ**, but frequently in this writer's usage pronoun references to deity can be taken equally as referring to God the Father or **His Son**. Since as we saw, the word **Him** is not separated by an "and" from the words **His Son Jesus Christ**, the **This** (Greek: *houtos*) might be taken as referring to both. Throughout his letter the apostle demonstrates his delicate grasp of the oneness of the Father and **Son,** never falling into the trap of equating them as though there was only one Person in the Godhead. The present verse demonstrates this delicate touch in that there is only one **true God**, yet we can speak of **Him/His Son** as being this very God.

But of **the true God** it may be said that He is also **eternal life**. The designation **eternal life** carries us back once again to the Prologue in 1:1-4, where we are told that the subject matter of John's letter is "that *eternal life* which was with the Father and was manifested to us" (1:2). We may also recall our Lord's own claim, "I am...the life" in John 14:6. This shows that the final statement is primarily a reference to **His Son Jesus Christ**, however much a reference to the Father is implicit in John's thinking.

Moreover, the reference to **eternal life** is the final *inclusio* of the epistle, tying prologue and epilogue together in this climactic affirmation. John has now fulfilled his intention to "declare" to his readers this "eternal life" (1:2). He has done so by showing to them that through "abiding" **in Him who is true**, which is also to abide **in His Son Jesus Christ**, they can possess always a vital experience of **eternal life**. That **life**, expressed in love toward their Christian brothers and sisters, springs out of the sinless inner self (verse 18). It is what marks their life and experience as being "of God" rather than of the world (verse 19), and it expresses the spiritual **understanding** which the Son of God came to give them (verse 20a).

Such an experience of **the true God and eternal life** must brook no rivals.

²¹Little children, keep yourselves from idols. Amen.

As noted previously in this Commentary, the earliest Christians, particularly in Asia Minor, had to contend with false teachers who rationalized or excused various forms of compromise with pagan idolatry and its immoral practices. It seems extremely likely that the Revisionists did so as well. In fact, this closing exhortation argues strongly that they did.

Whether they can be identified with the Nicolaitans mentioned in Revelation 2:6, 15 is debatable. But if they claimed to draw their doctrines from Nicolas, the proselyte of Antioch (Acts 6:5), then they must also have had roots in the Jerusalem church as 1 John 2:19 indicates that they did. That this godly man could have fathered such a movement seems unlikely, although every teacher experiences the misfortune of students who take his positions to an extreme. Still, the claim to such a link would have had resonance with the newly saved Christians of Asia Minor. Perhaps these heretics rationalized participation in pagan practices by means of a theology that claimed to be more "spiritual" than that which the new Christian churches taught.

But whether Nicolaitans or not, it is clear that this spiritualization had at its heart a heresy that denied that Jesus was the Christ (2:22); and it probably regarded the divine Christ as being beyond the suffering of death (cf. 5:6). This may have been accompanied by the claim that, once the true "Christ" was recognized as a spirit being, not the man Jesus, then the readers could identify with *this* Christ and regard mortal and physical experiences as morally indifferent. One could be "spiritual," therefore, and still participate in idolatrous feasts, since one knew himself to be beyond any set of "commandments" (2:4) pertaining to them. There was no such thing as eternal life imparted through a physical being whom one could see, hear, gaze at, and handle (cf. 1:1). Perhaps they also suggested that life should be lived for its *spiritual values*, not enslaved to a set of rules that governed earthly existence.

The precise, detailed form of the heresy John combats is not known to us. But we can glean enough about the antichrists to realize that their "spiritual descendants" have walked among the churches in every age since then. Their leading concepts always serve to undermine the Saviorhood of Jesus Christ and always they espouse compromise with the world around us. Always they are agents of Satan, promoting various forms of idolatry (whether literal or metaphorical) which blind men to "the true God and eternal life."

The First Epistle of John

The apostle's final words should therefore reverberate down the corridors of human history:

Little children, keep yourselves from idols.
Amen.

ENDNOTES

[1]G. Harder, *"nous,"* NIDNTT, Colin Brown, gen. ed., 3 vols. (Grand Rapids: Zondervan Publishing House, 1975-78), 3:127.

The Second Epistle of John

Protecting the Truth by Rejecting Error

CHAPTER 10

Protecting the Truth by Rejecting Error

(2 John 1–13)

As pointed out in the Introduction to First John, Second John is a personal letter written by John the apostle to a Christian church which is corporately personified as a "lady." This metaphorical way of referring to a Christian church is similar to Old Testament usage in which either Israel as a whole, or the cities of Israel, could have female personifications. So we meet expressions like "the daughter of Zion," "the daughter of Judah," "the daughter of my people," and "the daughter of Jerusalem" (e.g., Lamentations 1:6, 15; 2:11, 13; and many other places). In an extended parable, Ezekiel describes the city of Samaria as the woman Oholah, and Jerusalem as the woman Oholibah (Ezekiel 23:4).

In the New Testament, the Church as a whole is the "wife" or "bride" of Christ (Ephesians 5:23-24; Revelation 19:7-8; 22:17). Paul also describes the Corinthian church as a "chaste virgin" which is "betrothed...to one husband," that is, "to Christ" (2 Corinthians 11:2). In the early Christian context, therefore, there is nothing especially surprising about a Christian church being personified and addressed as an "elect lady" (2 John 1). John's purpose in the epistle is to warn this church against the "many deceivers" (antichrists) who "have gone out into the world" (2 John 7).

It is quite probable that this little epistle was brought to this church by the bearer of First John. If First John was a circular letter that was delivered to (and no doubt copied by) a circuit of churches, then Second John would have been dropped off at the church for which it was intended. Perhaps this was a church that John knew well, since he speaks of knowing some of its members, i.e., its "children" (2 John 4). One thinks readily of the circuit of the seven churches of Asia, to whom John wrote in Revelation 2 and 3. But even if the recipients of First John are the same seven churches, we do not know which one received Second John. However, since Christian tradition connected John personally with Ephesus,[1] the church there is the most probable recipient.[2]

As will be evident in the Commentary below, many ideas found in First John are touched on in Second John, but John feels no need to elaborate on these matters, since First and Second John reached this particular church together. First John, therefore, gave this church the full discussion that the apostle wanted them to have.

I. SALUTATION (1-3)

[1]**The Elder,**

To the elect lady and her children, whom I love in truth, and not only I, but also all those who have known the truth,

When writing this personal letter (as well as Third John), the writer is content to simply introduce himself as **The Elder**. In the New Testament "elders" are consistently identified as the leaders of a particular local church (cf., e.g., Acts 20:17).[3] In modern times the term has sometimes been thought to indicate "a disciple of the disciples of Jesus and thus a second-generation figure who served as a transmitter of the tradition."[4] But this usage is very doubtful, despite appeals to ancient writers to substantiate it.[5]

Most likely John uses the title in a self-effacing sense meaning simply, "the elderly one," much as a grandfather might say to his grandson, "This is your elderly granddad speaking." The readers, who are members of this church, would be for the most part younger than he. Of course, the recipients knew who this was, and would have accorded the elderly apostle appropriate respect, not merely due to his age but also to his long and distinguished role as a servant of Christ.

As already indicated, the expression **the elect lady and her children** refers to the church and its members.[6] The term **elect** (Greek: chosen) reminds the hearers/readers about the truth (more fully expressed by Paul) that they were chosen in Christ "before the foundation of the world" (Ephesians 1:4). This church was **elect** precisely because its members were **elect.** As Jesus had said to the apostles: "You did not choose Me, but I chose you" and again, "I chose you out of the world" (John 15:16, 19). The Scriptures do not seek to solve for us the mystery of the relationship between divine sovereignty and human responsibility, but all attempted explanations that downplay one at the expense of the other are to be rejected as extremes. The Scriptures testify clearly to both.

John now expresses his affection for the members of the church (**whom** is plural in Greek) with the declaration **whom I love in truth**. The words **in truth** might simply mean "truly," but in view of John's concern both here in this epistle and also in First John with God's **truth** over against falsehood and deception, the phrase is likely to suggest a love which not only is real and sincere, but also accords with the **truth** God has revealed in His Son.

Moreover his love for them is not an isolated love (**not only I**) but is shared by **all those who have known the truth**. The phrase **have known** (reflecting a Greek perfect participle, *egnōkotes*) conforms to John's usage in the first epistle where he several times employs the Greek perfect tense to express the knowledge of God which maturing Christians acquire (cf. 1 John 2:3-4, 13, 14). Since for John love is a product of such knowledge (1 John 4:7-8), no doubt the phrase here suggests that those who love this church have progressed into a vital experience of **the truth** by learning to obey it (cf. 1 John 2:3-4; 4:8 and discussions).

Evidently this congregation was progressing well in the truth (cf. verse 4), and John was confident that whoever knew about this progress would share his love for her, provided they also **have known the truth**. The simple principle here is that obedient Christians always rejoice in, and **love**, those who are likewise committed to **the truth**. Of course, obedient Christians also love every born again Christian brother and sister (cf. 1 John 5:1), but even God the Father and His Son have a special love for the *obedient* disciple (John 14:21, 23).

²because of the truth which abides in us and will be with us forever:

A reason is now stated why "all those who have known the truth" loved the Christians who constituted this church. They are loved **because of the truth**. Christian love is far from mere sentimentality, and it is far from mere humanism which "loves" humanity for its own sake. Instead, true Christian love is never separate from the Christian's love for the revealed **truth** of God.

Thus, love for our fellow Christians is rooted in the fact that they have believed **the truth** that "Jesus is the Christ" and so are "born of God" (cf. 1 John 5:1). We also love those who are "walking in truth" (cf. verse 4 and discussion above under verse 1). If our professed love has nothing to do with **the truth**, we may question whether it is genuine Christian love. On this point, Christians often deceive themselves about the emotions they feel toward others.

This **truth** (God's revelation in His Son) **abides in us**, John says. The words **in us** could also be rendered *among* us in view of the fact that John is addressing a whole church (the "elect lady"). He is probably not trying to describe the inward state of individual Christians so much as their corporate state. We could thus translate the phrase: *dwells among* **us**. Then the **us** will also include the writer himself and, by inference, all others in the larger Christian community. John's thought seems to be that God's revealed **truth** *makes its home* in the midst of the Christian church (or, churches) throughout the world.

This idea is quite similar to Paul's that "the church of the living God [is] the pillar and ground of the truth" (1 Timothy 3:15). God has ordained that His **truth** should dwell in the midst of the many Christian churches throughout the world which proclaim and support it.

But God's **truth** also **will be with us forever**. This is an astounding statement, especially since it was made more than 1,900 years ago! So many of the religions and cults of the Greco-Roman world of John's day have now passed off the scene and are mere historical memories. Yet Christianity, which must have seemed like a minor superstition to most of the cultivated citizens of the Roman Empire, has endured through the centuries and continues to **be with us** today. All over the contemporary world there are myriads of "elect ladies" (churches) where God's revelation in His Son is known and proclaimed just as it was in the church to which John writes.

The final **us** thus becomes fully corporate and embraces all Christians down through the ages of church history who have held to **the truth**. The Holy Spirit sees infallibly that so long as time continues, **the truth... will be with us**, and when time ends, this will still be true eternally. Thus, **the truth** will never be eliminated from this world—however fiercely it may be resisted—but will continue to offer its light to humanity **forever**.

³**Grace, mercy, *and* peace will be with you from God the Father and from the Lord Jesus Christ, the Son of the Father, in truth and love.**

As is common in the salutations in the New Testament epistles, John expresses a benediction, or wish, that his readers may enjoy God's **Grace, mercy, *and* peace**. To the extent Christians consciously experience God's **Grace** and **mercy**, they will also enjoy His **peace**.

The idea of **peace** here no doubt includes the hope that their external circumstances will be tranquil. But even if they are not, **peace** as an inner state is still available, just as Jesus said, "'These things I have spoken to you, that *in Me* you may have peace. *In the world* you will have tribulation; but be of good cheer, I have overcome the world'" (John 16:33; italics added). What may not be ours *outwardly* in the world can be ours *inwardly* as we abide in Him.

These benefits, John states, will come both **from God the Father** and also **from the Lord Jesus Christ, the Son of the Father**. The full title, **Lord Jesus Christ**, followed by the description **the Son of the Father**, is unique in the Johannine writings. Its use here is undoubtedly determined by the fact that the letter as a whole sounds a warning against those who deny the Person of Christ in some way (cf. verses 7, 9, 10). It serves as an emphatic affirmation of His lordship, messiahship, and deity.

Moreover, these benefits that John desires for them, and which come through both **the Father** and His **Son**, will come, John states, **in truth and love**. Not, as we might say in our truth-careless age, "in love and truth," (or even simply, "in love") but rather the reverse, thus giving priority to **truth**. Those who think in our day that **truth** can be comfortably downplayed in the interests of mutual **love**, do not share the New Testament point of view (see the discussion above under verse 2; cf. the same priority in 1 John 3:23; 4:21).

When divorced from **truth, love** is little more than sentimentality or humanism. If I truly care about my brothers, then I will want them to know, and live according to, God's **truth**. Thus God's **grace, mercy,** and **peace** must be experienced in an atmosphere shaped by the **truth**, which is the only atmosphere where genuine Christian **love** is found as well.

II. BODY OF THE LETTER: PROTECTING THE TRUTH BY REJECTING ERROR (4-11)

A. Practice the Truth as Originally Given (4-6)

> ⁴I rejoiced greatly that I have found *some* of your children walking in truth, as we received commandment from the Father.

The apostle somewhere encountered members of this church (**your children**) and was delighted (**rejoiced greatly**) to discover that they were living (**walking**) consistently with (**in**) God's **truth**.[7]

The pleasure that he finds in obedient Christians is an evidence of his concern to "make disciples" in accordance with our Lord's Great Commission (Matthew 28:18-20). Though he is the greatest of all writing evangelists in church history (the Fourth Gospel!), he knew that his task extended beyond evangelization. His emphasis in this passage on God's **commandment** also reflects his commitment to the task of the Commission, since the apostles were charged to teach Christian disciples "to observe all things that I have commanded you" (Matthew 28:20).

When John speaks here of **walking in truth**, he has in mind conformity to what God **the Father** had commanded (**as we received commandment**). As the following verses (5-6) make clear, this **commandment** is nothing less than the command to love one's fellow Christians. This is the only time in John's Epistles that he explicitly ascribes that **commandment** to God **the Father**. But as we have seen, for John, the words of Jesus are the words and witness of the One who sent Him (cf. 1 John 5:9 ff. and discussion); the command to exercise brotherly love is indeed a command that came from **the Father**. By putting it this way, the apostle implicitly affirms the authority of *the Son*, since his readers would know that the **commandment** was first spoken by Jesus Himself.

> ⁵And now I plead with you, lady, not as though I wrote a new commandment to you, but that which we have had from the beginning: that we love one another.

Although John was pleased with his encounter with some of the church's members, he takes nothing for granted. He pleads with the whole church, once again addressed under the title of **lady**, to adhere to the **commandment** to **love one another**. He is not asking them to pick up some **new** responsibility, but simply to fulfill an old one **which** he and they **had from the beginning**.

The idea expressed here, of course, is the same one that we met in 1 John 2:7 (see discussion there). Although the command was "new" when Jesus first spoke it (cf. John 13:34), it was no longer a **new commandment** for either the writer or the readership. Instead, it is a command that the writer had heard from the Lord Jesus Himself long ago when Christianity began, and which the readers **have** now **had from the beginning** of their Christian experience. It is not an innovation at all. The innovations were brought by the "many deceivers" about whom John wants this assembly to be warned (verses 7-8).

The command **that we love one another** is once again, as in all three of John's Epistles, a command for Christians. It is a command that only they can keep, or fail to keep. John is not concerned in any of the epistles with "love" directed toward the unsaved world. But he *is* concerned with evangelizing the lost (cf. 3 John 5-8) and he knows that when Christians **love one another** this is an effective witness to the world (cf. John 13:35).

> ⁶**This is love, that we walk according to His commandments. This is the commandment, that as you have heard from the beginning, you should walk in it.**

Once again, as in 1 John 5:2-3 (see discussion there), **love** for one's brother can be defined as obedience to God's commands. Thus, when **we walk according to His commandments**, we are in fact loving one another. There is absolutely nothing better that I can do for any of my brothers than to live obediently to God. My lifestyle will then have its maximum effect on them for good and, of course, will include reaching out to them in both their physical and spiritual needs (cf. 1 John 3:16-17; 5:16-17).

As he has done before (1 John 3:22-23), John summarizes God's **commandments** as a single **commandment**, but his use of this technique here is a little different. The single **commandment** is summarized by the words, **that as you have heard from the beginning, you should walk in it.** That is to say, **the commandment** constitutes a call to observe (**walk in**) what God commands in *the original form* in which His will was expressed. John is saying, in effect, that obedience to God's commands can be boiled down to a **commandment** to obey Him in exactly the way He *originally prescribed* this obedience. Thus, God says, "My command is to do the things I have told you to do in just the way I told you"!

The point of this statement is obviously to deter any suggestion that one can obey God's **commandments** *in some other form* than that in which they were originally given. In all probability, the Revisionists would not totally deny the command to "love one another." Instead, they would likely have revised the command in such a way as to justify any compromise they might want to make with idolatry. If, for example, they believed that a truly "spiritual" Christian could participate in the immorality that occurred in pagan temples (cf. 1 John 5:21 and discussion), they might also have said that in behaving in this way they were showing love to other Christians by teaching them about true freedom.

Needless to say, many in Christian history have done this. Efforts to "revise" God's commands so as to make them more palatable are prevalent in our own day as well. The establishment of gay and lesbian churches, or the ordination of gays and lesbians, are obvious examples. But there are many other examples, too. In any case, that John does have the Revisionists in mind is made plain by the following verses.

B. Protect Your Work By Rejecting Error (7-11)

> [7]**For many deceivers have gone out into the world who do not confess Jesus Christ *as* coming in the flesh. This is a deceiver and an antichrist.**

These words clearly reflect 1 John 4:1-3 (see discussion there). Here the "many false prophets" of 4:1 become **many deceivers.** The truth denied is also the same, and in both places the false prophets/**deceivers** are linked to the Antichrist. In 1 John 4:3, the false prophets speak in the "spirit of the Antichrist," while here the **deceiver** is called **an antichrist,** of which there are many examples (cf. 1 John 2:18). The underlying concept in both epistles is the same.

The opening word (**For**) connects with the preceding verse where the readers are warned to adhere to God's commands as they were originally given. Clearly John means that warning to be taken seriously in the light of the fact that **many deceivers have gone out into the world**. They must beware, therefore, of all efforts to "update" God's commandments in the light of a "new theology" of the Person of **Jesus Christ**.

If any of this sounds familiar in our own day, it should!

As in 1 John 4:2-3, once again the words **Jesus Christ *as* coming in the flesh** would be better rendered: *Jesus as Christ coming in flesh*. (There is no word for **the** in the Greek text here, as there is none in the comparable texts in First John.) No good reason exists not to take the whole expression here as the equivalent of the nearly identical expressions in 1 John 4:2-3 (see discussion there). The change from a perfect participle in the First John texts ("come") to a present participle here (Jesus Christ as **coming**) is not grounds for making out a significant difference in meaning. Such changes are to be expected in Greek authors, and the difference in meaning—if any—can only be a subtle one. Here we might see a nuance that the Revisionists denied this truth *in principle*, while in First John the denial is of the fact itself. But even this distinction might well escape a Greek reader or listener, especially as the two passages were not likely to be closely compared with each other, at least on first reading.[8]

The **deceivers** John had in mind are no doubt the same ones that concerned him in First John. Their theology involved the denial that **Jesus** was the **Christ,** a denial that marked them out as *antichrists* (cf. 1 John 2:22).

[8]Look to yourselves, that we do not lose those things we worked for, but *that* we may receive a full reward.

If for no other reason than this verse, the importance of Second John in the canon of the New Testament would be firmly established. No statement in the Scriptures makes clearer the integral connection between maintaining the truth and gaining eternal reward.

Unlike many contemporary preachers and expositors, the apostle does not connect the dangers of false doctrine with the loss of *eternal life*. John knew and affirmed that there can *be* no loss of eternal life (cf. John 6:35-

40). But loss of **reward** figures clearly in his thinking. The words **Look to yourselves** suggest the gravity of his concern. The Greek expression here (*Blepete heautois*) might even more suitably be rendered, *Watch out for yourselves*. The danger the apostle speaks of is real.

But what is that danger? The danger is that the intrusion of false teaching into the church can severely damage the work God has been doing among them. If this happens, the **reward** for that work will be diminished.

We must note here the interesting interplay of the pronouns: **that we do not lose...we worked for...*that* we may receive**. The repetition of **we** stands in sharp contrast with **Look to yourselves**. It is not going too far to say that the change from "you" to **"we"** strongly suggests that the apostle John had labored for the Lord in the very church and area where the recipients of this epistle were located. What was at risk, due to the threat of false doctrine, was not simply *their* work for God, but *the apostle's* as well. If the work of God in this church should suffer damage, therefore, it was not only *their* **reward** that would be affected, but *the apostle's* too.

This last idea is lost by most modern translations. For example, the NIV has: "Watch out that *you* do not lose what *you* have worked for, but that *you* may be rewarded fully" (italics added). However a very large majority of the manuscripts read **"we"** (as in NKJV) instead of "you," and appear to outnumber those reading "you" by well over two to one.[9]

It is worth noting that John does not say that to **lose the things we worked for** would mean the loss of *all* reward for them, but rather that the fullest possible reward would not be achieved. We should recall that the writer of Hebrews assured his readers, "God is not unjust to forget your work and labor of love which you have shown toward His name" (Hebrews 6:10). And the Lord Jesus Himself said, "For whoever gives you a cup of water to drink in My name, because you belong to Christ, assuredly, I say to you, he will by no means lose his reward" (Mark 9:41). Thus there is no question that at the Judgment Seat of Christ the Lord will compensate His servants for anything done for Him, however seemingly small or trivial. But the **full reward** that John speaks of here depends on more than the initial efforts.

A little reflection will show why this should be so. Since the task of evangelization should always be followed by the task of making disciples (cf. Matthew 28:18-20), winning souls to Christ is only the first step in a process that should go on in a Christian church as long as that church exists. When this process is carried forward properly, Christians will grow in their Christian experience and bear increasing fruit for God as time goes on. New souls will be won to Christ, will grow and produce fruit themselves, and so on. Only God knows the full potential of the work He is doing in any one Christian congregation. But if false doctrine is allowed to intrude, it has the potential to stop that church's progress or even to destroy the church. In that case, the full potential of the church is not realized, and the total value of previous labors in that church is thereby reduced.

In the case John is concerned with here, the denial that Jesus was "Christ come in flesh" struck at the very foundations of everything that the apostle and others in that church had labored for there. Since it fully subverted the way of salvation, it was a deadly poison indeed! Any church which adopted such a denial of truth would cease to be a truly Christian church and productive spiritual labors there would cease. No wonder John said, **Look to yourselves**! There was a real danger that a failure of vigilance by the church could **lose those things we worked for**. The whole edifice of Christian testimony in that particular place could be brought down with a crash, unless the Christians there were watchful.

We can also learn from the apostle's concern that we need to have an active interest in those who succeed us in any given ministry, since the way in which *they* protect the work of God can affect *our own* reward. Even though John was not currently on the scene in that locale (hence this letter), he had a lively interest in what was taking place there. Of course, he *did* love the Lord and His children in that assembly of believers. But a concern for a **full reward** is not in any way incompatible with this, as has sometimes been suggested. Some have even gone so far as to charge that a doctrine of rewards teaches Christians to think selfishly. But this charge has serious implications that those who espouse it have not considered.

No one spoke more frequently about heavenly rewards than our Lord Jesus Christ Himself. After all, it was He who told us, "Do not lay up for yourselves treasures on earth...but lay up for yourselves treasures in heaven...For where your treasure is, there your heart will be also" (Matthew 6:19-21). Needless to say, in encouraging His disciples to pursue heavenly treasure, Jesus was not encouraging anything *selfish*. Selfishness is not at all the same thing as enlightened self-interest. There is nothing sinful about that, for if we did not have valid self-interest we would have no instinct to preserve our lives or even any desire to avoid eternal damnation. Those who equate true self-interest with selfishness are ignoring reality and the Bible itself.

Equally to the point is the observation that, as our Lord's words disclose, laying up heavenly treasures is God's way of helping us to defocus from the world's material inducements and turn our hearts heavenward. It would be a form of self-righteous pride to say that, even though this is God's provision for this, we do not really *need* it and are willing to serve from gratitude alone. Anyone who would so speak is a naive student of his own nature. Besides, the words of our Lord in Matthew 6:19-21 are not a *suggestion*. They are a *command.*

So, in appealing to his readers to be careful in order that he and they may receive a **full reward**, John expertly employs a motivation which the Lord Jesus Himself often employed.

> **⁹Whoever transgresses and does not abide in the doctrine of Christ does not have God. He who abides in the doctrine of Christ has both the Father and the Son.**

These words are quite striking, coming as they do immediately after the warning to "Look to yourselves." If the Christians were impervious to false teaching, or at least to false teaching about the Person of Christ, John would have had no reason to warn them against the possible loss of a "full reward." According to some expositors, a true Christian could not succumb to heresies about Jesus Christ and, if someone does, it only proves that he was not a Christian to begin with. To others, of course, to give in to heresy would be to lose one's salvation. John shared *neither* viewpoint.

If the apostle had held either of the doctrines stated above, it was almost mandatory that he should warn the church that any acceptance of the false teaching placed them (or, showed them to be) in danger of eternal damnation. The fact that his concern is expressed in terms of losing a "full reward" is eloquent testimony that this alone is seen by him as the eternal consequence of failure to maintain the truth. The tendency of some modern theologians to frame every issue in the New Testament within the parameters of eternal salvation represents a massive misreading of the Scriptures.

Paul too understood the vulnerability of Christians to false teaching. He said, for example, that the teaching of Hymenaeus and Philetus that "the resurrection is already past" had overthrown "the faith of some" (2 Timothy 2:17-18). In 1 Timothy 1:19-20 he spoke of Hymenaeus (the same man?) and Alexander as individuals who "concerning the faith" had "suffered shipwreck" and whom Paul "delivered to Satan that they may *learn* not to blaspheme" (italics added). The Greek word for "learn" is *paideuō*, the word both Paul and the writer of Hebrews used to describe God's discipline of His own children (cf. 1 Corinthians 11:32; Hebrews 12:6-10). Paul elsewhere described Satan as an instrument in God's chastening (1 Corinthians 5:5). All wise pastors know what Paul and John knew, that Christians are not invincible in the face of cleverly concocted false doctrine.

Suppose, then, that the Christian church John was addressing was *not* vigilant as John has just warned them to be. Suppose one (or more) of its members gave in to the new theology. What had they done? John states it simply: that person **transgresses** (Greek: *parabainō* "to go aside") **and does not abide** (Greek: *menō* "to stay") **in the doctrine of Christ**.[10] That is to say, he *turns aside* from the truth instead of *remaining* in it. This form of expression can leave little doubt that we are talking about someone who once held to the truth but does so no longer.[11]

Of such a person it may be said that he **does not have God**. Since he did not *stay* **in the doctrine of Christ**, by *going aside* from it, he leaves **God** behind. He does not have **God** with him because he has abandoned **the doctrine** about **Christ** that God has revealed: namely, that "Jesus" is "Christ coming [or, come] in flesh" (cf. verse 7 and 1 John 4:2-3).

But this does not mean he is unsaved. If this person once held the truth that he has now abandoned, then that person is born of God. Contrary to the opinion of some theologians, we are not saved by *continuing* to believe, but by *believing*. When John states in 1 John 5:1, "Whoever believes that Jesus is the Christ is born of God," those words mean just what they say. There is not, as some claim, a hidden meaning derived from the Greek tense which indicates that the belief is ongoing. We have already dealt with the mistaken application of the Greek present tense under the discussion of 1 John 3:9 and do not need to repeat it here. Suffice it to say that nowhere in the New Testament is ongoing faith made a condition for eternal life.

For that matter, how could it be? At the moment of saving faith, the miracle of regeneration occurs and that miracle is irreversible (cf. John 6:35-40). To avoid the obvious conclusions to which this fact leads, some theologians affirm that though we are saved at the moment of true faith, whether we have *truly* believed or not can only be determined by whether we *remain* in the faith. The absurd idea is then advanced that we can "believe" without knowing whether or not we have *really* "believed." This tortured position is an affront to Scripture and common sense, and carries its own refutation on its face. (See the discussion under 1 John 2:3.)

As pointed out under our discussion of 1 John 5:12, statements about *having* God or *having* the Son, or *having* **the Father and the Son**, do not constitute a standardized, or fixed, concept in John's writings. First John 5:12 is the only place in Johannine literature where the expression is used in connection with eternal salvation. But in that place the phrase is chosen because of John's desire to locate eternal life in the Son of God, and in Him alone. In the whole of the Fourth Gospel, designed to bring people to faith in God's Son (cf. John 20:30-31), the idea of *having* **the Son** does not appear at all, although John frequently speaks about *having eternal life*.

Context must therefore dictate our understanding of the statements in this verse about not having/having **God** or **the Father and the Son**. The person who **does not abide in the** true **doctrine** about Jesus **Christ does not have God** with him in his new perspective and/or lifestyle. More bluntly, he is out of touch with **God**, while **he who abides in the doctrine of Christ** is vitally in touch with **God**, i.e., this person **has both the Father and the Son.** To be noted is the use of John's characteristic word for the experience of the disciple, namely the idea of "abiding." John is not talking here about mere creedal adherence to **the doctrine of Christ**, but about *staying* there in the sense of *living* in this truth. The natural implication about "remaining" somewhere which is found in the Greek word *menō* (*to abide, dwell, remain*) is ideally suited for this context which warns against "transgressing," or "going aside," from the truth.

¹⁰If anyone comes to you and does not bring this doctrine, do not receive him into your house nor greet him;

If the readers are to "abide" in the truth about Jesus Christ, they must be extremely wary of any traveling teacher who **comes to** them **and does not bring** (i.e., teach) **this doctrine**. They must offer him no hospitality or encouragement at all.

A common phenomenon in the Greco-Roman world of John's day was the familiar figure of the traveling teacher or philosopher who made his living by going from place to place and recruiting "students" who would pay for his instruction. The Christian church also had its traveling teachers, in particular, evangelists. As Third John shows, these men likewise needed to be supported if they were to carry on their work of evangelization. What John now enjoined on the members of the church was a determination to refuse all help for any professed Christian teacher who did not proclaim the truth about Jesus Christ.

Although not apparent in English, where **you** and **your** can be either singular or plural, in the Greek text these pronouns are plural, showing that the entire congregation is addressed. No one in the congregation was to furnish the false teachers with assistance of any kind. The words **do not receive him into your house** at the very least enjoined the refusal of such things as food or lodging. But the wisdom of not allowing such people even "to get in the door" has often been proved by those who have invited the representatives of cults to come in and talk. Letting them in is often easier than getting them out! Moreover, even the appearance of hospitality violates the spirit of this passage.

In fact, John tells the members of the church not even to **greet** such people. The reason for this is stated in the following verse.

¹¹for he who greets him shares in his evil deeds.

On first reading in English, this admonition may sound excessively harsh and overdrawn. An English reader is likely to wonder why a simple "hello" is a form of participation in the false teacher's **evil deeds**. But the Greek word for **greets** (*chairein*) is a standardized form meaning "rejoice." One might compare with it familiar expressions like "good luck" or "have a good day" in English, which are often substituted for "good-bye."

No doubt the Greek greeting "rejoice" was often said in a highly perfunctory way by the people who used it. The same may be said of the English "have a good day." But John here takes it for granted that Christians should not be superficial or insincere when they greet others. If a Christian is personally resistant to the common hypocrisies of the society round about him, then he should cultivate sincerity and genuineness in whatever he says. This affects how we greet people.

Would I really want to say "have a good day" to a man I knew to be an enemy of the truth? Suppose he really *did* have a good day! Would that not be a *bad* day for the truth? Thus, with such an expression, I must either speak hypocritically or actually wish him well in his spiritually destructive labors. The same obviously applies to the Greek greeting "rejoice," which no doubt approximated the English examples we have given, except that it might be used when meeting a person, or when that person departed. To say it genuinely to the bearer of a false message was to participate, however slightly, in what he was doing.

Some modern thinkers (e.g., C. H. Dodd) are offended by what they perceive to be "the elder's" intolerance (Dodd does not believe he was the apostle John!).[12] We can readily admit that this passage runs counter to modern and postmodern perspectives. Those who express judgmental attitudes toward another person's religious viewpoint or toward someone's lifestyle are condemned today as lacking in love. (Convictions held by theological and social conservatives often seem to be an exception to this general preference for tolerance!) But this contemporary mentality simply reflects a rejection of absolute truth. In what is called postmodernism, everyone's perspective may be regarded as "true" within his or her own frame of reference. But the New Testament makes claims of absolute truth. To reject the possibility of knowing absolute truth is tantamount to rejecting the New Testament as anything but a record of the early Christians' circumscribed, theory-laden interpretation of their experience. It is useless to argue with those who approach the New Testament this way about the degree of "tolerance" the author of Second John should have shown. The question for Christians, however, is whether or not we have been affected by the mentality of our age. Do we offer a measure of toleration and respect to those whom we know to be false teachers, even though this is inappropriate in the light of a passage like this?

It may be that we need a reminder that even casual remarks, like a greeting, may convey a measure of acceptance that the false teacher is unworthy to receive. It is solemn to realize that a failure in this area makes us, in a real sense, a facilitator of the false teacher's search for acceptance. To the extent that we play even a minor facilitating role with such teachers, we become persons who share in **his evil deeds**.

It should go without saying, of course, that John's advice here applies to people who are *teachers* or *promoters* of false doctrine (cf. Galatians 1:8-9) and not to those who have been deceived by them. These we should seek to rescue (cf. Jude 23). But the Western church needs a wakeup call on the very issue that John is discussing here. In a tolerant age, we must learn a true measure of *holy intolerance*.

III. FAREWELL (12-13)

> ¹²**Having many things to write to you, I did not wish *to do so* with paper and ink; but I hope to come to you and speak face to face, that our joy may be full.**

The last two verses of Second John are a personal "farewell" from the author, who clearly knew the recipients. He has **many things** he could **write** to them, but has decided to save these things for a future visit. This indirectly speaks volumes about the importance of the matters addressed in this letter, since he has chosen *not to wait* for a visit before communicating them. They were important enough to be put into writing immediately.

However brief, this epistle contributes significantly to our understanding of the way in which we should deal with false teaching (cf. the discussion above). The very fact that the apostle addressed this issue, while waiting on other matters, shows that he gave a high priority to protecting the Lord's sheep from error (cf. Paul's similar concern in Acts 20:28-31). Spiritual leaders are extremely derelict if they fail to defend their people from "wolves" (cf. Acts 20:29; Matthew 7:15).

The personal affection that John has for the recipients of his letter also comes through in his expressed intention to visit them **and speak**

face to face. He assures them that when he does come, it will be a joyful occasion. The words **that our joy may be full** indicate that seeing them **face to face** will be a source of mutual **joy**, both his and theirs. As the New Testament Scriptures consistently show, the apostles were very far from being "professional ministers" simply doing their "clerical duties." Instead they were men who sincerely loved their fellow Christians and genuinely enjoyed the company of those to whom they ministered the truth. No doubt it was a pleasure to be in *their* company as well!

¹³The children of your elect sister greet you. Amen.

If Second John were a personal letter to a particular woman, the question might be raised why only the children of her sister send their greetings. (The word for **greet** here is a standard one and different from the word in verses 10-11.) Of course, there are possible answers to this question: the sister was away; the sister was not a Christian; etc. But somehow this doesn't seem truly natural, especially since neither the **elect sister** nor "the elect lady" (verse 1) are given personal names. This stands in contrast to Third John where three personal names appear in the brief space of the epistle, while neither the "ladies" nor any of their "children" receive names in Second John.

On the other hand if, as we hold in this Commentary, the "elect lady and her children" of verse 1 are the church and its members, then **the children of your elect sister** simply refers to the members of the church where John is when he writes this letter. The bearer of the epistle would know the identity of that church so that the readership would recognize that John is sending the greetings of a sister church. (For the term **elect**, see the discussion under verse 1.)

It is definitely meaningful that Christian churches may be considered as "sisters" to one another in accordance with the electing grace of God. Like the members of one family, they should see themselves as mutual recipients of God's gracious gift of eternal life through His Son Jesus Christ. This perspective should lead to warm, supportive relationships between Christian churches even if, as may have been the case here, they are separated by a considerable distance. As Paul said of the Corinthian Christians, they were "called to be saints" not alone, but "with all who in every place call on the name of Jesus Christ our Lord" (1 Corinthians 1:2).

But as the apostle John has made so abundantly clear, both here and in First John, such a shared relationship is built on a common faith that Jesus is indeed the Christ come in flesh. Apart from belief in this truth there can be no true unity of heart, or real feeling of "family," among those who claim the name of Christian. Obviously the two churches shared this great truth, which included the realization that "whoever believes that Jesus is the Christ is born of God" (1 John 5:1). This was indeed a truth worth holding firmly.

With false doctrine in the air, both "the elect lady" and her **elect sister** needed to be on guard against it.

ENDNOTES

[1] According to Eusebius of Caesarea (ca. 262–ca. 339), after the outbreak of the Jewish War which led to the destruction of Jerusalem (A.D. 66–70), Asia Minor was to be John's sphere, "where," Eusebius states, "after continuing for some time, he died at Ephesus" (*H.E.* 3.1). The story of John's encounter with Cerinthus (see chapter 8, endnote 8) is said by Eusebius to have taken place at Ephesus (*H.E.* 4.14). For a fuller treatment of John's connection with Ephesus, see J. A. T. Robinson (*Redating the New Testament* [Philadelphia: Westminster Press, 1976], chap. IX, esp. pp. 256-59). Robinson dates the three Epistles of John somewhere between A.D. 60–65 (*Redating*, p. 307). In this Commentary, we give preference to this general time-frame for the writing of these letters. That, in turn, presupposes that John had contacts with Asia Minor, by epistle and perhaps in person, prior to A.D. 70. Eusebius's account could well be true since these earlier contacts made Asia Minor a natural sphere for John, following the fall of Jerusalem. (See next note.)

[2] Since, as we suggest, Second John was probably written and sent at the same time as the first epistle, John could simply be reporting an encounter with some of the church's members elsewhere than in Ephesus itself. Further, if John wrote from the Jerusalem church, as 1 John 2:19 can be taken to imply, he may have met some Ephesian Christians who had visited Jerusalem. But, since our knowledge of John's movements after about A.D. 33 or 34 is so slender, a visit by the apostle to the Ephesian church before the writing of these epistles is possible.

[3] Of course, Peter *does* call himself a "fellow elder" as he addresses the elders of the Christian congregations to whom he writes (1 Peter 5:1). But this shows clearly that he is thinking in terms of the same office as that held by the elders whom he addresses. No doubt Peter served as an "elder" in a church located wherever he was residing at this time. If "Babylon" in 1 Peter 5:13 is a

The Second Epistle of John

cryptogram for Rome (which seems likely), then 5:13 will be saying that Peter, his wife, and his son Mark are in that city with him. Thus Peter could call himself an "elder" of the church (or, a church, if there was more than one) in Rome. But in the text of 2 John 1, the simple, unadorned title of "the elder" does not quite sound the same as Peter's statement about being a *"fellow* elder," especially if, as we propose on the basis of 1 John 2:19, John is still resident at Jerusalem. In that church, at least, "the apostles and elders" were distinguished (cf. Acts 15:2, 4, 23). But of course the possibility cannot be finally excluded that John is using the title much as Peter did in order not to appear to assert his apostolic authority too blatantly. Naturally, the recipients knew that the author was an apostle and need not be told that he was not *only* an elder. But on balance, the explanation given in our commentary is probably better.

[4] Raymond E. Brown, *The Epistles of John,* AB (Garden City, NY: Doubleday, 1982), p. 651, supports this definition, in part, by appealing to Irenaeus, who "specifically mentions presbyters who saw John (*Adv. haer.* 5.33.3)," then adds: "Apparently Eusebius had a similar understanding of *presbyteros,* for he cites Irenaeus as mentioning the memoirs of a certain 'apostolic presbyter'" in *H.E.* 5.8. Neither text, however, can establish the quasi-technical use Brown wants. In Irenaeus, the reference need mean no more than that certain men (or, leaders) of advanced years had seen the apostle. In the case of Eusebius, the phrase "apostolic elder" could be adequately explained as a person whose experience reached back to apostolic times. But such ideas are a far cry from proving that the word "elder" itself had taken on such a semi-technical meaning that the new meaning was transparent when the word was used alone. "The elder" and "the elder who saw John" are differentiated precisely by the qualifying phrase, "who saw John."

[5] In connection with this issue, the often-quoted statement of Papias (ca. 60–ca. 130), as given by Eusebius (ca. 262–ca. 339), comes into play. Papias is quoted by Eusebius as saying: "But if I met with anyone who had been a follower of the elders any where, I made it a point to inquire what were the declarations of the elders. What was said by Andrew, Peter or Philip. What by Thomas, James, John, Matthew, or any other of the disciples of our Lord. What was said [or, what was being said] by Aristion, and the presbyter John, disciples of the Lord; for I do not think that I derived so much benefit from books as from the living voice of those that are still surviving" (*H. E.* 3.39). Eusebius thought, as have many others since his time, that a second John, called "the elder" (presbyter) is referred to here by Papias. Eusebius wished to assign the authorship of Revelation to this other John, while in modern times the authorship of the First, Second, and Third Epistles has often been ascribed to this supposed "alternative" John. But as is clear in Papias's statement, the term *elder* was used of the apostles

themselves. Papias's statement about "the presbyter John" is thus most naturally read as equivalent to "the apostle John" and thus the non-application of the title "elder" to Aristion indicates that he did not belong to the apostolic group. The change of verb tense in the statement about Aristion and John is then to be understood as referring to them as currently speaking, while the other named apostles must now be dead. Papias's point will be that he inquired of people who had heard the teachings of the apostles when many of them were alive, and he also inquired about the current teaching of the one remaining apostle as well as (the obviously prestigious) Aristion, who seems to have been an original hearer of Jesus about whom we know nothing except for Papias's remark. Although this statement (as given by Eusebius) is hardly a model of clarity, it is a foundation of sand for those who use it to establish the existence of a non-apostolic "elder" named John.

[6] This is clearly the prevailing view among the commentators (e.g., Brown, *Epistles*, pp. 651-55; Stephen S. Smalley, *1,2,3 John*, WBC [Waco, TX: Word Books, 1984], pp. 318-19; I. Howard Marshall, *The Epistles of John*, NICNT [Grand Rapids: Wm. B. Eerdmans Publishing Co., 1978], pp. 60-61; J. L. Houlden, *A Commentary on the Johannine Epistles*, HNTC [New York: Harper & Row, 1973], pp. 141-42; Rudolf Bultmann, *The Johannine Epistles: A Commentary on the Johannine Epistles*, Herm [Philadelphia: Fortress Press, 1973], pp. 107-108; C. H. Dodd, *The Johannine Epistles*, MNTC [New York: Harper & Row, 1946], pp. 143-45; John R. W. Stott, *The Letters of John: An Introduction and Commentary*, rev. ed., TNTC [Grand Rapids: Wm. B. Eerdmans Publishing Co., 1988], pp. 203-205; Marianne Meye Thompson, *1–3 John*, IVPNT [Downers Grove, IL: InterVarsity Press, 1992], pp. 150-51).

[7] The words *some of your children* have been thought to suggest an implicit rebuke of "others of your children" who were *not* **walking in truth** (so Dodd, *Epistles*, p. 147; Smalley, *1,2,3 John*, p. 323). But nothing necessitates this inference and we do not know enough about the relationship between John and this church to draw any such conclusion. It seems more probable that Marshall (*Epistles*, p. 65), is correct to say that "it is more likely that the elder [apostle, in our view] is thinking of the personal contact which he has had with some members of the church."

[8] Some commentators fall into the trap of overrefinement in attempting to articulate a difference between the perfect tense in 1 John 4:2-3 and the present tense in 2 John 7. For example, A. E. Brooke, *A Critical and Exegetical Commentary on the Johannine Epistles*, ICC (Edinburgh: T. & T. Clark, 1912), p. 175, writes: "In the First Epistle stress was laid on the historical fact and its permanent consequences. Here the writer regards it as a continuous fact. The Incarnation is not only an event in history. It is an abiding truth." This is no more correct

The Second Epistle of John

than to say that in John 6:38 the perfect tense of "I have come down from heaven" is historical, while the present tense of the same verb in 6:33 (in participle form) shows that the coming is a "continuous fact." Indeed, the present participle of this verb is used again in John 6:50 and is repeated by the crowds with an aorist participle in 6:51. Still less should we concur with Stott, *Epistles*, p. 212, when he says of the present participle: "In strict grammar this should refer to a future coming, and some have wondered if a reference to the parousia...is intended." Of course, "strict grammar" indicates nothing of the sort. Those who search for significant distinctions in John's use of verb tenses are pursuing a will-o'-the-wisp. (See our discussion of the present tense in both text and notes under 1 John 3:9.)

[9] Naturally the implication that the apostles could lose reward did not sit well with some ancient scribe or editor, leading to a change of persons in the two offending verb forms (*apolesōen* becomes *apolesēte* and *apolabōmen* becomes *apolabēte*). This probably occurred in some ancient text now reflected in the mss. Aleph, A, B and others. The changes eliminate any suggestion that the apostle can suffer any loss in this situation and are a typical manifestation of the hagiographic tendencies scribes not infrequently display. The reading with the first person plural in both verbs is found in 69.5 percent of the mss examined by W. L. Richards (*The Classification of the Greek Manuscripts of the Johannine Epistles*. No. 35: Society of Biblical Literature Dissertation Series [Missoula, MT: Scholars Press, 1977], p. 269) and is read by Hodges/Farstad, *MajT*.

[10] The Greek phrase translated "the doctrine of Christ" (*tē didachē tou Christou*) can be understood either as "the doctrine about Christ" or "the doctrine from Christ." In the latter case, it might be taken to refer to Christ's command to love, mentioned in verse 5, or more generally to Christian doctrine that originates with Him. The meaning "from" is favored, e.g., by Brown, *Epistles*, pp. 674-75, Brooke, *Epistles*, p. 177; F. F. Bruce, *The Epistles of John: Introduction, Exposition and Notes* (Old Tappan, NJ: Fleming H. Revell, 1970), pp. 141-42; Stott, *Epistles*, p. 214. The meaning "about" is preferred by Marshall, *Epistles*, pp. 72-73; Smalley, *1,2,3 John*, p. 332; and Bultmann, *Epistles*, p. 113. Bultmann states the case well: "...it is more probable, however, that 'of Christ' is an objective genitive, since the author hangs everything on his Christology, i.e., on the doctrine about Christ, as v 7 shows." He then points to the similarity between verse 7 and 1 John 2:23, where Christology is in view. In light of the concern of verses 7-8 with Christology, surely "doctrine *about* Christ" is the correct interpretation.

[11] The critical editions of the Greek New Testament here read *proagōn* ("to go before," "lead the way") instead of *parabainōn* ("go aside," "transgress"). A metaphorical and sarcastic sense is generally assigned to *proagōn* by the commentators (cf. Brown's translation [*Epistles*, p. 645]: "Anyone who is so

'progressive' that he does not remain rooted in the teaching of Christ does not possess God"). However, the "strangeness" of this use of the Greek verb cannot be entirely ignored. One might suspect a corruption of the text, especially if in some early exemplar *parabainon* was smudged or otherwise illegible, so that only the first and the last two letters were legible (i.e., *p.......on*) forcing a scribe or editor to guess at the word. The manuscript support for *proagon* is exceedingly slim: according to Nestle-Aland (27th), only Aleph, A, B, and 0232. As our various textual discussions, taken together, suggest, the very ancient base text (or, Ur-text) of these Egyptian manuscripts had suffered various scribal disturbances, which must then have been remedied by someone fairly facile in Greek, but without the resources to check his basic manuscript. This "restored" text formed the substantial basis of what can properly be called the Egyptian text, best exemplified in Aleph, B, Ᵽ75 and a few others.

[12] Cf. Dodd, *Epistles*, pp. 151-53, where he writes: "This 'short way with dissenters' strikes a harsh note in our ears. To ostracize people whose opinions we dislike is natural enough, but to find it recommended as a Christian duty is another matter" (*Epistles*, p. 151). Obviously, a 'great gulf fixed' stands between this mentality and the New Testament perspective on false teaching. The modern spirit of toleration toward variant religious convictions is possible only where a belief in the working of Satan has receded far into the background. That there have been excesses and errors done in the name of truth in no way diminishes the dangers of satanic delusion. Indeed, Satan can trade on such failings to create a tolerant atmosphere in which error can stand on an equal footing with truth. So, for example, in our own day homosexuality is no longer considered a gross perversion of morality, but merely a "lifestyle choice"! We are urged to accord legal protections to those who commit a sin for which God judged Sodom and Gomorrah with fire and brimstone. Since society willfully forgets that God is a Judge, they will be dramatically reminded of this with the advent of the Day of the Lord (cf. Revelation 14:6-7).

The Third Epistle of John

Upholding the Truth by Supporting Its Representatives

CHAPTER 11

UPHOLDING THE TRUTH

(3 John 1-14)

Unlike Second John, which is really a letter to a church, Third John is a true personal letter. Its addressee is named and the man on whose behalf the letter was written is likewise named.

As with Second John, we do not know where this little epistle went. It may well be that its bearer was the same person who carried the first two epistles to their destinations. But this is a guess and the letter does not offer us enough information to settle on a specific place. If First John went to Asia Minor, an area for which John may have felt special responsibility (cf. Revelation 2 and 3),[1] the recipient, Gaius, may well have been a member of one of the seven churches of Revelation. We can hardly say more than this.

The apparent purpose of Third John seems to have been to encourage Gaius to offer hospitality to Demetrius, who was evidently a traveling evangelist, known and approved by the apostle. In the course of writing on Demetrius's behalf to Gaius, John explains why he had not made the same request of Gaius's church. The reason was the imperious behavior of a leader in that church, Diotrephes.

Despite its brevity, Third John offers us a revealing and helpful glimpse of life in a church of the apostolic period. For this reason, its presence in the canon of New Testament Scripture is to be fully respected. The very fact that it has been passed down to us through the centuries argues that its first readers, beginning with Gaius, were able to recognize its spiritual worth and power. As with all canonical Scripture, it is not a council of the church that determines a book's acceptability for inclusion in Scripture. Rather, all genuine Scripture has survived precisely because of its inherent character. The Word of God carries its own authority with it, and spiritual people down through the centuries simply acknowledge that authority.

Third John, then, is inspired by the Holy Spirit and, like all Scripture, "is profitable for doctrine, for reproof, for correction, for instruction in righteousness" (2 Timothy 3:16).

I. SALUTATION (1)

¹**The Elder,**

To the beloved Gaius, whom I love in truth:

Once again the apostle writes under the self-effacing title of **The Elder** (probably "the older one," "the senior"; see comments under 2 John 1). The intended recipient is a man named **Gaius** for whom John expresses Christian **love.** This man is **beloved** to John (and no doubt to others, cf. verse 3) and the apostle can say that he loves him **in truth,** that is, both "truly" and in accord with Christian **truth** (cf. this phrase and the discussion under 2 John 1).

The name **Gaius** was common in the Greco-Roman world of John's time. Several men bearing this name appear in the New Testament:

1. A Macedonian who was a traveling companion of Paul and involved in the riot at Ephesus (Acts 19:29);

2. A man of Derbe who waited to meet Paul at Troas for the trip to Jerusalem (Acts 20:4, 5) and possibly the same as (1);

3. A Corinthian whom Paul baptized and who was his host when Paul wrote Romans from Corinth (1 Corinthians 1:14; Romans 16:23); and

4. The man addressed here.

There is nothing to indicate that the **Gaius** of Third John should be identified with any of the others. However, in the case of Gaius of Corinth, he like this **Gaius** was apparently a man of means, since "the whole church" met in his house (Romans 16:23). If we had reasons for thinking that John had a connection with the Corinthian church, this identification would be tempting. As it is, we must confess that we do not know where the **Gaius** of John's letter resided.

II. BODY OF THE LETTER: UPHOLDING THE TRUTH BY SUPPORTING ITS REPRESENTATIVES (2-12)

The body or main portion of this letter is divided into three subunits, each of which begins with the word "beloved." Fundamentally, the letter appeals to Gaius to do what Diotrephes was unwilling to do: i.e., support the truth by supporting its representative, Demetrius.

A. Commendation of Gaius's Walk in the Truth (2-4)

²Beloved, I pray that you may prosper in all things and be in health, just as your soul prospers.

The apostle begins this commendatory section by expressing the wish that Gaius may do as well in temporal matters as he is doing spiritually.

The word rendered **prosper** by the NKJV (Greek: *euodousthai*) is equivalent to our English expression "get along well" and does not contain a necessary reference to material prosperity. The apostle wants things to go well for Gaius and for him to **be in** good **health**. Since he regards Gaius's **soul** as "getting along well" (**prospers**, same Greek word as before), he expresses the hope that Gaius's temporal well-being might match his spiritual well-being.²

It has been suggested that if the same wish were made (and realized) for some Christians in our churches, they would probably be in the hospital!

Just how well Gaius was doing in his Christian life is indicated in the following verse. Obviously, the apostle wanted Gaius to know that he was writing him about Demetrius precisely because Gaius was the kind of man who could be counted on for help.

³For I rejoiced greatly when brethren came and testified of the truth *that is* in you, just as you walk in truth.

John now states that he has received information from certain Christian **brethren** that Gaius conducts himself consistently with **the truth**. Specifically, they **testified** to the fact that Gaius was a man in whom **the truth** was a dynamic force. (For this idea, cf. 1 John 1:8 and discussion there.) Its power and effectiveness **in** Gaius was evidenced by (**just as**) the fact that he walked **in truth**; i.e., he obeyed God's commands. As always when John deals with the "abiding" life of the disciple, the inward and outward realities correspond. If Gaius walked **in truth**, it was precisely because **the truth** lived effectually within him, and vice versa.

Since no doctrinal errors are addressed in Third John, **the truth** is likely to refer to the substance of the Christian revelation as made in and through God's Son. But as we have seen, for John **the truth** cannot be separated from the fundamental reality that Jesus is Christ come in flesh (cf. 1 John 4:3-4; 2 John 7), and any denial of that places one outside of any valid partnership with **the truth**. It may thus be taken for granted that **the brethren testified**, among other things, to Gaius's "orthodoxy" which lay at the root of his support of, and obedience to, **the truth**.

> **⁴I have no greater joy than to hear that my children walk in truth.**

John is delighted with the reports of Gaius's adherence to the **truth** and expresses the thought that **to hear** such a report brings him a superlative **joy**.

The possibility certainly exists that Gaius was a convert of the apostle John, but the words **my children** (Greek: *ta ema tekna*) do not prove this conclusively. The expression "my little children" (Greek: *teknia mou*) occurs in reference to the recipients of First John in 2:1 and 3:18 (and without "my" at 2:12, 28; 3:7; 4:4; 5:21), and it expresses the apostle's paternal feelings for them. All of them are not likely to have been his converts. However, the expression here is not quite the same and the differentiation *could* signal the way John might speak in reference to an actual convert.

In any case, John's joy in those for whom he has a father's heart is an inspiration. He is saying to Gaius, in effect, "I can't imagine anything making me happier than hearing about your consistent Christian walk." To **walk in truth**, of course, meant that Gaius *lived in conformity* to *the* **truth**, and every spiritual "father" knows how richly meaningful it is to have one's "spiritual children" living in obedience to God.

Thus John conveys at the very beginning of his letter his personal delight in Gaius. Even if he had been so inclined, Gaius would have found it hard to turn down the request which this caring spiritual father would shortly make of him.

B. Encouragement of Gaius's Support for Those who Proclaim the Truth (5-8)

> **⁵Beloved, you do faithfully whatever you do for the brethren and for strangers, ⁶who have borne witness of your love before the church. *If* you send them forward on their journey in a manner worthy of God, you will do well,**

As is clear from these verses and from verses 7 and 8, **the brethren** referred to here are Christian missionaries (i.e., itinerant evangelists), and Gaius is being encouraged to continue to assist them as he has evidently done in the past. Whether "the brethren" referred to in verse 3 were also itinerant evangelists is not certain, but quite possible. In any case, John has moved on from his general commendation of Gaius's Christian walk to the more specific subject of the assistance he renders to such men as these.

The phrase **for the brethren and for strangers** is difficult.[3] It could refer to Gaius's hospitality to the missionaries *and* to Christian travelers otherwise unknown to Gaius. The option does not appear to be open to take **strangers** to mean non-Christians, since the statement **who have borne witness…before the church** appears to refer to both categories. Sometimes, however, in the New Testament, the term *brother* or *brethren* seems to refer to specific people known to the Christians who are addressed (cf. 1 Corinthians 16:12; 2 Corinthians 9:3, 5; 12:18). In that case, **the brethren** may indicate traveling evangelists from the general area where John is, and whom both John and Gaius knew, while **strangers** refers to evangelists from other places who were unknown to Gaius before their arrival in his area of residence. This latter conclusion is strengthened by the fact that the Greek text (at least, the majority of the manuscripts) adds an article, i.e., literally, **for the brethren and for *the* strangers**, suggesting specific individuals, rather than a general category. Thus the phrase may equal "for the evangelists you know and for those you don't know."

Gaius it seems was a truly open-handed man when it came to the matter of assisting those who traveled in service to the gospel. The apostle applauds this activity as an expression of fidelity to the Lord and His truth. The words **you do faithfully** might be more literally rendered, "you do a faithful thing," and John's point is that **whatever** Gaius might **do** (Greek: *ergasei* "do, accomplish") **for** these servants of Christ is an act of faithfulness to God.

But such acts were not only expressions of faithfulness, but also of love for these traveling missionaries. Thus when any of them had **borne witness…before the church** where John was located, it was to Gaius's **love** that they testified.[4] Obviously, Gaius was a host whose hospitality was warm and ungrudging, so that he conveyed a true spirit of Christian **love** to those whom he entertained and assisted. He was what Paul would call a "cheerful giver" (2 Corinthians 9:7).

Verses 5 and 6 are actually one sentence in Greek. Thus the words, *If* **you send them forward on their journey in a manner worthy of God, you will do well**, may better be rendered, "whom (referring back to the brethren and strangers) you will do well by sending [them] on their journey in a manner worthy of God." Here John gently makes a transition from what Gaius had done (as reported in John's church) to what John expects he *will do* under the present circumstances. Thus the initial words of verse 5, **whatever you do**, refer both to what has been done and to what will be done by Gaius in assisting **the brethren and strangers**.

To **send them forward on their journey in a manner worthy of God** encompasses all that Gaius needs to do to be an ideal Christian host. Thus he will need to furnish the missionaries with appropriate food and lodging, taking care to see that all their needs are attended to. He should also provide them with whatever supplies or assistance they may require when the time comes for them to set forth on their travels once more. It is indeed a high standard to set for any Christian host that his treatment of those who travel in the service of the Lord should be of such a quality that it can be deemed **worthy of God**. In other words, **God** is to be in no way disgraced by meager, half-hearted, or grudging hospitality to those who serve Him. In John's day, the need for such hospitality was magnified by the poor quality of the inns in the Roman Empire, as well as by the hostility that Christian evangelists might expect to encounter in their travels.

> **⁷because they went forth for His name's sake, taking nothing from the Gentiles.**

This verse actually begins a new sentence (as indicated in *MajT*). The word **because** renders the Greek, *gar*, which normally introduces a new statement or sentence, and can be translated here as "For."

The reason why Gaius should do what the apostle is asking him to do for these men is that they have gone out on their mission without seeking any assistance from unsaved **Gentiles**. By the term **Gentiles** (Greek: *ethnē*) John cannot possibly mean *all ethnic* **Gentiles**. Instead, he here uses that word to describe those who are outside the Christian church, much as Paul could say, "Give no offense, either to the Jews or to the Greeks or to the church of God" (although there were both Jews and Greeks within the church, 1 Corinthians 10:32; cf. also Matthew 18:17). These evangelists, therefore, avoided the unseemly practice often engaged in today, in which preachers of the gospel solicit financial assistance from everybody, whether saved or not. But as is indicated by the words **taking nothing**, these New Testament preachers apparently refused to *accept* such help, which is more than simply not *asking* for it.

These evangelists had, in fact, gone out on their mission **for His name's sake, taking nothing from the Gentiles**. The words **for His name's sake** could be rendered "for the sake of the Name." (There is no word for **His** in the Greek text, and though it could be implied by the Greek article, a reference to our Lord's uniquely holy and exalted Name is perhaps preferable: i.e., **the Name** par excellence.) The clear implication of this, under either translation, is that to have sought material assistance from the unsaved would have been unworthy of **the Name** in which these preachers **went forth**. Since the One who sent them had "all authority…in heaven and on earth" (Matthew 28:18), it would be truly embarrassing to suggest implicitly that without the assistance of the unregenerate, He could not sustain His servants.

We are reminded here of the statement of Ezra about being "ashamed" to ask the Persian king for an escort for the Jews returning to the land: "For I was ashamed to request of the king an escort of soldiers and horsemen to help us against the enemy on the road, because we had spoken to the king, saying, 'The hand of our God is upon all those for good who seek Him, but His power and His wrath are against all those who forsake Him'" (Ezra 8:22).

Needless to say, a preacher who grovels for money, whether before the saved or the unsaved, does not have a true sense of the dignity of **the Name** under which he serves.

> **8We therefore ought to receive such, that we may become fellow workers for the truth.**

In the light of the lofty Name under which these missionaries serve, John says, and in view of their commendable refusal to take help from the unsaved, **We** Christians (i.e., John, Gaius, or anyone else who could do so) **ought** to offer them generous hospitality.

The word **receive** (Greek: *apolambanein*) could be used in the sense of "welcoming," e.g., welcoming a guest into one's home (cf. Luke 15:27),[5] and this is no doubt its sense here. When Christians "welcomed" and offered hospitality or help to such servants of the Lord, they became **fellow workers** (Greek: *synergoi,* "co-workers") **for** (or, with) **the truth** proclaimed by them. In other words, they became *partners with* the preached word! Christians should always value highly the privilege of facilitating **the truth** of God in any way they can, however humble or mundane the means of doing so may be. Any involvement in this undertaking is of eternal significance before God.

> [9]**I wrote to the church, but Diotrephes, who loves to have the preeminence among them, does not receive us.**

The question might possibly have arisen in Gaius's mind as to why this request was put to him instead of to the church to which he belonged. (The simple reference to **the church** is best taken as a reference to his particular church fellowship.)[6] It would be most natural if the normal custom was to send a letter along with the traveling evangelist to the church in the city to which he was heading. Then the church could arrange for his accommodations with whoever desired to or was able to provide them. John's remark here implies that his procedure was a bit unusual and so he wishes to explain it to Gaius.

John states that he *has* written **to the church**. Whether this was in fact the same church to which Second John was written cannot be determined. Certainly there is nothing in Second John to suggest that the church addressed there had a problem of the kind mentioned here. But since the apostle had already determined to deal with the problem in person (cf. verse 10), no mention of this concern was to be expected. The possibility exists that Second John *is* the letter referred to here, but it is only that— a possibility.[7]

The problem in Gaius's church was the presence there of a dominant leader named **Diotrephes** who is very pointedly described as a person **who loves to have the preeminence among them**. This withering indictment by the apostle does not in the least suggest that **Diotrephes** held to some doctrinal error; still less is there the slightest hint that he was not a Christian. Instead, John "capsulizes" this personality with what is functionally almost a title: "the lover of being first" (Greek: *ho philoproteuon*).

As is well known to all who are realistic about Christian experience, it is sadly possible in the church for someone who assumes a place of leadership to fall into the trap of always wanting their way, or always wanting to be "in charge." Such people may be born again and perfectly orthodox, but they have brought into the church the spirit of the world, specifically "the pride of life" (cf. 1 John 2:16). They have completely missed the spirit of servanthood that the Lord Jesus enjoined on His disciples (Luke 22:24-27). To love **to have the preeminence** is exactly the opposite of our Lord's model of humble service! To desire **the preeminence** is also to assume in the church a position that Christ alone should fill, even as Paul has written, "And He is the head of the body, the church…that in all things He *may have the preeminence*" (Colossians 1:18, italics added). The Greek verb used by Paul is the simple form (*proteuo*) of the one used here by John. Thus, a person like **Diotrephes** is guilty of usurping a position in the church that belongs to the Lord Jesus Christ alone!

We must not conclude that **Diotrephes** was the "pastor" of this church, since that office is unknown to the New Testament. (In the New Testament, *pastor* is a *gift*, not an *office*. See Ephesians 4:11.) Instead, he was most likely one of the elders of **the church** since the elders (or, bishops) of New Testament churches seem always to be referred to in the plural (Acts 14:23; 15:2; 16:4; 20:17; Philippians 1:1; for the equivalence of the terms "elders" and "bishops," compare Acts 20:17 with 28, and Titus 1:5 with 7). The organization of the early church differed from what is common today. No New Testament text can be given to support the view that the New Testament churches each had a single man as its "pastor." Still less do we find support for a "priest" in these local churches. Instead, the New Testament supports the idea (indicated in the passages just referred to) that each church was ruled by a body of elders who functioned together as equals. There is no sign of a "pastor," or even a "chairman of the board," in Paul's encounter in Acts 20 with the Ephesian elders!

Diotrephes, therefore, would have been simply one of a number of elders. But the rise of **Diotrephes** to **preeminence among** the Christians of his church undoubtedly suggests that the other elders allowed him to have his way. This often happens, even today, when a strong personality sits on an elder board where the rest of the elders tend to be passive.

Thus, we can find in **Diotrephes** the earliest known precursor of the so-called "monarchical bishop," i.e., an elder who had assumed authority over the rest of the elders. In time this led to the creation of a distinction between *the* bishop and the elders who were under his direction.[8] This development seems to have initiated a process that led to an ecclesiastical hierarchy, such as is found in Catholicism, but which is foreign to New Testament thought. **Diotrephes** provides us with our one New Testament glimpse of hierarchical Christianity, with a sobering reminder of the self-seeking which ecclesiastical hierarchies so easily foster.

Of **Diotrephes**, the apostle affirms that he **does not receive us**. Margaret Mitchell has convincingly shown that the Greek verb (*epidechomai*) was widely used in diplomatic contexts in the Greco-Roman world and has argued that here it refers to Diotrephes's refusal to **receive** the emissaries and letters of the author.[9] But though **Diotrephes** may have dared to do this, John seems serenely confident that he can put this man in his place if he goes to that church in person (verse 10). Most likely the apostle means by the word **us** those who formed a part of his immediate circle. Assuming that Third John was written at or near the time of First John, the reference may be to John and the other apostles (cf. 1 John 2:19 and the discussion there), whose communications and representatives were not "accepted" by this local dictator. For this reason, John does not expect Demetrius (verse 12) to be received by him either. That is why he is writing Gaius, rather than the church, to request hospitality. (The letter mentioned here *may* have requested hospitality and **Diotrephes** had refused it, but this seems less likely than that John simply refrained from making such a request when he wrote to **the church**.)

What exactly **Diotrephes** gave as a reason for his conduct we do not know. But in view of verse 10, a categorical rejection of apostolic authority appears improbable. Perhaps **Diotrephes** simply refused to accept any credentials, like a letter, which missionaries authorized by the apostles brought with them. He could have argued that there was no way to check on the authenticity of such documents. It is certainly true that traveling teachers from other places could be a source of trouble for the infant New Testament churches (cf. Acts 15:1; Revelation 2:2). Perhaps he also insisted on the "autonomy of the local church" and refused to accept any interference from the apostles within what he thought to be his own sphere of authority. In any case, as verse 10 discloses, whatever his excuse or excuses may have been, the apostle regarded them as "prattle."

> **[10]Therefore, if I come, I will call to mind his deeds which he does, prating against us with malicious words. And not content with that, he himself does not receive the brethren, and forbids those who wish to, putting *them* out of the church.**

We are not sure where the apostle was when he wrote this letter to Gaius. As we have been suggesting in this commentary, he might have been still in Jerusalem where all three epistles could have been written. If so, the situation in Judea may well have become volatile as the Jewish War (A.D. 66–70) loomed closer. Thus, if the apostle wrote Third John in 65 or early 66, the Lord Jesus' prophecies about Jerusalem's destruction would soon find fulfillment. The apostles may already have made plans to leave, with John planning a trip to Asia. If so, the words **if I come** would then suggest that a trip to Asia Minor by John could well bring him to the very church where Diotrephes was. (But see our comment under verse 13.)[10]

John assures Gaius that **if** he does **come** to Gaius's church, he will **call to mind** the **deeds** that Diotrephes does. The statement might be more lucid if rendered as "*I will bring up what he is doing.*"[11] The apostle had no intention of sweeping Diotrephes's misconduct under the rug, even though Diotrephes himself would have been relieved if he did so. John's intention here is deliberately understated. In saying, "I will bring these things up," it seems clear that he means, "I will deal with them." Confronted by the revered apostle himself, it is unlikely that Diotrephes could have offered any meaningful resistance.

By the term **his deeds**, the apostle no doubt has in mind Diotrephes's cavalier refusal to recognize any emissaries and/or messages that had come to him from the apostles. Such rejections had been accompanied by **prating against us** (the apostles) **with malicious words.** The verb for **prating** (Greek: *phlyareō*) occurs only here in the New Testament and signifies the kind of talk that is foolish or senseless, as well as **malicious** (which is a felicitous translation of the Greek word *ponērous:* "wicked").

The word *phlyaros* (related to *phlyareō*) occurs in 1 Timothy 5:13 in the sense of "gossips" (NKJV), "tattlers" (KJV).

Diotrephes, we may gather, dredged up whatever negative things he could about the apostles, however trivial or founded on rumor and gossip. Perhaps he suggested that they were getting a bit too old to be careful about whom they sent, or that they were too trusting and their representatives might be dangerous scoundrels whom they had not detected, etc. The possible specifics are endless, nor should we think that the apostles were immune to all sorts of negative criticism, even while those who criticized might hold their doctrines. Paul's critics mocked his appearance and public speaking ability: 2 Corinthians 10:10!

But Diotrephes's offenses were not confined to a personal rejection of those who represented the apostles, or who came with their approval or authorization. In an icy expression of irony, John suggests that Diotrephes's "prattle" did not "satisfy" him (he was **not content with that**). Whereas he ought to have been deeply ashamed of these **malicious words** with which he demeaned the apostles, he actually added to **that** (Greek: "to these things," i.e., to the words he spoke) the additional sins of both rejecting the traveling preachers **himself** and then also preventing others (**those who wish to**) from doing so. The words of the NKJV **he himself does not receive the brethren, and**... indicate: "neither does he *personally* receive the brethren, and *in addition*..."[12] Diotrephes' overweening lust for power did not allow him to tolerate others who refused to follow his lead.

The very missionaries whom Gaius was praised for assisting (verses 5-6) got nothing from Diotrephes personally, nor did Diotrephes allow others to extend the hospitality that he himself refused to give to these servants of Christ. Instead, he ordered those who might **wish to** show them hospitality not to do so, and, presumably when defied, he dealt with their defiance by **putting *them* out of the church**. Diotrephes was clearly an autocrat of the first magnitude who had such a hold on the church that he could rid the church of those members who didn't bow to him.

If, as we suggest, Gaius belonged to the same church as Diotrephes,[13] then Gaius was risking the displeasure of this dictatorial leader if he acceded to John's request. John knew this, of course, and the following verse seems to contain a warning against allowing Diotrephes to influence him in this matter.

C. Exhortation to Continue this Support in Regard to Demetrius (9-12)

> [11]Beloved, do not imitate what is evil, but what is good. He who does good is of God, but he who does evil has not seen God.

In this final subunit of the body of the epistle, John gets down to the central purpose of this letter. He wants Gaius to behave differently from Diotrephes and to receive Demetrius as he has received so many other servants of Christ (cf. verses 5-6).

Gaius might reasonably be expected to be somewhat daunted by the prospect of challenging the policy Diotrephes tried to enforce on the church. John obviously does not want any potential conflict with Diotrephes to deter Gaius from doing the right thing. On the other hand, Gaius already has received the brethren (verses 5-8), something which Diotrephes has refused to do (verse 10). It seems quite possible that in Gaius's case, Diotrephes looked the other way. If Gaius was a man of some means, as his penchant for hospitality implies, he may also have been a major source for the financial support of the church. If so, Diotrephes would not be the last leader to make special allowances for a well-to-do Christian brother whose generous giving he wished to retain!

Alternatively, Diotrephes may only recently have begun his policy of excommunicating those who wanted to help the traveling evangelists, so that a confrontation over anything Gaius did now would loom large on the horizon. Like many gracious individuals in our own day, Gaius may have abhorred confrontation—especially with willful people like Diotrephes—so that he may well have needed these words from John to instill in him the necessary backbone.

Gaius, therefore, is told **not** to **imitate what is evil**. It would be utterly absurd to suggest that, since he was obviously a born again believer, he could not possibly have done so. Such a suggestion would be ridiculous on its face. But if he *did* **imitate...evil**, it could then be said of him that he had **not seen God**! Conversely, if he did the right thing, it could be said that he was **of God**.

We have already met these types of expressions in First John. To be **of God** is a fluid expression signifying usually that the action of the person in question has its source or inspiration in God (cf. 1 John 3:10b and discussion). We are likewise told in 1 John 3:6, "Whoever sins has neither seen Him nor known Him;" that is, sin is always an act performed in spiritual ignorance and darkness. The sinner acts sinfully precisely because he has lost sight of God (cf. the discussion under 1 John 3:6).

As we have noted, especially under the discussion of 1 John 3:9, it is no longer tenable to appeal to the Greek present tense to evade the straightforward meaning of such statements and to water them down with a meaning like "continues to" or "keeps on doing" this or that. Here the Greek articular present participle is used in the phrases translated **He who does good** (Greek: *Ho agathopoiōn*) and **he who does evil** (Greek: *ho kakopoiōn*), but these expressions imply no more than that the action is performed. Such participles can express actions that occur only once (e.g., John 6:33, Greek: *ho katabainōn* "He who comes down") or actions that no longer are occurring (e.g., John 9:8, Greek: *ho kathēmenos kai prosaitōn* "he who sat and begged"). The nature of the Greek construction used by John is such that the statements remain true whether **good** or **evil** is done once or many times. To claim otherwise is to appeal to inaccurate, spurious grammar.

Gaius, therefore, is being told that if he refuses to **imitate** the **evil** which Diotrephes does, and instead **does good** by receiving Demetrius (verse 12), then in so acting he will be **of God**. That is, he will be behaving in such a way that **God** Himself is the Source of what he is doing. Alternatively, if he **imitates** Diotrephes and **does evil**, he will be acting out of spiritual blindness and will have had no vision or perception of God before his heart. **God** has been lost sight of, He has not been **seen,** when someone **does evil**. In other words, such a person is "walking in darkness" (cf. 1 John 1:6).

This forceful way of putting the choices that confront Gaius is clearly intended to instill in him the determination to keep his eyes on **God** and to allow **God** to be the true Source of what he does. In this light, there can be no question that Demetrius must be received and Diotrephes ignored!

> [12]**Demetrius has a *good* testimony from all, and from the truth itself. And we also bear witness, and you know that our testimony is true.**

Gaius should have no concerns about Demetrius's character or worthiness to receive hospitality in Gaius's home. He had **a *good* testimony from all** who knew him. These words render a Greek phrase that might be better handled by: *is testified to by all* (*memarturetai hypo pantōn*), that is, all those in a position to do so had given it as their "testimony" that **Demetrius** was a worthy servant of Christ.

But beyond that, **Demetrius** received "testimony" **from the truth itself.** By this John probably meant that **Demetrius** proclaimed **the truth.** By doing so he demonstrated his "orthodoxy" and this made him worthy to receive support in his travels from other Christians (cf. 2 John 10!).[14] Thus, **the truth** testified *to him* as he proclaimed it.

In the case of false prophets, Jesus Himself had taught that a tree could be known by its fruits (cf. Matthew 7:15-20). This has nothing to do with the popular, but false, notion that a man's salvation can be determined by his good works. The fruits in question are *words* (cf. Matthew 12:33-37) and a false prophet can be tested only by the *words* he speaks, since by his deeds he *seems* genuine because he comes in "sheep's clothing." The validity of a man's ministry must be tested by his message. **Demetrius** could survive such scrutiny since his loyalty to **the truth** constituted a testimony **from the truth itself.**

Still a third "witness" was available to **Demetrius.** (For the Old Testament rule about having "two or three witnesses," see discussion under 1 John 5:7-8.) John now states, **And we also bear witness.** This can hardly be anything but a reference to the apostles, whose "witness" Diotrephes was unwilling to accept (at least in this indirect form). As a spokesman for the rest (as he was also in 1 John 1:1-4 and elsewhere), John knows how the apostolic circle evaluated this man and he adds their weighty testimony to the "witnesses" already mentioned. He is confident that Gaius, unlike Diotrephes, will accept this testimony, adding **and you know that our testimony is true.**

Gaius thus has every reason to receive this highly commended traveling evangelist and the preservation of this letter suggests that he did. After all, the epistle went to Gaius in the first place and it could have become public property only through him or his family. Had he refused to honor the apostolic request, we might never have heard of it. But the Spirit who inspired this little letter was well able to move its recipient to do "what is good" (verse 11)!

III. FAREWELL (13-14)

> **[13]I had many things to write, but I do not wish to write to you with pen and ink; [14]but I hope to see you shortly, and we shall speak face to face. Peace to you. Our friends greet you. Greet the friends by name.**

The farewell of Third John is quite similar to that of Second John. The apostle has a lot to say to Gaius, but he prefers to do this in person. Earlier he had used the words "if I come" (verse 10), and now he expresses the hope that he will be able to do this **shortly**. No doubt Demetrius was coming to Gaius's area ahead of John, hence this letter of recommendation which was needed to procure him Gaius's hospitality. Other matters can wait to be discussed **face to face** (literally "mouth to mouth," see 2 John 12 and discussion there).

The statement of this verse, if made by John from Jerusalem, suggests that a trip to Asia Minor had already been decided on. Alternatively, the suggestion that First, Second, and Third John were all written at the same time cannot be proved, so perhaps Second and Third John were written later than First John, after the apostle had already reached Asia Minor.

It would be extremely interesting to know if John did come and how he dealt with Diotrephes when he did. But in the sovereign wisdom of God, we have not been granted this knowledge. Yet it is highly instructive to catch the glimpse this epistle affords us of a church that, for a time at least, had fallen under the sway of a single individual.

It is not for nothing that the New Testament presents us with the normative picture of local churches led by a body of leaders, not by just one, except for the situation here. The Lord's people ought therefore to be encouraged to seek multiple leadership in the form of a group of elders. More often than not, one-man leadership is deeply flawed, if not in the way Diotrephes was flawed, in other ways that can be just as bad. In our own time, we have witnessed the devastating effects on a church when a single, preeminent leader falls into immorality.

The distinctive feature of John's farewell in this epistle is his reference to **friends**, both those who are with him and who **greet** Gaius, and those whom John wants Gaius to **Greet**. Ideally, *all* Christians should be

friends of one another. But as this epistle shows, such an ideal may well fall short of attainment.

Clearly Diotrephes was not a *friend* to the apostle in any legitimate sense of that word. In all probability John felt that Gaius need not be enjoined to **Greet** everyone in the church, whether they sided with Diotrephes or not. To **Greet** everyone might very well be falsely interpreted as a "ploy" by the apostle to undermine the standing of Diotrephes with his allies in the church, and it might have needlessly embroiled Gaius in controversy with the Diotrephes party.

John does not want this. Instead he wishes **Peace to** Gaius and tactfully suggests that he confine the passing on of John's greetings to those whom Gaius knows to be well-disposed toward the apostle.[15] After all, why trouble Gaius on this matter? As John has made clear (verse 10), he will handle this himself in person. Thus, even in this simple farewell, we can detect the spirit of love which the great apostle of love demonstrated to those whom he shepherded for his Lord. If the apostle John had any great "signature" to his ministry to God's sheep, it would surely be these words: "Beloved, let us love one another" (1 John 4:7)!

> "And now abide faith, hope, love, these three;
> But the greatest of these is love."
> —1 Corinthians 13:13

ENDNOTES

[1] Cf. note 1, chapter 10 (p. 257).

[2] Rudolf Bultmann: "Such a wish as this is common at the beginning of private letters in late antiquity" (*The Johannine Epistles: A Commentary on the Johannine Epistles,* Herm [Philadelphia: Fortress Press, 1973], p. 97 n 1). See his note for his reference to the sources. Marshall shrewdly suggests that Gaius "may have lived at some distance from the church," and wonders whether Gaius might not have been in the best of health so that, "although he could entertain guests at home, he was not able to make the journey to the church to confront Diotrephes" (I. Howard Marshall, *The Epistles of John,* NICNT [Grand Rapids: Wm. B. Eerdmans Publishing Co., 1978], p. 89). This is possible but beyond demonstration.

[3] The phrase is even more difficult as read in the critical editions of the Greek New Testament (Nestle-Aland [27th] and UBS [4th]), where the wording

kai touto xenous replaces *kai eis tous xenous*. The critical text is supported by Aleph, A, B, C and a number of other mss. W. L. Richards (*The Classification of the Greek Manuscripts of the Johannine Epistles*. No. 35: Society of Biblical Literature Dissertation Series [Missoula, MT: Scholars Press, 1977], p. 275) finds 14.6 percent of the mss he examined in support of *touto*, while 79.3 percent reflect the reading *eis tous*, which is printed by Hodges/Farstad, *MajT*. The critical reading is awkward Greek, a fact concealed by Raymond E. Brown, *The Epistles of John*, AB (Garden City, NY: Doubleday, 1982) in his translation: "for the brothers, even though they are strangers" (p. 701). More literally, he renders it "for the brothers—and this [these] strangers" and cites 1 Corinthians 6:6 as a parallel (*Epistles*, p. 709). But Paul's text is not truly parallel because it contains a proposition (*kai touto epi apistōn*), which is precisely what is needed to improve the "barbarous" Greek of the critical editions (i.e., we need: *kai touto eis xenous*). The critical reading has no stylistic precedent in John's Gospel or Epistles, and we are within reasonable bounds again to suggest the possibility of an early emendation to correct a corrupted exemplar. It is possible that in transcribing the words *ADELPHOUCKAIEICTOUCXENOUC* an early scribe skipped from *OUC* (1) to *OUC* (2) (*homoioteleuton*) and thus created the truly awkward text: *ADELPHOUSXENOUC* which a reviser subsequently glossed by adding *kai touto*. Perhaps *kai touto* was initially a marginal gloss that was later included into the text itself.

[4]The reference to **the church** might well be to the Jerusalem church itself since, as Paul's own journeys in Acts show us, travel between Asia Minor and Jerusalem by sea, was apparently not uncommon (cf. Acts 18:21-22; 19:21). It is in no way implausible that in the pre-70 A.D. period to which we assign the epistle (see Introduction), Christian missionaries sent out from Jerusalem could have returned with glowing reports of Gaius's hospitality.

[5]Cf. BGD, p. 94.

[6]It has indeed been maintained that the church in question was not the one Gaius belonged to. Brown, *Epistles*, p. 717, thinks the phrase **among them** makes it unlikely that Gaius was a member of this church, since he is always "addressed in the second person." But against this is the simple reference **to the church** rather than "the church at…" or some other qualifying phrase. Further, Diotrephes is introduced as if he were known to Gaius, not as, e.g., "One of their elders, Diotrephes, does not…" No doubt, if the apostle had written **among you** it would have sounded a bit like Gaius was implicated in that. John's **among them** is scarcely different from saying, "I wrote to the church, but Diotrephes, who loves first place among its members…" Marianne Meye Thompson, *1–3 John*, IVPNT (Downers Grove, IL: InterVarsity Press, 1992), p. 160, wonders: "…why does the Elder have to tell Gaius what Diotrephes is doing if they

294

belong to the same fellowship?" There could be many reasons why. A man of Gaius's nature might be tempted to rationalize what Diotrephes was doing as "well-intentioned" but misguided, while John sees him as a self-willed authoritarian whom Gaius needs to recognize as such. Gaius will need backbone if he is to resist this man, as John urges him to do in verse 11. There is no reason to think that Diotrephes made himself out to be what he really was, but like all would-be church dictators he must have argued that his actions were in the best interests of the congregation (see the commentary discussion).

[7] Thompson, *1–3 John*, p. 161, states: "Few commentators today argue that what the author is referring to...is either 1 or 2 John... Most take it as another letter, now lost."

[8] The monarchical bishop finds its earliest documentation in the writings of Ignatius (d. 98/117), bishop of Antioch, who promotes a threefold ministry of one bishop, plus a plurality of elders (presbyters) and deacons in the local church. Rudolf Schnackenburg, *Die Johannesbriefe*, 2nd ed., HTKNT (Frieburg, Germany: Herder, 1963), p. 329, regards it as possible that Diotrephes was a monarchical Bishop, but prefers to see him as part of a transitional period which led to the state of affairs we meet in the epistles of Ignatius: "Wir befinden uns in einer Übergangszeit, in der sich der monarchische Episkopat festigt, wie wir ihn aus den Ignatiusbriefen kennen."

[9] Margaret M. Mitchell, "'Diotrephes Does Not Receive Us': The Lexicographical and Social Context of 3 John 9–10," *JBL* 117 (1998): 299-320.

[10] Brown, *Epistles*, pp. 718-19, goes way too far in detecting hesitation in the clause **if I come**, when he writes that it "indicates that he [the writer] has no desire to come in such a hostile way and subtly expresses his hope that he will not have to do so." Since Brown does not think of an apostle here, he attributes to the "Presbyter" an unlikely reluctance for religious confrontation, a mood more characteristic of the 20th century than the 1st (cf., e.g., Galatians 2:11-14 ff., Acts 15:2, 5; etc.).

[11] As suggested by BGD, p. 846.

[12] Cf. Brown, *Epistles,* pp. 701 and 719, "and furthermore."

[13] See verse 9 and note 6 above.

[14] Various ideas have been proposed to explain the words **from the truth itself**. C. H. Dodd, *The Johannine Epistles*, MNTC (New York: Harper & Row, 1946), p. 167, suggests: "The Truth itself testifies to Demetrius in the sense that his whole way of life so manifestly embodies the Christian ideal (as we might put it) that no one who is acquainted with him needs any further testimony" (similarly, Brown, *Epistles*, pp. 723-24; and Thompson, *1–3 John*, p. 163). This broader sense includes the one we propose in the Commentary and could well be right. F. F. Bruce, *The Epistles of John: Introduction, Exposition and Notes* (Old

Tappan, NJ: Fleming H. Revell, 1970), p. 155, thinks (improbably) that there is a direct reference to the Lord and that we should translate: "the Truth Himself." Stephen S. Smalley, *1,2,3 John,* WBC (Waco, TX: Word Books, 1984), p. 361, thinks that we should "understand the 'testimony of the truth' to Demetrius as an acknowledgment that his whole way of life expressed a commitment to the truth of Christ which constantly resulted in 'good' (loving) conduct." In any case, it seems quite wrong against the background of the three epistles to downplay any allusion to Demetrius's loyalty to the truth that "Jesus is the Christ come in flesh." Christian character may well be included, but a reference to his orthodoxy seems unavoidable.

[15] In the standard critical editions of the Greek New Testament (Nestle-Aland [27th] and UBS [4th]) the words **Peace** through **by name** constitute verse 15 (followed also by the Jerusalem Bible).

Scripture Index*

Boldface type indicates extended discussion of text

301

Subject Index

Notes

Notes

Notes

Notes

Notes

Notes

Notes

Notes